Britain and Africa in the twenty-first century

Manchester University Press

Britain and Africa in the twenty-first century

Between ambition and pragmatism

EDITED BY DANIELLE BESWICK,
JONATHAN FISHER AND STEPHEN R. HURT

Manchester University Press

Copyright © Manchester University Press 2019

While copyright in the volume as a whole is vested in Manchester University Press, copyright in individual chapters belongs to their respective authors, and no chapter may be reproduced wholly or in part without the express permission in writing of both author and publisher.

Published by Manchester University Press
Altrincham Street, Manchester M1 7JA
www.manchesteruniversitypress.co.uk

British Library Cataloguing-in-Publication Data is available

ISBN 978 1 5261 3413 4 hardback
ISBN 978 1 5261 6033 1 paperback

First published by Manchester University Press in hardback 2019

This edition first published 2021

The publisher has no responsibility for the persistence or accuracy of URLs for any external or third-party internet websites referred to in this book, and does not guarantee that any content on such websites is, or will remain, accurate or appropriate.

Typeset by Servis Filmsetting Ltd, Stockport, Cheshire

Contents

List of figures and tables	*page* vii
List of contributors	viii
Foreword – Chi Onwurah MP, Chair, All-Party Parliamentary Group for Africa	x
Acknowledgements	xii
List of abbreviations	xiii

    Introduction: UK Africa policy in the twenty-first century: business as usual? – *Danielle Beswick, Jonathan Fisher and Stephen R. Hurt*   1

Part I: Africa in UK international relations: trade, aid, development and security

1 The evolution of UK policy to Sub-Saharan Africa, 1997–2019 – *Alex Vines*   15

2 Africa's trade with Brexit Britain: neo-colonialism encounters regionalism? – *Mark Langan*   35

3 The UK and Africa relations: construction of the African Union's peace and security structures – *Kasaija Phillip Apuuli*   54

4 The securitisation of UK aid and DFID programmes in Africa: a comparative case study of Cameroon, Central African Republic, Ethiopia, Kenya and Uganda – *Ivica Petrikova and Melita Lazell*   73

5 The UK and peacekeeping operations on the African continent – *David Curran*   99

Part II: Africa and UK actors: parties, publics and civil society

6 Rehabilitating the 'nasty party'? The Conservative Party and Africa from opposition to government – *Danielle Beswick*   121

7 Labour, international development and Africa: policy rethinking in opposition – *William Brown*   139

8 The mixed fortunes of African development campaigning under
   austerity and the Conservatives – *Graham Harrison*   161
9 British campaigns for African development: the Trade Justice
   Movement – *Stephen R. Hurt*   179
10 International development NGOs, representations in fundraising
   appeals and public attitudes in UK–Africa relations – *Danielle Beswick,
   Niheer Dasandi, David Hudson and Jennifer vanHeerde-Hudson*   196

   Conclusions: aspects of continuity and change after New Labour –
   Danielle Beswick, Jonathan Fisher and Stephen R. Hurt   214

Index   223

Figures and tables

Figures

1.1	The UK's share of Africa's bilateral trade, 2016	19
4.1	The effect of strategic interest on UK provision of conflict prevention and resolution, peace and security (CPS) aid to conflict-affected countries	78
4.2	UK aid provision to the five case-study countries, 2002–15	80

Tables

4.1	Key statistics about the five African case-study countries	79
4.2	UK provision of aid to democratisation and CPS activities between 2002 and 2015	82
4.3	Five highest-funded democratisation activities	84
4.4	Four highest-funded conflict, peace and security activities	87

Contributors

Kasaija Phillip Apuuli is an Associate Professor in the Department of Political Science and Public Administration at Makerere University, Uganda.

Danielle Beswick is Senior Lecturer in the International Development Department at the University of Birmingham.

William Brown is Senior Lecturer in Government and Politics at the Open University.

David Curran is Assistant Professor in the Centre for Trust, Peace and Social Relations at Coventry University.

Niheer Dasandi is Senior Lecturer in Politics and Development in the International Development Department at the University of Birmingham.

Jonathan Fisher is Reader in African Politics in the International Development Department at the University of Birmingham.

Graham Harrison is Professor in the Department of Politics at the University of Sheffield.

David Hudson is Professor of Politics and Development in the International Development Department at the University of Birmingham.

Stephen R. Hurt is Reader in International Relations at Oxford Brookes University.

Mark Langan is Senior Lecturer in International Politics at Newcastle University.

Melita Lazell is Senior Lecturer in International Political Economy at the University of Portsmouth.

Ivica Petrikova is Senior Lecturer in International Relations at Royal Holloway, University of London.

Jennifer vanHeerde-Hudson is Professor of Political Behaviour at University College London.

Alex Vines OBE is Head of the Africa Programme and Director for Area Studies and International Law at Chatham House and an Assistant Professor at Coventry University.

Foreword

As Chair of the All-Party Parliamentary Group for Africa, I am delighted to support this important edited collection. It provides us with a number of timely reflections on the direction of travel of UK–Africa relations since the election of the Coalition Government in 2010. In doing so, it builds on some of the key findings of a seminar series on 'British Africa policy after Labour', which concluded with a meeting in Nairobi, Kenya in June 2016. The All-Party Parliamentary Group for Africa supported this series and the book provides a rich and complex account of the dilemmas and tensions shaping recent British engagement with Africa. The analysis covers both a range of different actors including political parties and non-governmental organisations and policy areas including aid, trade and peacekeeping. As such, it represents an original and important contribution that will be of interest to both scholars and policymakers alike.

The individual chapters engage with a coherent set of important questions, framed by the editorial team, which focus on the drivers and power dynamics underpinning contemporary UK engagement with Africa. Given the recent work done by the All-Party Parliamentary Group for Africa in our 2017 report on the future of Africa–UK trade and development cooperation, it is pleasing to see how this book addresses these issues from a number of perspectives.

The domestic context within which UK policymakers are currently operating is unpredictable given the result of the Brexit referendum. This has provided an opportunity to ask important questions about what kind of trade relationship with the UK might best serve African development in the future. Two of the chapters in this collection offer some important insights in this respect. First, a consideration of the developmental impacts of a continuation of the existing EU scheme of Economic Partnership Agreements (EPAs) with African sub-regions leads to the conclusion that they will perpetuate colonial patterns of trade. By contrast, there is also analysis of the ongoing work of UK civil society organisations which support a more progressive alternative to the reciprocal free trade that is central to EPAs.

Although the book focuses in the main on UK policy towards Africa, it also acknowledges that across a number of different policy spheres African actors are able to exert varying degrees of agency in the relationship. For example, in the realm of trade it is clear that African countries are far from passive recipients of policy and they will be able to draw important lessons from their experience of negotiating EPAs with the EU.

UK–Africa relations also need to take account of the changing global context where we see a range of players, including India and China, taking a much greater interest in what is a diverse continent. As this book effectively demonstrates, UK engagement with Africa has taken on a more pragmatic tone in recent years. With Africa's population predicted by the UN to increase to 2.5 billion by 2050, this book makes a convincing case for the UK to rethink where Africa features within the hierarchy of its foreign policy agenda.

Lastly, the book provides some thoughtful reflections on the perceptions of Africa that shape the public imagination. One can only hope that this collection stimulates wider self-reflection among a range of UK actors upon the need for new ways of thinking about and engaging with Africa.

Chi Onwurah, MP
Chair, All-Party Parliamentary Group for Africa

Acknowledgements

The editors would like to thank the Economic and Social Research Council for their generous funding of the Research Seminar Series on 'UK Africa policy after Labour' between 2014 and 2016 (Reference ES/L000725/1), at which many of the chapters collected here were first presented. We are grateful to all of the speakers and participants in the events which made up the series, in both the UK and Kenya, for their engagement and enthusiasm in bringing this project to fruition. We would also like to acknowledge the contributions of all of our series partners, for hosting and otherwise supporting the events and the seminar team, including: the Royal African Society, All-Party Parliamentary Group for Africa, British Institute in Eastern Africa, Chatham House, Institute for Public Policy Research, the University of Birmingham, Oxford Brookes University, the University of Warwick and the University of Sheffield. Finally, thanks are due to the two anonymous reviewers for their support for this manuscript and thorough reading of drafts, and to Rob and Tony at Manchester University Press for helping to ensure we made it across the finishing line.

List of abbreviations

ACP	African, Caribbean and Pacific Group of States
ACPP	Africa Conflict Prevention Pool
AMIS	African Union Mission in Sudan
AMISOM	African Union Mission in Somalia
APF	African Peace Facility
APSA	African Peace and Security Architecture
ASF	African Standby Force
AU	African Union
BDS	British Defence Staff
BOAG	British Overseas Aid Group
BOND	British Overseas NGOs for Development
BPST	British Peace Support Team
BPST(EA)	British Peace Support Team for East Africa
CAFOD	Catholic Agency for Overseas Development
CAR	Central African Republic
CDC	Commonwealth Development Council
CfA	Commission for Africa
CFTA	African Continental Free Trade Area
CPS	Conflict Prevention and Resolution, Peace and Security
CRS	Creditor Reporting System
CSOs	Civil society organisations
DFID	Department for International Development
DIT	Department for International Trade
EASF	East African Standby Force
EBA	Everything But Arms
ECOWAS	Economic Community of West African States
EDF	European Development Fund
EEC	European Economic Community
EFIF	Enough Food If
EPAs	Economic Partnership Agreements
FCO	Foreign and Commonwealth Office

FDI	Foreign Direct Investment
GNI	Gross National Income
GSP	Generalised System of Preferences
ICAI	Independent Commission for Aid Impact
LCID	Labour Campaign for International Development
MoD	Ministry of Defence
MONUC	United Nations Mission in the Democratic Republic of Congo
MPH	Make Poverty History
NATO	North Atlantic Treaty Organisation
NGO	Non-governmental organisation
NHS	National Health Service
NPF	National Policy Forum
NSC	National Security Council
OAU	Organisation of African Unity
OECD	Organisation for Economic Co-operation and Development
ONUC	UN Mission to the Congo
PSOs	Peace Support Operations
RECs	Regional Economic Communities
RUF	Revolutionary United Front
SADC	Southern African Development Community
SAIH	Norwegian Students' and Academics' International Assistance Fund
SDGs	Sustainable Development Goals
SLM	Sudan Liberation Movement/Army
TCCs	Troop Contributing Countries
TJM	Trade Justice Movement
TNCs	Transnational Corporations
TTIP	Transatlantic Trade and Investment Partnership
UHC	Universal Healthcare
UKIP	UK Independence Party
UNAMIR	United Nations Assistance Mission for Rwanda
UNAMSIL	United Nations Assistance Mission in Sierra Leone
UNCTAD	United Nations Conference on Trade and Development
UNEF	UN Emergency Force
UNMISS	United Nations Mission in South Sudan
UNPROFOR	United Nations Protection Force
UNSC	United Nations Security Council
UNSOS	United Nations Support Office in Somalia
WTO	World Trade Organization

Introduction: UK Africa policy in the twenty-first century: business as usual?

Danielle Beswick, Jonathan Fisher and Stephen R. Hurt

Fifteen years after Tony Blair placed Africa at the heart of British foreign policy in his famous 'scar on our consciences' speech at the 2001 Labour Party Conference (Blair, 2001), the place of Africa in UK international relations could hardly be more ambiguous. For some in Whitehall, Africa represents 'an exciting trading opportunity' for a post-Brexit world (Price, 2017); for others a source of 'marauding' and 'desperate' migrants who represent a 'threat' to British security (Perraudin, 2015). Africa is also the main focus of the UK's international development efforts, albeit an investment framed by ministers more around British 'global leadership' than the Blair era's 'one noble cause' (Patel, 2017; Wintour and Watt, 2004). If twenty-first-century Britain has an Africa policy, its shape and focus appear to elude its designers and implementers.

The UK relationship with Africa is, nevertheless, more complicated and multi-faceted than a strategy document or prime ministerial call to action. For better or worse, the British and African peoples have a deep, complex and contradictory history, which encompasses social, cultural, economic, political and linguistic linkages. These comprise not only relationships between governments and leaders but also between political parties, advocacy coalitions, civil society organisations and populations themselves. 'Africa' – whether as a romanticised site of exoticism and adventure, a brutal, and brutalising, 'heart of darkness' (Conrad, 1899; 2007), or a place of moral imperatives and charitable impulses – has long existed as an idea in the minds of the British people and their governments. Consequently, an analysis of contemporary UK Africa policy viewed through the lens of the Blair era tells us only one – incomplete – part of the story.

The purpose of this book is therefore to explore what drives UK Africa policy today, focusing particularly on the period since the Labour Party's 2010 departure from office. This edited collection, which brings together substantial and significant new material from policymakers, practitioners and scholars from different disciplines, addresses four main questions:

1. What are the domestic and foreign policy determinants of contemporary UK Africa policy?
2. How far do these build on or challenge the conclusions of previous analyses of UK Africa policy and relations, particularly those that focused on the periods of Labour government from 1997 to 2010?
3. What are the potential implications of these continuities and emerging trends for the UK and for Africa, in relation to each other and to wider developments in the sub-fields of security, development, trade, party identity, civil society campaigning and regionalism?
4. What are the power dynamics within UK–Africa relations? To what extent is the UK's relationship with Africa forever shaped by its colonial past?

Drawing on discussions developed in a 2014–16 seminar series funded by the UK Economic and Social Research Council,[1] our point of departure is the literature on the Blair era and Africa. The high profile afforded to the continent by the 1997–2010 Labour Government – seen in military interventions (the 2000 Operation Palliser intervention in Sierra Leone), unprecedented levels of aid provision and major diplomatic initiatives (the 2005 G8 Summit in Gleneagles) – has led many scholars to re-interpret UK Africa policy through focusing on this somewhat extraordinary period. A particular emphasis in this regard has been placed on Blair's language and how policy framings of Africa have spoken to domestic, political interests while purporting to speak to broader, more humanitarian ambitions. Rita Abrahamsen, for example, detects in Blair's 2001 'scar' speech part of a more general securitisation of the African continent in line with post-9/11 Global War on Terror logics (Abrahamsen, 2005). Similarly, Ian Taylor has argued that the professed ethical focus of Labour policy on Africa in theory was, in fact, undermined by far less ethical practices in reality – notably in trade and arms sale policies (Taylor, 2005, 2012 – see also Porteous, 2008).

Julia Gallagher's influential work on Blair and Africa explores how the Blair Government constructed the African continent as an apolitical space where the British polity could come together and enact an idealistic, moral agenda, focusing on Blair's 'pursuit of the good [British] state' by portraying Africa as simply a normative cause (Gallagher, 2009, 2011). This collection, however, seeks to take the discussion beyond Blair and the 1990s to consider the contours of UK

Africa policy in a quite different domestic and international context which has included global financial crisis, Coalition and Conservative government and the commandeering of UK foreign policymakers' attention by the June 2016 Brexit vote and its consequences.

Our authors seek, in part, to understand how the Blair legacy has been institutionalised or recalibrated in the contemporary era (Chapters 1, 6 and 7) but also to go beyond this conceptual framework to focus on issues and contexts hardly envisaged in the 1990s (Chapters 2, 3 and 5). The book also examines important continuities in the UK–Africa relationship, which link the Blair and Gordon Brown Governments to their predecessors and successors, as well as long-standing or new relationships between UK institutions/organisations and Africa which go beyond prime ministers and governments (Chapters 6, 8, 9 and 10). Our original contribution – beyond bringing the study of UK Africa policy out of Blair's shadow – is to analyse this range of both domestic and international elements of UK Africa policy and how these reflect mutual dependencies and contingencies cutting across often very separate spheres of research and policy.

In doing so, we focus on three key dimensions of the UK–Africa relationship outlined below.

Instrumentalisation

UK Africa policy has, for many scholars, long been determined by realist motivations – engaging the continent in order to maximise Britain's political, economic and military advantage and, at one point, supremacy on the global stage. In the eighteenth and nineteenth centuries, these interests were expressed through the exploitative and extractive practices of colonialism and slavery. In more recent times, British interests in Africa have been argued to be focused around economic ties and trade relations – on promoting UK companies and businesses, publicly and privately, and the shaping of accessible and open African markets. As Paul Williams (2004) notes, despite evolving rhetoric and international contexts, this was a central preoccupation of both the 1979–97 Conservative Government and the 1997–2010 Labour Government. Emma Mawdsley, Simon Lightfoot and Balász Szent-Iványi have further demonstrated how this trend has continued – even been strengthened – under more recent Conservative-led administrations (Lightfoot et al., 2017; Mawdsley, 2015;), though – as Peg Murray-Evans cautions – Britain's membership of the European Union has fundamentally transformed the architecture and substance of these economic relationships in a manner which contemporary actors in Whitehall have perhaps not fully taken on board (Murray-Evans, 2016).

Security interests have also been argued to be a long-standing pivotal driver of UK Africa policy. London's relations with many of its former colonies during the Cold War, it is suggested, were based primarily around bolstering anti-communist governments in the context of a wider foreign policy aimed at opposing and weakening the Soviet Union (Brown, 2004; 2007). This support was offered, alongside that of the US and other Western states, regardless of the democratic credentials of the regime in question and became a key element of regime maintenance strategies of leaders such as Hastings Kamuzu Banda of Malawi and Daniel arap Moi of Kenya. The post-9/11 Global War on Terror has led to similar dynamics, albeit with the threat of communism exchanged for that of Islamic terrorism (Abrahamsen, 2005). Counter-terrorism imperatives, it is argued, have dominated UK Africa policy under Blair, Brown, Cameron and May with discursive commitments to promoting human rights and democratisation undermined by the provision of extensive, direct aid and military support to increasingly authoritarian regimes which can claim to be firewalls against Islamic fundamentalist influence, or guarantors of order in opposition to George W. Bush's infamous 'ungoverned spaces' (Fisher and Anderson, 2015; Hagmann and Reyntjens, 2016).

Britain's extensive aid programme in Africa – with a genealogy stretching back to colonial-era 'Development and Welfare' grants – is, it is suggested, subject to these instrumental logics, in spite of policy statements and laws since 1997 reframing UK aid as aimed at eradicating global poverty. Whether UK aid to Africa has been 'hijacked' – to use Ngaire Woods's (2005: 393) words – in the name of security since 9/11 is an open question, though the linking of British aid to British global policy goals has been increasingly hard to ignore (see Chapter 4). Andrew Mitchell, Secretary of State for International Development from 2010–12, described the UK in 2011 as a 'development *superpower*' (Norton-Taylor, 2011; emphasis our own), while the 2015 UK aid strategy – the first since 2009 – was subtitled 'tackling global challenges in the national interest' (Her Majesty's Treasury and Department for International Development, 2015; Norton-Taylor, 2011). In its 2017 election manifesto, the Conservative Party argued for a renegotiation of the definition of 'Overseas Development Assistance' ('changing the rules') within the Organisation for Economic Co-operation and Development's (OECD's) influential Development Assistance Committee – widely interpreted as the first step to incorporating counter-terrorism operations into formal OECD pronouncements on what aid includes (Conservative Party, 2017: 39; Chapter 6).

Ultimately, though, notions of Britain engaging Africa for its own interests focus less on what London *does* do and more on what it *does not*. Africa, it is argued, ranks low on the list of priorities for most British prime ministers, rendering the Blair era even more unusual in a long history of neglect and disinterest. Britain's failure to intervene during the 1994 Rwandan Genocide is viewed by many as a clear example of London's strategic disregarding of moral obligations on the basis of a country's, and region's, perceived insignificance to national interests; a charge levelled, of course, at many other Western governments, including the US (Melvern and Williams, 2004). Indeed, one of the reasons that the Blair Government's prominent engagement with African issues attracted so much attention is because Africa has tended to be largely ignored by British prime ministers, at least in relation to other continents and foreign policy arenas. Even under Blair, Whitehall's attention was fleeting. Chris Mullin, UK Africa Minister 2003–5, recalls that he was unable to attract government interest in engaging with northern Uganda's humanitarian crisis for the better part of a year until 'a conversation with [Blair] on the plane home from Abuja' sparked the Prime Minister's interest and 'the entire machine ... suddenly sprung to life' (Mullin, 2009: 445–7; also Porteous, 2005: 289–90).

The first part of this book therefore examines how critical these instrumental agendas have remained in the post-2010 era. The UK's growing interest in supporting African peacekeeping and development of peace support architecture is scrutinised by Apuuli (Chapter 3) and Curran (Chapter 5) in this regard, while both Vines (Chapter 1) and Langan (Chapter 2) consider the impact of the Brexit vote on UK relations with Africa – a foreign policy crisis which places Europe, once again, at the heart of UK foreign relations but which also arguably opens up new space for UK–Africa engagement (see also below). To begin with, then, our collection considers how far UK Africa policy since 2010 has returned to what might be considered 'business as usual'.

Identity

We argue, however, that contemporary UK–Africa relations cannot be understood through a purely pragmatic lens. Africa is an arena in which ideas about UK identity and the role and position of the UK on a global stage, as well as ideas about what characterises Africa and Africans, are nurtured and projected to both domestic and international audiences. Our contributions suggest that this remains as true since 2010 as it was under the previous Labour Governments.

Previous analyses of the Blair and Brown administrations emphasised the extent to which UK Africa policy had become personalised and infused with particular values which, in some cases, these leaders sought to link directly with the Labour Party. There is, therefore, a need, addressed in this collection, to consider the extent to which prioritisation of Africa by UK political leaders continues to be a purely Labour conceptual project. The contributions by Brown (Chapter 7) and Beswick (Chapter 6) examine this issue, namely the direct impacts of domestic party political developments on engagement with Africa. Brown considers the Labour Party's search for a coherent Africa strategy in opposition since 2010, led by a succession of shadow ministers and against a backdrop of leadership and identity crises within the Party. Beswick's account of Conservative Party engagement with Africa highlights the importance of David Cameron's leadership, in opposition and government, in pushing Africa up the foreign policy agenda of the Party. It also, however, notes that this did not emerge in a vacuum, arguing that efforts to separate the identification of Labour with Africa in the minds of the UK public began in opposition under Michael Howard. Both Beswick and Brown locate engagement with Africa in relation to processes of transformation within the two parties, from opposition to government or its reverse, and through changes of leadership – after Blair, Brown and Cameron – that arguably led to a fall in Africa's profile within both parties.

Beyond parties and leaders, the UK has seen significant and sustained campaigns by civil society organisations and coalitions, seeking to raise the profile of Africa in UK public consciousness and generate support for their activities. These have primarily focused attention on aid, including both humanitarian and development assistance, trade and debt. Chapters 8 and 9 by Harrison and Hurt respectively, consider two examples of high-profile campaigns since 2010: the Trade Justice Movement (TJM) and Enough Food If (EFIF), respectively. Harrison suggests that the Make Poverty History (MPH) campaign during Blair's tenure led to reflection on how development charities might pursue campaigns which avoided the Africanisation of poverty in the eyes of the British public. He examines the EFIF campaign, launched in 2013, finding that despite professed commitment to change campaigning strategies and imagery used to attract support, no substantive difference was visible in the way Africa was portrayed. Instead, he suggests that there was a symbiotic relationship between the campaign and the Conservative Party in government, which precluded critical engagement. The closeness of the campaign and the government allowed each to claim a form of victory and legitimacy; the government claimed global leadership in campaigns against hunger, largely based on their promotion of business and science solutions to hunger and malnutrition, and EFIF were able to claim – somewhat unconvincingly – that campaign efforts led directly to the commitment to spend 0.7 per cent of Gross National Income on overseas development assistance. Hurt's analysis of TJM tells a different story. This one of the three pillars of MPH has persisted beyond 2005, but it has seen its influence reduced in the post-2010 period due to a lack of connections with members of the incoming government.

The two chapters show how the closeness that developed between New Labour and campaign organisations and coalitions up to 2010 may have supported the presentation of particular images of Africa and Africans to the British public. The subsequent scramble for new connections with government following the defeat of Labour, and the simultaneous impacts of the financial crisis, also seem to have contributed to a crisis of confidence and funding concerns within these campaigns. It is suggested that these developments have curtailed many of the high ambitions expressed after MPH to address the Africanisation of poverty and the images of Africa and Africans being presented by development organisations to the UK public. Hurt and Harrison's contributions, on the leitmotifs and strategies used by civil society in Africa campaigning in the UK, thus help us to make further sense of the findings presented by Beswick, Dasandi, Hudson and vanHeerde-Hudson (Chapter 10) on UK public attitudes to aid and Africa. Their analysis of the presentation of Africa and Africans in fundraising campaigns demonstrates the persistence of images of Africans, often children, in positions of helplessness and hopelessness. Their analysis of an Oxfam campaign does however suggest that there are efforts to get beyond these stereotypes and to change the way the UK public sees and engages with Africa. The experiments reported in their chapter also highlight the long-term dangers of existing campaign strategies, which reduce feelings of efficacy in potential donors, and signpost ways to design campaigns around more positive emotions. This could, if taken further, signal the start of more complex and contextualised campaign materials, supporting better – and potentially more critical – conversations about, and presentations of, UK relations with Africa.

Agency

Finally, while our primary focus is on UK policy towards Africa, our authors also consider the role of African agency in the UK–Africa relationship. Building on recent scholarship which has sought to move away from mainstream International Relations narratives on African dependency, we consider the nature of power dynamics across different dimensions of contemporary UK–Africa engagement (Beswick and Hammerstad, 2013; Brown, 2012; Brown and Harman, 2013). As Vines notes in Chapter 1, in tracing the evolution of UK policy towards Sub-Saharan Africa, the UK relationship with, and influence across, the continent is part of its claim to 'punch above its weight' in the international arena. The UK–Africa relationship is a key element of the case for Britain's place as a permanent member of the UN Security Council, its role in international peace and security, and in defining and promoting the Sustainable Development Goals.

Since the Brexit vote in 2016, Africa has also been touted as a potential beneficiary of a re-focusing of UK foreign policy. The Commonwealth, over a third of whose members are African states, has also enjoyed an increased profile in UK foreign policy discussions. The uncertainty unleashed by the Brexit vote has thus arguably created an opportunity for African actors to influence the shape and content of their relations with the UK. The contributions from Apuuli (Chapter 3), Petrikova and Lazell (Chapter 4), and Langan (Chapter 2) speak to the ways in which African actors have sought to engage with and shape UK engagement with Africa, and in Langan's case may seek to do so in future. In particular, Langan cautions against a division of the Commonwealth into Francophone and Anglophone factions for the purpose of trade negotiations. Nevertheless, while we recognise that the policies and approaches described in this book are not unidirectional, and that African actors are able to resist, shape, initiate, influence and potentially reject UK engagement in specific arenas, the uniting focus of this collection is on how UK–Africa relations are shaped and driven by ideas, organisational logics and practices emanating from the UK. For a more detailed discussion of African agency in these processes and others which constitute relations between the UK and the continent we would highly recommend Brown and Harman (2013), Brown (2012) and Beswick and Hammerstad (2013).

Structure of the book

In outlining our arguments, the collection is organised into two sections. The first section takes a thematic approach to examine how Africa features in UK foreign policy, and whether, and to what extent, this reveals any significant shifts from what was visible under New Labour from 1997–2010. This section begins with an overview chapter from Alex Vines, Head of the Africa Programme at Chatham House. Vines reflects on the values and interests which have influenced the thinking of UK politicians on relations with Africa, including domestic factors such as concentrations of UK voters with ties to Africa, visa and immigration arguments, Africans in the UK prison population and those working in UK public services, particularly the health sector. He provides an overview of these topics before delivering a chronological analysis, which highlights changes over time and the role of domestic factors, including political personalities, in these shifts. In Chapter 2, Mark Langan examines options for UK–Africa trade relations following the Brexit vote, drawing parallels between 'Brexit discourse' and a longer-standing imperial romanticism associated with previous UK administrations, including those of New Labour. Chapters 3 and 5 examine UK engagement with peace and security challenges in Africa, through Apuuli's examination of the UK role in African Union peace and security structures and Curran's chapter on the UK's 'consistently inconsistent' contributions to peacekeeping in Africa. In Chapter 4, we turn to development, with Petrikova and Lazell deploying a new framework to analyse the extent to which UK development engagement with African states has become securitised, comparing five cases to test their hypotheses.

The second section of the book focuses on domestic influences on UK relations with Africa since 2010. Chapters 6 and 7, by Beswick and Brown respectively, analyse the influence of party leadership and party position in government/opposition on relations with Africa. Both chapters draw on new empirical research to demonstrate how the changing political fortunes of the Labour and Conservative parties have affected the priority afforded to Africa and the ways in which engagement is framed by party leaders for a domestic and international audience. The following two chapters, by Harrison and Hurt, examine the legacy of the MPH campaign for two subsequent campaign efforts that sought to push Africa into UK public consciousness and to spur government action on issues which strongly affect Africa, namely trade justice and hunger. Taken together with Chapter 10, by Beswick, Dasandi, Hudson and vanHeerde-Hudson, these contributions highlight dissatisfaction with the ways in which Africa has been portrayed in civil society campaigns. They also show the significant impact of the 2008 financial crisis and the 2010 Labour election defeat, which ruptured links between campaign organisations and government, on Africa campaigning in the UK.

Finally, the Conclusion reflects on the research questions posed at the start of this chapter, by considering the extent to which UK policy towards Africa has changed since 2010 and what this tells us about the drivers of engagement and prospects for the future.

Note

1   See www.researchcatalogue.esrc.ac.uk/grants/ES.L000725.1/read and www.open.ac.uk/socialsciences/bisa-africa/uk-africa-policy for more information on the Series and its outputs [accessed 2 February 2018].

References

Abrahamsen, R. (2005) 'Blair's Africa: the politics of securitization and fear', *Alternatives: Global, Local, Political*, 30:1, 55–80.

Beswick, D. and Hammerstad, A. (2013) 'African agency in a changing security environment: sources, opportunities and challenges', *Conflict, Security & Development*, 13:5, 471–86.

Blair, T. (2001) 'Full text: Tony Blair's speech (part one)', *Guardian*, 2 October 2001, www.theguardian.com/politics/2001/oct/02/labourconference.labour6 [accessed 2 February 2018].

Brown, S. (2004) '"Born-again politicians hijacked our revolution!" Reassessing Malawi's transition to democracy', *Canadian Journal of African Studies*, 38:3, 705–22.

Brown, S. (2007) 'From demiurge to midwife: changing donor roles in Kenya's democratisation process', in G. Murunga and S. Nasong'o (eds), *Kenya: The Struggle for Democracy* (London: Zed Books), 303–31.

Brown, W. (2012) 'A question of agency: Africa in international politics', *Third World Quarterly*, 33:10, 1889–908.

Brown, W. and Harman, S. (eds) (2013), *African Agency in International Politics* (London: Routledge).

Conrad, J. (2007) *Heart of Darkness* (London: Penguin Classics, new edition, 2007; originally published 1899).

Conservative Party (2017) *Forward Together: Our Plan for a Stronger Britain and a Prosperous Future* (London: Conservative Party).

Fisher, J. and Anderson, D. (2015) 'Authoritarianism and the securitization of development in Africa', *International Affairs*, 91:1, 131–51.

Gallagher, J. (2009) '"Healing the scar?" Idealizing Britain in Africa, 1997–2007', *African Affairs*, 108:432, 435–51.

Gallagher, J. (2011) *Britain and Africa under Blair: In Pursuit of the Good State* (Manchester: Manchester University Press).

Hagmann, T. and Reyntjens, F. (eds) (2016), *Aid and Authoritarianism in Africa: Development without Democracy* (Chicago, IL and London: University of Chicago Press and Zed Books).

Her Majesty's Treasury and Department for International Development (2015) *UK Aid: Tackling Global Challenges in the National Interest* (London: Her Majesty's Treasury and Department for International Development).

Lightfoot, S., Mawdsley, E. and Szent-Iványi, B. (2017) 'Brexit and UK international development policy', *Political Quarterly*, 88:3, 517–24.

Mawdsley, E. (2015) 'DFID, the private sector and the re-centring of an economic growth agenda in international development', *Global Society*, 29:3, 339–58.

Melvern, L. and Williams, P. (2004) 'Britannia waived the rules: the Major Government and the 1994 Rwandan Genocide', *African Affairs*, 103:410, 1–22.

Mullin, C. (2009) *A View from the Foothills: The Diaries of Chris Mullin* (London: Profile Books).

Murray-Evans, P. (2016) 'Myths of Commonwealth betrayal: UK–Africa trade before and after Brexit', *The Round Table: The Commonwealth Journal of International Affairs*, 105:5, 489–98.

Norton-Taylor, R. (2011) 'Fox v Mitchell, armed forces v development aid', *Guardian*, 13 June 2011, www.theguardian.com/politics/defence-and-security-blog/2011/jun/13/aid-development-military [accessed 2 February 2018].

Patel, P. (2017) 'Speech at "What the world needs from Global Britain" event', 29 June 2017, www.gov.uk/government/speeches/priti-patel-speech-at-what-the-world-needs-from-global-britain-event [accessed 2 February 2018].

Perraudin, F. (2015) '"Marauding" migrants threaten standard of living, says foreign secretary', *Guardian*, 10 August 2015, www.theguardian.com/uk-news/2015/aug/09/african-migrants-threaten-eu-standard-living-philip-hammond [accessed 2 February 2018].

Porteous, T. (2005) 'British government policy in sub-Saharan Africa under New Labour', *International Affairs*, 81:2, 281–97.

Porteous, T. (2008) *Britain in Africa* (London: Zed Books).

Price, M. (2017) 'UK–Africa trade will be even better after Brexit', *City Press*, 13 August 2017, www.fin24.com/Economy/Africa/uk-africa-trade-will-be-even-better-after-brexit-20170811 [accessed 2 February 2018].

Taylor, I. (2005) '"Advice is judged by results, not by intentions": why Gordon Brown is wrong about Africa', *International Affairs*, 81:1, 299–310.

Taylor, I. (2012) 'Spinderella on safari: British policies towards Africa under New Labour', *Global Governance*, 18:4, 449–60.

Williams, P. (2004) 'Britain and Africa after the Cold War: beyond damage limitation?', in I. Taylor and P. Williams (eds), *Africa in International Politics: External Involvement on the Continent* (London: Routledge), 41–60.

Wintour, P. and Watt, N. (2004) 'Blair's mission on Africa', *Guardian*, 8 October 2004, www.theguardian.com/politics/2004/oct/08/uk.world1 [accessed 2 February 2018].

Woods, N. (2005) 'The shifting politics of foreign aid', *International Affairs*, 81:2, 393–409.

Part I

Africa in UK international relations: trade, aid, development and security

1
The evolution of UK policy to Sub-Saharan Africa, 1997–2019

*Alex Vines**

This chapter examines the key drivers behind the UK Government's Africa policy from 1997 to 2018 (under Labour from 1997–2010; under the Liberal Democrat Coalition and the majority Conservative Government of 2010–17 and under a minority Conservative Government from 2017). The chapter also assesses developments after the EU referendum (Brexit) and evaluates how the UK's strategy towards Africa might evolve.[1] Overall, political interest remains firmly based upon humanitarianism but African security and trade have also become secondary drivers to protect the UK's position as a permanent member of the United Nations Security Council (UNSC) and more recently EU and particularly French relations. Free trade is also of mutual UK–African increased interest, as this chapter will show. A final key driver is the UK's African diaspora and its impact on domestic politics. This has already resulted in Somalia, Nigeria and Zimbabwe being of increased importance to the UK. Yet, competing global priorities will require hard choices, and UK policy ambition underpinned by a new Africa strategy agreed by the National Security Council in early 2018 has unlocked £50 million for a UK network upgrade of personnel and infrastructure in Africa. There has increasingly been recognition of UK decline in Sub-Saharan Africa as other nations have upgraded and invested more deeply in their Africa networks. In January 2018, Martin Kettle in the *Guardian* observed that:

> In some respects Britain is not a global leader but a global laggard. Macron has only been president of France for eight months, but he has made six visits to Africa in that time. By contrast no British prime minister has set foot on any part of Africa since 2013. There is either no diplomatic presence, or only a vestigial one, in some 16

African countries. Japan now has more embassies in Africa than Britain, and Germany more aid workers. (Kettle, 2018)

This may be an unfair caricature but it is partly correct, as this chapter shows, and the UK's preoccupation with migration and particularly its visa policy is also demonstrably impacting its Africa ambitions. The chapter will bring together these different elements of UK Africa policy to show how the key drivers have changed over time and to assess the current state of, and challenges for, UK–Africa relations. It begins by outlining the specific interests and values which have featured strongly in contemporary UK–Africa relations, before presenting a chronological analysis which demonstrates how domestic political dynamics have interacted with these drivers to produce specific policy outcomes and shifts over time.

Evolving interests and values

As highlighted in the Introduction, Africa has been important in maintaining the UK's claim to be a global player. The UK has been able to draw on its sphere of influence in Africa to help shore up its claim to a permanent seat on the UNSC, and to enhance its status in Europe up to Brexit. The UK has also, at times, seen Africa as a continent on which it can take the lead internationally, as the examination of the Commission for Africa (CfA) later in this chapter demonstrates. For the UK, Africa is a place where it can demonstrate its military might and its unrivalled capacity to promote international development through its Department for International Development (DFID). The fight against Ebola in Sierra Leone was but one way of demonstrating this military might and developmental capacity.[2] The UK also has other tangible strategic and economic interests in Africa. The most obvious areas are immigration, crime and counter-terrorism – particularly in relation to those countries from which the UK already has large immigrant (and until recently emigrant) populations, such as in Nigeria, Somalia and Zimbabwe. These issues have been discussed elsewhere (see Vines, 2011: 26);[3] by contrast little attention has been paid to the ways that Africans in the UK have become an important driver of innovation and developed a stronger voice in UK politics.

The importance of the diaspora

The UK's 2001 census found that Sub-Saharan Africans constituted Britain's fastest-growing minority group during the 1990s, with 486,000 respondents recording their ethnicity as black African, outnumbering Britain's Caribbean population (*ibid.*: 27). Yet illegal migration and related underreporting suggest that this figure is a significant underestimate. Many new British citizens are of African origin, and this is reflected in the importance of Africans in UK economic activity, service delivery, and national and local politics.

The African diaspora has helped focus parts of the UK economy. An Institute for Public Policy Research study in 2007 showed that official Nigerian migrants were the second most successful immigrant group in Britain by salary. South Africans, Ghanaians and Zimbabweans did well too, earning significantly above the British average (Sriskandarajah *et al.*, 2007). Despite visa challenges, significant numbers of African students also choose to study in the UK – in 2015 Nigeria was the third largest non-European supplier of students (over 30,000) to UK universities. The UK is a world leader in fintech and innovative technologies and has cleverly married British expertise and financing with African ingenuity and understanding of local markets. UK fintech start-ups have done well in East Africa since 2008, followed by M-Pesa, M-Kopa and Azuri technologies.

In a similar vein, the UK's employment of African health professionals in the National Health Service (NHS) has generated particular concern and publicity about Britain's African engagement. A survey suggests that almost a quarter of new overseas-trained physicians recruited into the NHS came from Sub-Saharan Africa. In 2014, the fifth and sixth largest contributors of staff to the NHS were Nigeria and then Zimbabwe; South African doctors were 2.1 per cent of NHS staff followed by Nigeria (1.6 per cent) (Siddique, 2014). In 2002 the Government drew up a voluntary code to prevent poaching of nurses from Africa by the NHS (Styan, 2007: 1180). This reluctance to pursue hard-nosed strategic and commercial interests in Africa was also no doubt at least partly a consequence of a growing appreciation on the part of policymakers of the changing nature of domestic political and, indeed, electoral constituencies. Over 80 per cent of Africans live in Greater London, with four significant concentrations in four of London's poorest boroughs: Southwark, Newham, Lambeth and Hackney. A second significant characteristic is the diversity of Britain's African population, which no longer comprises Anglophone West Africans; rather there is significant Francophone African settlement in addition to large inflows from the Horn of Africa and expansion of the long-established Somali population (*ibid.*: 1186). It is not just in London that African communities prosper in Britain; there are concentrations of Angolans in Coventry and Manchester, and a large Somali community in Cardiff, for example.

The African diaspora in the UK also plays an important role in remittance flows. The World Bank (2016) ranked the UK as the world's tenth largest remittance-sending country and Nigeria is the UK's second largest recipient of remittances after India (*ibid*.: 22). The fragmentary official data available suggest that total remittances into Sub-Saharan Africa were around $9 billion in 2006 (*ibid*.: 22).[4] While this represented barely 5 per cent of global remittances, it is significant to African economies. Though now dated, the Black and Minority Ethnic Remittance Survey found that black British Africans had the highest propensity to remit of any migrant population in the UK (Boon, 2006: 5).

Three British MPs elected in the 2010 elections were of African origin, which has been reflected in increased debate in Parliament on African issues and chairing of All Party Parliamentary Groups (Africa, Angola and Nigeria, for example). A number of other MPs have needed the African vote to maintain healthy majorities and this makes understanding African issues more important, not only for British foreign policy but also in Britain's domestic politics. Africa will become increasingly important because significant communities of British African origin care about the continent and lobby for attention. This is also reflected in the devolved administrations, with the Welsh Assembly developing its own aid projects in Lesotho and Somaliland and the Scottish Parliament in Malawi and Uganda (Anyimadu, 2011).

Trade and investment

As regards economic interests, these are meaningful but by no means vital. Figures from the United Nations Conference on Trade and Development (UNCTAD) show UK total exports to Sub-Saharan Africa valued at $11.6 billion in 2008 (up from $9.7 billion in 2007), and total imports to the UK from sub-Saharan Africa at $15.1 billion in 2008 (up from $13.7 billion in 2007) (UNCTAD, 2009). Arguably, only South Africa plays a significant commercial role in this trade relationship, as it was the UK's top export market in Africa in 2009 (and the UK's twenty-fifth largest overseas market) with sales (in finished goods only) totalling £2.1 billion; the UK is also the largest single investor in South Africa.[5] Nigeria is the UK's second largest trading partner in Africa and its thirty-third largest overseas market for goods. UK exports of goods to Nigeria were worth £1.2 billion in 2009, and total exports of services were worth £1.3 billion in 2008.

Moving forward to 2014, Africa accounted for 4.3 per cent of the UK's trade deficit in 2014, down from 5.1 per cent in 2004. The UK's overall trade balance with Africa was in deficit in all periods between 2004 and 2008, before briefly turning into surplus between 2009 and 2011, due to an increase in UK exports and a fall in imports. The UK's trade balance with Africa returned to a deficit in 2012 following an increase in imports. Figure 1.1 shows the UK's

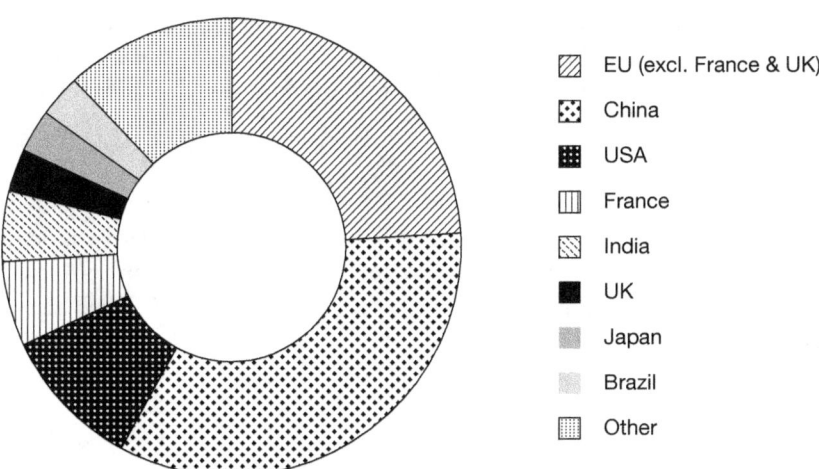

Figure 1.1 The UK's share of Africa's bilateral trade, 2016.
Source: Adapted from Intracen (2017).

share of Africa's bilateral trade in 2016. The majority of the UK's trade with Africa is in goods, which accounted for 68 per cent of total trade between the two regions in 2014, with the remainder accounted for by services (Office for National Statistics, 2016). South Africa remains the UK's largest export and import market in Africa. The Office for National Statistics (*ibid.*) notes that the UK ran a trade in goods and services deficit averaging £1.2 billion with South Africa 2004–10, until an increase in UK service exports in 2011 saw the UK begin recording a trade surplus, totalling £0.6 billion in 2014 (*ibid.*).

In 2014, the value of the UK's outward foreign direct investment (FDI) in Africa was £42.5 billion and the amount the UK invested in Africa more than doubled between 2005 and 2014 from £20.8 billion to £42.5 billion (Intracen, 2017). South Africa was the largest recipient of UK FDI in Africa, accounting for 29.8 per cent of total UK FDI in the continent in 2014. Mining, quarrying and financial services were the main industrial groupings in receipt of UK FDI, representing 54.4 per cent and 34.3 per cent of total UK FDI into Africa in 2014 respectively (Office for National Statistics, 2016). The UK was Sub-Saharan Africa's sixth largest trading partner in 2016, with total flows of $20.8 billion. FDI from the UK to Africa was $2.4 billion in 2016 according to a report by accounting firm EY. EY (2017: 20) noted that since the 2016 EU membership referendum there had already been a measurable decline in UK FDI to Africa:

The UK, which has led Western European investment in Africa since 2010, saw its share of FDI projects ease from 10 per cent in 2015 to 6.1 per cent in 2016. The more notable decline was in FDI jobs, down by a significant 81.4 per cent. The Brexit vote at the end of June 2016 and the resulting uncertainty seem to have had an immediate impact on UK investment into Africa. Governments across the continent will need to redefine their trade and investment relations with a post-Brexit UK.

The importance of London as a source of FDI, however, is increasingly understood by African policymakers. Since 2014, a number of African Governments (Burundi, Guinea, Togo, Madagascar and Mauritania) have opened or re-opened diplomatic missions in London, aimed partly at trying to attract funding and to diversify away from France.[6]

Importance of aid

Aid rather than trade was the prime focus of British efforts in Africa during the Labour Government, but this has radically changed since May 2010, with the Conservative–Liberal Democrat Government insisting that trade needs to be prioritised, a situation that the FDI figures echo. Although the outright expression of UK mercantilist interests in Africa remained there was always a bit of a taboo towards the end of Labour's term of office, despite a growing readiness to make the UK's strategic interests more explicit.

It would be wrong, however, to overstate the extent to which relative power and strategic interests were driving UK Africa policy. A good example of this point might be the case of Zimbabwe, where ideological and domestic pressures interact. From a purely strategic point of view, what happens in Zimbabwe is of limited interest to the UK, yet domestic pressure forces engagement – dramatically illustrated in UK policy and press focus on the country around the departure of Robert Mugabe as president in November 2017 (Vines, 2018). Ironically, this engagement has rarely been thoughtful or strategic, lacking as it does the framework of a broader awareness of interests and opportunities among many of Zimbabwe's neighbours (Cargill, 2007).

The UK's interests in Africa, under Labour from 2004, were upgraded by policymakers for the first time since the end of decolonisation, keen as Labour was to emphasise the moral dimension of the UK's approach and to engage younger voters. This approach was facilitated by the downgrading of the Foreign and Commonwealth Office (FCO) and the upgrading of DFID, with a near exclusive focus on development and poverty reduction. Labour politicians and government officials underscored the symbolic role that Africa policy has come to play in the UK's self-perceptions as a 'moral' power willing to do good; these politicians and officials were able to do so since they were operating in an arena where there was limited party political or media dissent (Gallagher, 2009).

Indeed, surprisingly given Britain's finances, all the main political parties in the 2010 elections defended ring-fenced international development from future cuts, and maintaining the UK's commitment to provide 0.7 per cent of Gross National Income (GNI) for international development. This promise was upheld by the Coalition of the Conservative–Liberal Democrat Government and enshrined into law in March 2015. Given the depth of public spending cuts in other areas, this commitment to development assistance and the new Government's signalling that poverty reduction would remain core to DFID were remarkable. Although debated in 2017 through the media, this commitment survived and all the main parties recommitted to the 0.7 commitment in the run-up to the June 2017 elections. Given the diminished popularity of the Conservative Government following the elections, 0.7 is now regarded by government ministers as an important instrument to demonstrate to the electorate that the Conservatives do care about humanitarian 'values'.

Understanding how UK policy towards Africa has evolved since 1997 can only be understood through analysis of British domestic politics. The following section examines the rise of Africa policy under Labour, its subsequent decline and the current drive up to early 2018 to develop a new Africa strategy. Understanding this evolution is best done by examining episodes marked by changes in political fortunes of the party in office.

The rise of Africa policy under New Labour, 1997–2005

For much of the 1990s, Britain was largely uninterested in Africa, except as a destination for aid and managing post-colonial legacy disputes. However, this was to change (Clapham, 2002: 87; Vines, 2011: 30). Blair authorised British troop support for UN and regional peacekeeping efforts in Sierra Leone in May 2000 (Ero, 2001: 60; Leboeuf, 2003). He also began promoting Africa's causes at international gatherings, starting with the G8 summit in Genoa in 2001 (Porteous, 2005). By the beginning of Labour's second term, in 2001, a discernible UK policy on Africa was emerging (Vines, 2011: 30; Williams, 2004). At the Labour Party Conference of September 2001, Blair made his much-quoted pronouncement that Africa was a 'scar on the conscience of the world' that would become 'deeper and angrier' without action to heal it. Blair announced that Africa would be a policy priority for his new Government, although the war in Iraq made this impossible for much of 2004.[7] Although officials in the Prime

Minister's Office were not surprised, Blair's speech on Africa caught the Africa specialists in the FCO off-guard.

As I have argued elsewhere (Vines, 2011), the increasing importance of Africa policy under Labour in these years is most clearly reflected in the emergence and growth of DFID. Establishing this cabinet-level ministerial department, under the outspoken Clare Short, signalled a powerful and not entirely unwelcome shift given past FCO priorities in Africa (Kampfner, 2004). Under Labour, international development became an area where Britain punched well above its weight. Aid spending tripled in real terms and DFID enjoyed a reputation as a progressive, innovative and effective donor (Vines, 2011: 32–3). This gave Britain a strong voice in debates on the Millennium Development Goals, as well as in the G8 and international institutions.

By 2001 DFID had a larger budget and greater influence than the FCO. It enjoyed relative ministerial stability under Clare Short, Baroness Amos, Hilary Benn and Douglas Alexander. However, this period saw a downplaying of the role of traditional diplomacy and politics and an exaggeration of the humanitarian and development agenda in Africa. This emphasised the role of aid and de-emphasised the need to understand politics, history and context (see Gallagher, 2009), a shift which helped politicians feel more comfortable with Africa policy. It can be argued that in many ways DFID took on the role of a Ministry for Sub-Saharan Africa. Bilateral and regional programmes in Sub-Saharan Africa increased from £300 million in 1997–8 to £1.5 billion in 2008–9, and by 2005 DFID was providing direct budget support to seventeen African countries, drawing questions about whether these governments were committed to good governance and poverty reduction.[8]

The Commission for Africa: the anti-climax of Labour's Africa policy

It was in 2005 that the single most visible action of Labour on Africa was effected, namely the hosting of its CfA report for its presidency of the G8. The establishment, process and publication of the report spoke as much about Britain and its own politics and perceptions of Africa as about Africa itself. The CfA was established by Blair in February 2004 (see Brown, 2006; Hurt, 2007; Williams, 2005). The aim of the Commission was to take a fresh look at Africa's past and its present as well as assess the international role in its development path (see Brandt Report, 2006).

The CfA, and by extension the UK Government, developed a reputation for being loftily out of touch, an image not helped when a key figure in the Commission reportedly claimed at a dinner for senior international diplomats that 2005 would be the year when 'Africa was discovered on the international agenda' (Vines, 2011: 32–3). The blunders surrounding the CfA were widely noted (see *ibid.*), and the Commission dissolved in September 2005. Blair claimed that the report's recommendations had been integrated into UK foreign policy, but many key recommendations failed to have an impact. The UK's presidency of the EU in the second half of 2005 saw little progress, although a new EU Strategy for Africa was agreed by the European Council in December 2005.

A degree of retrenchment: UK Africa policy, 2005–10

During the Labour Government's third term, the focus on Africa seemed to fade (*ibid.*: 33–6). In a keynote speech in Abuja in 2006, Foreign Secretary Jack Straw had outlined a series of key pillars of UK engagement towards Africa: development, governance, conflict, terrorism, migration, crime and drugs, energy security, environment, Islam and China (Straw, 2006). David Miliband, Straw's successor, insisted: 'By no stretch of the imagination is it possible to argue that the UK's influence in Africa is lower today than it was ten years ago. In fact, it is massively enhanced' (Lunn *et al.*, 2008: 105). Despite this claim, Miliband showed little interest in Africa, engaging only in relation to Kenya's post-election crisis in December 2007, the Democratic Republic of the Congo and Zimbabwe (BBC News, 2008). Brown as Prime Minister did seek to maintain an aid focus with specific reference to Africa, including during the 2010 election campaign.

British policy towards Africa may have appeared to display a high degree of continuity, but it was coming under closer scrutiny and when we examine this period tensions become clear. During 2005, significant Whitehall restructuring was underway. Africa was officially a government priority, but dramatic contradictions lay behind this rhetoric. The high costs of British engagement in Iraq fuelled calls to cut costs, and this came alongside a review of security of British diplomatic and aid missions abroad. During 2005, government departments working on Africa were being downsized and the FCO faced a 20 per cent cut in personnel, with diplomatic missions in Lesotho, Swaziland and Madagascar closed by the end of 2005 (Vines, 2011: 34).[9]

Africa at the FCO under Labour did not enjoy stability of leadership. By the 2010 elections, eight ministers under Labour had overseen Africa policy.[10] Under Labour, the FCO was not assigned to house expertise but rather tasked to implement policy. Increasingly, the UK's country policies were decided by the diplomatic missions on the ground, except where there were strategic interests such as energy security or a domestic angle, such as in Zimbabwe or Somalia (which both had dedicated FCO housed units attached to them).

The closure of High Commissions in Lesotho and Swaziland in 2005 passed largely without remark, and this represented a break in British commitment to maintain a Commonwealth network (*ibid.*). At the same time, it should not be forgotten that the drive for personnel and expertise cuts inside the DFID was equal to that of the FCO. A number of DFID offices were downsized and positions merged, although unlike the FCO a number of other DFID programmes were expanded. Countries such as Nigeria, due to population size, were seen as strategic and maintained significant levels of investment. At the other end of the spectrum, as in the FCO, small programmes were vulnerable. For example, DFID closed its Gambia office in early 2010 and the Lesotho office in late 2010.[11] DFID's overall budget under Labour did not suffer, but cuts in personnel resulted in increased outsourcing.

The elections in 2010 brought an end to closing of UK programmes and embassies in Africa and saw a greater focus on trade promotion, as will be examined in the next section. British diplomacy and aid efforts in Africa were from now on to focus more on promoting UK interests.

Interests more than values: the Coalition Government, 2010–15

Given the acute British budget deficit in 2010, the Conservative-led Coalition sought to prioritise trade and investment opportunities in Africa for British businesses. Some twenty FCO prosperity officers were appointed to complement fourteen existing UK trade and investment offices on the continent. High-level 'prosperity partnerships' with Angola, Côte d'Ivoire, Ghana, Mozambique and Tanzania were launched, though in practice this resulted in little material difference and by 2017 they had been quietly dropped. The Government also established prime ministerial trade envoys for Angola, Nigeria and South Africa. These were further expanded following the 2015 elections, and in December 2018 there were nine trade envoys covering the following sub-Saharan countries: Angola, Democratic Republic of Congo, Ethiopia, Ghana, Guinea, Kenya, Mozambique, Nigeria, Rwanda, South Africa, Tanzania, Uganda and Zambia.

Since 2012 the UK Government has re-opened embassies in Côte d'Ivoire, Madagascar, Liberia and Somalia, and opened a new embassy in South Sudan. These, with the exception of Madagascar, were closely linked to security and aid responses. The governments of the UK and Somalia also co-hosted two international summits on Somalia in London in 2012 and 2013 to encourage increased international engagement on Somalia, and a further summit on Somalia was held in May 2017.

As Foreign Secretary, William Hague visited Mogadishu in 2012 to highlight the UK's engagement with Somalia, and visited South Africa in 2013. He received more African leaders and ministers than had his Labour predecessors, although his key interest was combating sexual violence in conflict and he visited eastern Congo as part of this campaign. His successor as Foreign Secretary, Philip Hammond, rarely focused on Africa. In August 2015, Hammond caused a stir by claiming that the UK's 'number one priority' was to find a way to make it easier to send would-be asylum seekers back where they came from and adding that Europe could not 'absorb millions of migrants from Africa'. His visits to Tripoli and Mogadishu and Nairobi in 2015 and 2016 all focused on migration and counter-terrorism.

David Cameron visited Africa only twice as Prime Minister, on a two-day visit in July 2011 to South Africa and Nigeria and to Nelson Mandela's funeral in South Africa in 2013. It was an important political statement that Cameron did not cancel his 2011 trip to South Africa, as the then Foreign Secretary William Hague had cancelled his visit there in early 2011 because of the Arab Spring. An additional cancellation by Cameron would have seriously damaged bilateral relations, which had recently improved following the ninth bi-annual UK–South Africa Bilateral Forum in London in June 2011, despite disagreements over Libya strategy. This Africa visit was supposed to symbolise the shift to a more trade-focused approach by Britain in Africa, but also that London was reinvesting in its diplomatic network on the continent.

A third Cameron trip to Africa had been planned for August 2016, to Nigeria, Kenya, Ethiopia and Somalia, but due to the 'Brexit' referendum this was postponed; after the referendum a shortened Kenya and Somalia trip was also cancelled. Originally, David Cameron had also planned to make Africa a legacy priority of his final years in government, including the unveiling of a new UK strategic vision for partnership. Brexit ended this ambition.[12]

Legacies of the Coalition and Cameron Governments

There are a number of lasting legacies of the Coalition and Cameron Governments besides the re-booting of trade promotion and the re-building of the UK diplomatic network in Africa. The first was the UK's support of the Libyan intervention in 2011. Like Tony Blair's legacy on Iraq, this legacy will haunt David Cameron. The planning, execution and narrative around this intervention showed a low level of awareness among UK policymakers of the broader African context. The use of UNSC Resolution 1973 to authorise the use of force to protect civilians in Libya – but which was in reality used as a justification for North Atlantic Treaty Organisation (NATO) military support of the rebels – has not been forgotten (Landsberg, 2011).

A second legacy was the UK's much-deepened engagement on Somalia. Possibly, in an attempt to compensate for an unsatisfactory Libyan outcome, David Cameron prioritised Somalia policy, greatly strengthening UK engagement, including the re-opening of a British embassy in Mogadishu in 2013. He saw this as key for his legacy, though his planned trip to Mogadishu in July 2016 did not occur as he was quickly replaced as UK Prime Minister by Theresa May.

Linked to Somalia is the UK's decision in 2015 to double its UN peacekeeping contribution through deployments to Somalia as well as South Sudan (see Chapter 5). The UK hosted an international Defence Ministerial conference in September 2016, co-hosted with Rwanda and Ethiopia, to build military capabilities and champion peacekeeping reform. Until 2016, the UK was the fifth highest provider of assessed contributions for UN peacekeeping. In 2016 its position dropped to sixth.

Britain's military is also engaged in capacity-building. There is the British Peace Support Team for East Africa in Kenya; the International Military Advisory and Training Team in Sierra Leone; and the BPST in South Africa (which ended in December 2017 and has been merged with the Kenya operation). West Africa/Sahel activities have been clustered out of Abuja, Nigeria and there are also *ad hoc* peacekeeping training activities in other countries, such as The Gambia, and anti-poaching support in Gabon and Malawi. Britain's Defence attaché network has also been expanded since 2015, with new staff in Senegal, Botswana and Cameroon.

Kenya remains strategic for Britain for a number of reasons but particularly for the leasing of training facilities for the British military, through the British Army Training Unit Kenya. This is a permanent training support unit based mainly in Nanyuki and providing logistical support to visiting UK units. Under an agreement with the Kenyan Government, renewed in 2016, six infantry battalions per year carry out six-week exercises in Kenya. There are also three Royal Engineer Squadron exercises that carry out civil engineering projects, and two medical company group deployments that provide primary healthcare assistance to the civilian community. These military engagements are framed by the 2015 Strategic Defence and Security Review, which spelled out a vision of a 'secure and prosperous United Kingdom, with global reach and influence' (see Curran and Williams, 2016).

This section has highlighted how UK politics have impacted upon Africa policy. The next section now draws upon lessons learned and how these can help frame future policy efforts such as the new Africa strategy, scheduled to be adopted by the National Security Council on 27 February 2018.[13]

Learning from the past

In terms of UK Africa policy, the Labour Governments left an important legacy that the Conservative–Liberal Democrat Coalition and its successor Conservative Government built upon. Labour left behind DFID and the start of a process to define UK strategic interests in Africa. DFID is undoubtedly Labour's main legacy that impacts Africa, and the Coalition Government's commitment to maintain it as a separate cabinet-level-led ministry was welcomed by the wider donor community. Britain's finances in 2010 forced clearer thinking and less waste. In September 2010, the UK Foreign Secretary, William Hague, admitted to the Foreign Affairs Committee that 'the reduction and withdrawal of this country's diplomatic presence – something that we know has taken place in large parts of Africa – is a mistake'. As noted in this chapter, although there has been some re-building of the UK diplomatic network in Africa, Britain needs to become less reliant on small posts and needs to scale up and also merge DFID and FCO offices in more countries (Cargill, 2013).

Britain has been a leading international development partner and its commitment to devote 0.7 per cent of GNI to such development allowed it to maintain a strong voice in multilateral aid efforts such as meeting the Sustainable Development Goals. As other DFID programmes globally wind down, Africa will become more important for DFID spend. Britain is also scaling up through supporting the CDC Group plc. In 2017, the CDC was the largest single investor in private equity funds in Africa, supporting fifty-eight funds investing in thirty-two out of the fifty-four countries on the continent.[14]

Through Labour, Coalition and Conservative-led government there has been a common refrain that the gravest national security threats originate not in strong states but in states marked by poverty, fragility and weakness, as found in parts of Africa. The Conservative–Liberal Democrat Coalition's efforts to build on this and create a new stabilisation and reconstruction force are therefore relevant to Africa. Aligning aid with security brought new challenges, such as integrating poverty reduction and security within a framework for defence. With the creation of the NSC, regional analysis, including of Africa, has featured less.

The biggest single challenge to future UK Africa policy came from within British politics. On 23 June 2016 the UK voted to leave the EU and this had some short-term impact directly on Africa, particularly on currencies that were already volatile, such as the South African Rand. UK officials are reviewing Britain's international partnerships, including in Africa: South Africa, Kenya, Nigeria will be more important in UK foreign policy because of trade but other

African countries may suffer given Britain's limited resources and capacity and the need to determine priorities. In late 2017, a review of Africa policy began aimed at drawing up a new strategy and seeking an additional £50 million for the UK network in Africa (drawn from the aid budget).

Following the UK elections of June 2017, Rory Stewart was appointed as a joint FCO and DFID junior minister with area responsibility for Sub-Saharan Africa. Although he lacked Africa background, appointing him jointly responsible for Africa at DFID and the FCO was an experiment in how to bring the FCO and DFID closer. Stewart also spearheaded the successful initiative to obtain more resources for the UK government network in Africa and win prime ministerial backing for a longer-term, decade-long strategy. However, after just six months in post, Stewart was promoted to prisons minister and Harriett Baldwin was appointed as Minister of State for Africa at the FCO and Minister of State at DFID on 9 January 2018. The review continued and a new UK Africa strategy was adopted by the NSC in February 2018, unlocking £50 million to create up to three hundred new Africa-focused UK government jobs and open new diplomatic missions in Chad, Djibouti and Niger and re-open missions in eSwatini (formerly Swaziland) and Lesotho.

Building up to this new Africa strategy, there were already some perhaps surprising high-profile UK engagements with Africa during the 2016–17 Government of Theresa May. She committed to hold the May 2017 Somalia conference in London, her Chancellor Phillip Hammond visited South Africa in late 2016 and her Secretary for International Trade, Liam Fox, visited Ethiopia, South Africa, Mozambique and Uganda in 2017. More surprising was that her then Foreign Secretary, Boris Johnson, visited Ethiopia, Gambia, Kenya, Liberia, Nigeria, Uganda and Somalia in 2017 and attended in Abidjan the AU–EU summit (in December 2017) – the most visits in Africa by a senior UK government official in many years. Also between October 2016 and November 2017 the then Development Secretary, Priti Patel, visited Kenya, Sierra Leone, Ethiopia and Nigeria (and was en route in Kenya to visit Uganda and Ethiopia when she was recalled to London and subsequently resigned).

The British Government in September 2017 also published a position paper that advocated for continued support of EU military operations and sanctions after Brexit. There was in effect a British pivot to the Sahel in 2018 because of its increasing importance region for UN and EU–UK and France–UK diplomatic and security cooperation in a post-Brexit context. For example, in 2018 British diplomats have been stationed in Chad for the first time preparing for a full embassy and the UK in early 2018 also committed to send three Chinook helicopters to Mali to support French counter-terrorism operations in the Sahel. Since 2016, the Royal Air Force has provided transport flights in support of

France's Operation Barkhane, and the FCO set up in 2018 a cross-Whitehall Sahel Unit. The UK is also considering contributing troops to the UN peacemaking mission in Mali and also contributes to several EU military programmes, including those countering migration from Libya and piracy off Somalia.

Prime Minister Theresa May's trip to South Africa, Nigeria and Kenya in August 2018 was an important signal of renewed British political and economic interest in Africa. She was convinced to make the visit following her interaction with African Heads of state at the Commonwealth Heads of Government Meeting in April 2018 in the UK. Despite the mixed press coverage (including over her dancing skills), the most notable commitment was her statement that the UK would host an African Investment Summit in 2019 and that the UK seeks to become the largest G7 investor in Africa by 2022.

Senior members of the British Royal Family also increased their footfall in Africa in 2018, with the Prince of Wales and Duchess of Cornwall visiting Gambia, Ghana and Nigeria; the Duke of Cambridge going to Tanzania, Kenya and Namibia, and the Duke of Sussex to Zambia.

Overall though, despite these high-profile engagements, core political interest in Africa has actually declined. The party manifestos of both Labour and the Conservatives for the 2017 elections hardly specified Africa. The Conservatives dropped their reference to Zimbabwe (seen in their previous manifesto). They recommitted to 0.7 per cent of GNI for international development, but allowed for the possibility of changing the rules of definition which govern how that money is allocated.

Still, Brexit could provide the UK with opportunities regarding Africa. Liberated from the constraints of the EU's Economic Partnership Agreements (EPAs), the UK could open up its markets to African trade. For simplicity, UK officials are looking for future agreements that closely resemble the EPAs. While this might work with South Africa (the UK is a major importer of South African wine and fruit), it is unlikely to be so straightforward in countries like Nigeria and Tanzania that are unhappy with the EPAs and want greater import protectionism to enhance their industrialisation ambitions. EPAs may be a good place to start negotiations, but they are not templates in themselves (see Chapter 2).

In an environment of declining risk appetite by banks towards Africa, post-Brexit the UK could also seek to increase its financial services and FDI in Africa. It could continue to boost its trade facilitation efforts, aid for trade and project finance. This requires strategic thought by UK government agencies. The biggest single impediment to improving bilateral relations remains visas and – with the Conservatives in their 2017 party manifesto committed to significantly reducing migration to the UK – imaginative thinking is also needed on this.

Conclusions

The rise of the UK's Africa policy under Labour arguably was aid-focused and culminated in the anti-climax of the CfA, with the third term of the Labour Government seeing a degree of retrenchment in Africa policy as it recognised that aid on its own did not bring global influence. The Conservative-led Coalition Government that followed, and its Conservative successor, pursued a more clearly business promotion and defence re-engagement strategy, with Nigeria, Kenya and Somalia becoming strategic priorities for the UK.

Africa represents a means by which the UK has tried to enhance its international standing and promote its strategic and economic interests. The shaping of Africa policy reflected the readiness of the UK's Labour politicians to respond to British non-governmental organisations, the media and public opinion on Africa. Under the Conservatives there was a more openly mercantilist policy following the 2016 EU membership referendum and the key question will be whether the UK has significant human and financial resources to engage comprehensively with Africa, or will choose a small number of strategic partners and greatly deepen its engagement only with them. Without the EU, burden-sharing is less possible, although the United Nations, the Commonwealth, G7 and G20 and NATO offer some scope for multilateralism.

Any future Africa policy will require consistent financial and human resources – the 'more for less approach' has reached its limits. The new Africa strategy of 2018 will make a difference because it unlocks £50 million to create up to three hundred Africa-focused government jobs and paves the way for the opening and re-opening of diplomatic missions and providing more staff for small sized and medium posts so that the UK can upscale its Africa partnerships. What is clear is that UK Africa policy will in the future have an even more explicit emphasis on the UK's commercial and security strategic interests and the Government will be required to better define what its priorities are. There needs to be some sort of measurable policy objective spine (a summit, for example) to measure progress in UK–Africa relations over the coming decade or at least more clearly defined bilateral strategic partnerships if a post-colonial pan-African strategic ambition remains achievable in practice, and not just on paper.

Notes

* Alex Vines is Head, Africa Programme, Chatham House and Assistant Professor, Coventry University. Claudia Wallner, during her placement at Chatham House, assisted in providing some research support. This chapter links to two others, referenced where appropriate: 'To Brexit and beyond: Africa and the United Kingdom', in D. Nagar and C. Mutasa (eds), *Africa and the World: Bilateral and Multilateral International Diplomacy* (Farnham: Ashgate, 2018), 25–39 and 'Africa and the United Kingdom: Labour's legacy, May 1997–May 2010', in T. Chafer and G. Cumming (eds), *From Rivalry to Partnership? New Approaches to the Challenges of Africa* (Abingdon: Routledge, 2011), 25–40.

1 The chapter benefited from insights from regular meetings on UK–Africa relations at Chatham House, in Whitehall and in Africa and beyond over this period.
2 For a much more detailed examination of this see Vines (2018).
3 Home Office figures discussed in Vines (2011) show that Africans from across the continent still find Britain an attractive country in which to live. Despite emotive reports about crime, Africans represent a relatively small proportion of the 10,000 jailed foreign nationals in 2016. Europe accounted for the greatest proportion of all foreign nationals within the prison population (51 per cent); those from Africa (19 per cent) and Asia (16 per cent) contributed the second and third largest proportion respectively. In 2016 Somalis were 3.4 per cent of the African total, followed by Nigerians at 3.3 per cent (Allen and Watson, 2017: 13). Zimbabwe in 2009 was one of the largest sources of asylum applicants to the UK but almost a decade later in 2017, the prime source was from Eritrea.
4 All dollar references are to US dollars throughout this book.
5 In 2006, 351,000 South Africans visited the UK; in 2007, 498,474 Britons visited South Africa. Some 700,000 Britons live in South Africa and some 350,000 South Africans reside in the UK. South Africa was the twenty-first largest importer of goods to the UK in 2009, worth £3.6 billion.
6 There has not been a similar swing of Anglophone openings in Paris. This is partly because France maintained a bigger and more stable diplomatic network in Africa although in 2017 The Gambia opened an embassy in Paris and France an embassy in Banjul in 2018.
7 The terrorist attack on the US of 11 September 2001 also convinced Blair that dealing with Africa's failing states was important for international security.
8 For a more detailed account see Vines (2011).
9 The Mali mission had already closed in 2003, releasing funds for a British diplomat to be stationed in Monrovia (Liberia) housed at the US embassy. A number of DFID offices in Africa were also closed in 2005, such as in Botswana. See Vines (2011).
10 Labour Africa ministers were: Tony Lloyd MP, 1998; Peter Hain MP, 2000; Bill Rammell MP, 2001; Baroness Amos, 2002; Chris Mullin, MP, 2003; Lord Triesman, 2005; Lord Malloch-Brown, 2007; Baroness Kinnock, 2009. Conservative Africa ministers to 2018 have also been numerous and had short tenures. From 2010–18 the role has been held by eight individuals: Henry Bellingham MP, 2010; Mark Simmonds MP, 2012; James Duddridge MP, 2014; Grant Shapps MP, 2015; James Duddridge MP, 2016; Tobias Ellwood MP, 2016; Rory Stewart MP, 2017; Harriett Baldwin MP, 2018.

11 DFID decided that obvious aid cuts during 2005 – the 'Year of Africa' – would be too embarrassing, but cuts did occur, including for middle-income countries like Botswana.
12 Author interview with UK Government representative, London, May 2017.
13 The UK government has commissioned a number of studies internally to feed into this policy refresh and held consultation meetings including at Chatham House. The British Council in Nairobi also held a consultation in February 2018 titled 'Our Future Africa: The British Council's Role in Africa's Trajectory'.
14 See CDC Group, www.cdcgroup.com/ [accessed 1 February 2018].

References

Allen, G. and Watson, C. (2017) 'UK prison population statistics', House of Commons Library Briefing Paper, No. SN/SG04334, 20 April 2017, http://researchbriefings.parliament.uk/ResearchBriefing/Summary/SN04334#fullreport [accessed 1 December 2017].

Anyimadu, A. (2011) *Scotland and Wales in Africa: Opportunities for a Coordinated UK Approach to Development* (London: Royal Institute for International Affairs).

BBC News (2008) 'Brown appeals for unity in Kenya', *BBC News*, 1 January 2008, http://news.bbc.co.uk/1/hi/world/africa/7165999.stm [accessed 30 January 2018].

Boon, M. (2006) *BME Remittance Survey: Research Report* (London: Department for International Development).

Brandt Report (2006) 'The Brandt Report: a summary', January 2006, www.sharing.org/information-centre/reports/brandt-report-summary [accessed 30 January 2018].

Brown, W. (2006) 'The Commission for Africa: results and prospects for the West's Africa policy', *Journal of Modern African Studies*, 44:3, 349–74.

Cargill, T. (2007) 'Tony Blair and the United Kingdom's Africa policy', *South African Yearbook of International Affairs 2006/2007* (Johannesburg: South African Institute of International Affairs), 323–33.

Cargill, T. (2013) 'Back to business? UK policy and African agency', in W. Brown and S. Harman (eds), *African Agency in International Politics* (London: Routledge), 65–79.

Clapham, C. (2002) *Africa and the International System: The Politics of State Survival* (Cambridge: Cambridge University Press).

Curran, D. and Williams, P. D. (2016) *The UK and UN Peace Operations: A Case for Greater Engagement* (Oxford: Oxford Research Group).

Ero, C. (2001) 'A critical assessment of Britain's Africa policy', *Conflict, Security & Development*, 1:2, 51–71.

EY (2017) 'Attractiveness Program Africa: connectivity redefined', May 2017, www.ey.com/Publication/vwLUAssets/ey-attractiveness-program-africa-2017-connectivity-redefined/$FILE/ey-attractiveness-program-africa-2017-connectivity-redefined.pdf [accessed 19 May 2017].

Gallagher, J. (2009) 'Healing the scar? Idealizing Britain in Africa, 1997–2007', *African Affairs*, 108:432, 435–51.

Hurt, S. R. (2007) 'Mission impossible: a critique of the Commission for Africa', *Journal of Contemporary African Studies*, 25:3, 355–68.

Intracen (2017) *Africa International Investment Report*, http://itemsweb.esade.edu/wi/Prensa/TheAfricaInvestmentReport2017.pdf [accessed 21 February 2017].

Kampfner, J. (2004) *Blair's Wars* (London: Free Press).

Kettle, M. (2018) 'Theresa May's vision of a global Britain is just a Brexit fantasy', *Guardian*, 31 January 2018.

Landsberg, C. (2011) 'Fractured continentally: undermined abroad: African agency in world affairs', paper presented to the seminar African Agency: Implications for IR Theory, London, 14 September 2011, www.open.ac.uk/socialsciences/bisa-africa/files/africanagency-seminar4-landsberg.pdf [accessed 1 December 2017].

Leboeuf, A. (2003) 'L'engagement britannique en Sierra Leone: du volontarisme externe à l'appropriation', *Afrique contemporaine*, 207, 99–113.

Lunn, J., Miller, V. and Smith, B. (2008) 'British foreign policy since 1997', House of Commons Library Research Paper 08/56, June 2008.

Office for National Statistics (2016) 'The UKs trade and investment relationship with Africa', 23 May 2016, www.ons.gov.uk/economy/nationalaccounts/balanceofpayments/articles/theukstradeandinvestmentrelationshipwithafrica/2016 [accessed 26 February 2018].

Porteous, T. (2005) 'British government policy in Sub-Saharan Africa under New Labour', *International Affairs*, 81:2, 281–97.

Siddique, H. (2014) 'Top 10 non-UK nationalities working for NHS', *Guardian*, 26 June 2014, www.theguardian.com/society/2014/jan/26/nhs-foreign-nationals-immigration-health-service [accessed 1 December 2017].

Sriskandarajah, D., Cooley, L. and Kornblatt, T. (2007) *Britain's Immigrants: An Economics Profile* (London: Institute for Public Policy Research).

Straw, J. (2006) 'Africa: a new agenda', Abuja, 1 March 2006, www.oyibosonline.com/africa-a-new-agenda-foreign-secretary [accessed 1 December 2017].

Styan, D. (2007) 'The security of Africans beyond borders: migration, remittances and London's transnational entrepreneurs', *International Affairs*, 83:6, 1171–91.

UNCTAD (2009) *UNCTAD Handbook of Statistics 2009* (New York: United Nations).

Vines, A. (2011) 'Africa and the United Kingdom: Labour's legacy, May 1997–May 2010', in T. Chafer and G. Cumming (eds), *From Rivalry to Partnership? New Approaches to the Challenges of Africa* (Farnham: Ashgate), 25–39.

Vines, A. (2017) 'What Britain can do for Zimbabwe in the post-Mugabe era', *Prospect*, 23 November 2017, www.prospectmagazine.co.uk/world/what-britain-can-do-for-zimbabwe-in-the-post-mugabe-era [accessed 20 January 2018].

Vines, A. (2018) 'To Brexit and beyond: Africa and the United Kingdom', in D. Nagar and C. Mutasa (eds), *Africa and the World: Bilateral and Multilateral International Diplomacy* (London: Palgrave Macmillan), 119–42.

Williams, P. (2004) 'Britain and Africa after the Cold War: beyond damage limitation?', in I. Taylor and P. Williams (eds), *Africa in International Politics: External Involvement on the Continent* (London: Routledge), 41–60.

Williams, P. D. (2005) 'Blair's Commission for Africa: problems and prospects for UK policy', *Political Quarterly*, 76:4, 529–39.
World Bank (2016) *Migration and Remittances Factbook 2016* (Washington, DC: World Bank).

2

Africa's trade with Brexit Britain: neo-colonialism encounters regionalism?

Mark Langan

The Brexit campaign for the UK to leave the EU was predicated upon a number of policy claims from the leading 'Brexiteer' politicians, notably Liam Fox, Michael Gove and Boris Johnson. One particularly interesting claim was that a Brexit decision to leave the EU would offer a progressive opportunity for improved, 'pro-poor' ties with Commonwealth countries in Africa (Lowe, 2016; Murray-Evans, 2016; Plummer, 2015; UKIP, 2016). According to the Brexiteer discourse, EU trade and aid policies are skewed against the economic and social interests of poorer countries, especially those of Anglophone former British colonies. Brexit and the re-establishment of an independent UK trade policy would therefore offer new scope for assisting Commonwealth allies through enhanced trade and aid ties.

In this vein, Brexiteer politicians articulate(d) and envisage(d) what might accurately be termed the *moral economy* of trade and development ties between Brexit Britain and Commonwealth African countries (see Langan, 2016). Namely, they embedded legitimating norms and ethical claims within an envisaged economic relationship with developing countries in former parts of the British Empire. In this fashion, the Brexiteer campaigners legitimised not only their intentions to enhance economic ties between Britain and Commonwealth nations, but more broadly they also legitimised the Brexit project itself as a progressive contribution to global politics. By delinking Britain from the EU, UK voters apparently would be chastising an uncaring European Commission for its failed 'development' interventions, while at the same time offering hope to poorer people in African former colonies (Express, 2016).

Accordingly, this chapter first explores the moral economy of Brexit Britain's envisaged trade and aid ties with Commonwealth African nations. It explores the narrative themes and claims within the Brexiteer discourse and how this created legitimising images of a renewed Britain doing 'good' on the international stage. Certain historical parallels are drawn here between Brexiteers' imperial romanticism and that espoused in pre-Brexit times, particularly by New Labour politicians. The chapter then explores whether this moral economy of pro-poor relations is likely to be realised in a material sense. That is, whether the realities of Brexit Britain's interventions via trade and aid policies in Africa will deliver the progressive vision promised by politicians such as Boris Johnson. The chapter particularly draws attention to concerns about the tying of UK aid monies to trade deals, as well as the entrenchment of UK corporate involvement in Africa's strategic sectors such as oil and gas. Thirdly, the chapter considers possible African responses to the potential neo-colonial interventions of Brexit Britain. Chiefly, it examines the role of African Regional Economic Communities (RECs) and the African, Caribbean and Pacific (ACP) group of states as potential vehicles for resisting some of the overt machinations of British institutions (namely, the Department for International Trade (DIT) under Liam Fox and the Department for International Development (DFID) formerly under Priti Patel, and now Penny Mordaunt). In so doing the chapter queries whether Brexit trade ties will be 'good' for African countries as per the imperial romanticism of Brexiteer discourse.

The moral economy of Brexit Britain's trade and aid ties with Commonwealth Africa

The term *moral economy* has gained renewed intellectual traction in the study of International Relations following interventions from Andrew Sayer (2000; 2007; 2015; 2016). The concept relates to the fact that *all* economic structures are established and maintained through discursive overture to norms and ethics pertaining to the perceived functions of the economic system in question. Sayer (2000: 79–82) usefully explains that the use of the term 'moral economy' does not denote that we as researchers agree that a system is in fact moral. Rather that we are investigating the way in which certain economic activities are legitimised, rationalised and perpetuated through actors' recourse to strategic moral narratives. Sayer (2007: 262–3) explains that the purpose of a critical political economy should be to deconstruct such 'moral economies' and to juxtapose ethical discourse with the material realities of economic structures for their perceived beneficiaries. In so doing, a critical political economy may challenge the ways in which (oftentimes) dominant economic structures are maintained – and accepted by economic actors – as being legitimate, natural or deserved (Sayer, 2004).

The concept of moral economy is particularly useful when considering Brexit Britain's envisaged trade and aid linkages with African developing countries, particularly those states that belong to the Commonwealth (largely those of the former British Empire). The Brexit campaign was fought on numerous distinct policy fronts, including trade and development issues. Leading Brexiteer campaigners explicitly referred to the re-establishment of an independent UK trade competency as a necessary step forward for both British and African affairs (Express, 2016). Politicians such as Liam Fox and Boris Johnson fiercely condemned what they perceived to be the recalcitrant and regressive behaviour of the European Commission in its own trade dealings with African countries (*ibid.*). In particular, they pointed to the EU tariff schedule that allows unprocessed agricultural goods from Africa into Europe with zero duty; whereas processed goods are often taxed at punitive rates (*ibid.*). This state of affairs, for the leading Brexiteers, indicated that the EU was acting in bad faith in its relationship with African countries. Namely that the EU sought chiefly to protect its own agricultural producers and manufacturing industries from African competition, while at the same time encouraging colonial patterns of raw material extraction (see Monteith, 2017). Brexit Britain on the other hand – given its 'natural' instinct for free trade – would apparently ensure a fairer playing field for business people in African countries, particularly those of the Commonwealth.

This chief element of the 'moral economy' of Brexit Britain's envisaged trade and aid ties with African countries was repeated time and again within the statements of the leading Brexiteers during the referendum campaign of 2016. Importantly, it continues to be firmly stated within the post-campaign period of Brexit implementation. One of the most explicit instances of this narrative, during the campaign itself, was expressed by James Cleverly MP. He explained during a 'Leave' campaign event that EU trade policies punished African producers and that EU aid was used as a means of alleviating Europeans citizens' guilt:

> We can put a sticking plaster over our collective guilt [regarding Africa] through aid payments and charitable giving and I'm not saying we shouldn't do those things, but what we have seen time and time again is the only sustainable and effective way of lifting people out of poverty is buying their stuff, buying the produce that they grow and they develop [through trade].If we don't do that, or more importantly if we don't give them the chance to sell to us, then we are condemning them to prolonged poverty and that's something that I can't subscribe to. (Express, 2016).

Interestingly, this perspective echoes certain concerns in the academic literature on EU–Africa trade and development ties (cf. Hurt, 2016; Langan, 2014; Price and Nunn, 2016; Siles-Brügge, 2014;). Namely, that the EU's Economic Partnership Agreements (EPAs) with sub-regions of the ACP group do not sufficiently cater for the economic needs of the developing country signatories. In particular the EPAs stipulate that ACP countries must liberalise their tariff schedules in relation to goods emanating from EU member states. The EU, meanwhile, simply promises to maintain its current tariff schedule, which discriminates against value-added goods from Africa such as processed cocoa (as opposed to the raw cocoa beans). In short, there does appear to be considerable evidence to support the central thrust of this Brexiteer claim – that EU trade policy is regressive in character and damaging to Africa's long-term economic development.

This narrative thread of a wider Brexit discourse on Commonwealth Africa continues in the post-referendum phase, as recently underscored by interventions from Daniel Hannan MEP in July 2017. This high-profile Eurosceptic Conservative politician stated that the EU treats Africa 'as an economic colony', further explaining that:

> Brussels applies tariffs to tomato sauce, but not to tomatoes; to chocolate, but not to cocoa beans … Africa, in other words, is expressly discouraged from developing secondary industries that would add value to its commodities … [whereas the lifting of tariffs by the UK would lead to] cheaper food [which …] would boost our entire economy, freeing up spending power … We'd be promoting social justice at home and development abroad at no cost. (Millar, 2017)

This narrative is sustained within the statements of UK government ministers themselves – notably of Liam Fox and of Boris Johnson in their roles as International Trade Minister and (former) Foreign Secretary. Dr Fox has continued to laud the benefits of free trade for developing countries. In a post-speech discussion at the American Enterprise Institute, he laid down a challenge to apparent left-wing opposition to free trade policies:

> And I would issue a challenge to them, which is if you don't like free trade, which they say they don't, which countries in the world would you like to remain poor? Which countries in the world would you like not to have access to the global markets? Because that is, in effect, what you are talking about. If you're talking about that we raise protectionist barriers, that we refuse to consider further global trade liberalizations, what are the impacts going to be on developing countries? And what will happen to the stability in those countries that might come back to bite us in terms of security? (American Enterprise Institute, 2017: 15)

Boris Johnson, meanwhile, while Foreign Secretary, concluded a visit to Ghana in which he promised that West Africa would benefit from new free trade arrangements with Britain. Once more, according to the Brexit discourse, the decision to leave the UK will open new progressive opportunities for poverty eradication via trade (Express, 2016).

Interestingly, Murray-Evans (2016) identifies another distinct strand within the Brexiteer trade discourse on Africa. Namely, that the UK is perceived to have 'betrayed' or 'abandoned' Commonwealth Africa (and India) upon its original decision to join the European Economic Community (EEC) in the 1970s. Brexiteer campaigners alluded to the fact that Britain had chosen to join the EEC family at the expense of its obligations to its former colonies in the Commonwealth community. Murray-Evans (*ibid.*) convincingly points to the fact, however, that the majority of Commonwealth nations were integrated into a preferential trade relationship between the EEC (including newly joined Britain) under the ACP–EEC Lomé Conventions. The discourse, or 'myth' of a British Europhile betrayal of the Commonwealth is therefore deemed to be highly dubious.

Moreover, a British – or perhaps more properly, English – imperial romanticism for the Commonwealth (as embodied in the narrative of Europhile betrayal in the 1970s) is now cemented in the post-referendum phase through Brexiteer discourse regarding a paternalistic duty of care towards former colonies. Not only does this relate to the narrative of free trade and open markets *per se*, but it also embraces a wider narrative of Britain's paternalistic duty to guide both social and economic development in Africa. Tobias Ellwood, while Under Secretary of State at the Foreign and Commonwealth Office (FCO) was a notable proponent of such narrative themes. In a speech in 2017, he outlined the need for the UK to provide a paternal eye over African economic development, given the continent's apparently endemic failings:

> we have to be frank and we have to be honest. At the moment, productivity in Africa is poor – the economic output of one billion people in Sub-Saharan Africa is lower than that of 82 million people in Germany. For all the reasons I mentioned earlier, the UK is uniquely placed to help. We are working to boost productive investment in Africa, including by UK firms. (Chatham House, 2017: 4)

Interestingly, however, a section of Whitehall officialdom baulks at imperial romanticism and a paternalistic UK interest in economic development in former colonies. British media reports that these officials have despairingly labelled such Brexiteer interest as 'Empire 2.0' (Farand, 2017). It should be stated, however, that paternalistic discourse – often expressed as part of an imperial romanticism

– has a much longer discursive lineage. Recent New Labour Governments, for instance, regularly invoked a sense of British paternalistic care towards former colonies in Africa. Prime Minister Tony Blair's notorious reference to Africa as a 'scar on the conscience of the world', and then Chancellor Gordon Brown's political overtures to the Jubilee 2000 campaign, stand as immediate examples of a paternalistic instinct within British–Africa ties that pre-dates current Brexit discourse (BBC News, 2000; McGreal, 2002). Such historical parallels are important as context when assessing the contemporary discursive stance of Brexiteer politicians. It should also be said that the moniker 'Empire 2.0' appears apt when the likely material realities of Brexit trade and development cooperation with Africa are considered in closer detail.

Empire 2.0: the realities of the 'moral economy' of Africa–UK trade after Brexit

Brexit discourse continues to present UK trade policy as a likely spur for African development. Influential voices such as Daniel Hannan MEP express sympathy with the need to open up UK markets to African agricultural produce, while also removing UK tariffs that hinder African diversification into value addition via processing and manufacturing (Millar, 2017). In terms of concrete policy options available to UK decision-makers that might achieve such aims, there has been open discussion among certain UK civil society groups about the prospect of extending Duty Free and Quota Free access to least developed countries on a unilateral basis.[1]

The UK, in this scenario, would offer equivalent market access to African countries as promised by the EU under its Everything But Arms (EBA) scheme (Razzaque and Vickers, 2016: 61). Poorer countries, through dint of a World Trade Organization (WTO) exemption, would be allowed to access British markets on a low-tariff basis without having to liberalise in return. This would, in theory, provide a spur to value addition in Commonwealth African states, as promised by Brexit campaigners – by enabling them sufficient policy space to protect their nascent industry via protectionist tariffs against UK competition. At the same time, due to UK liberalisation, African agriculturalists could enjoy access to UK supermarkets and the consumer base therein (*ibid.*: 61).

In practice, however, what might be deemed the 'Brexit–EBA' scenario appears unlikely to offer sustainable grounds for pro-poor growth in Commonwealth countries, or Africa more broadly. This style of unilateral trade regime would remain vulnerable to future WTO challenges. Meanwhile, it would only be open to least-developed African countries. Those that are middle-income states – or that later 'graduated' to middle-income status – would see their preferential market access revoked. The 'Brexit–EBA' scenario, much like the EU's EBA scheme itself, would also not include processes for removing non-tariff barriers to Africa–UK trade (Deb, 2007). Strict phytosanitary requirements would notably remain in force, effectively hampering African agricultural and horticultural producers who are often unable to fulfil costly plant hygiene protocols (Nimenya et al., 2009). In addition, the political will for such a scenario among Brexiteer political elites (as discussed further below) remains somewhat in doubt. Similarly, an adjacent proposal for the UK to simply offer non-discriminatory access to all developing countries (and to other third parties such as China) via the Generalised System of Preferences (GSP) would also seem a flawed option in terms of achieving the moral goals embraced within Brexiteer discourse. The Centre for Global Development (2016: 10), for example, states that it would be possible for the UK to

> replace EU Economic Partnership Agreements with simple nondiscriminatory trade preferences for countries ineligible for Everything But Arms ... the UK could seize the opportunity to offer GSP preferences (beyond LDCs) that are genuinely nondiscriminatory and generalized in application. Starting with a clean slate, the UK could offer a unified regime marked by simplicity, openness, and nondiscrimination.

Strikingly, however, the Ramphal Institute (2017), linked to the ACP Secretariat, has condemned such a policy option on the basis that it would whittle away the current preferences that African countries enjoy. Namely, that if the UK were to open its markets to all third parties on the same low-tariff basis, then the current preference margin that African countries enjoy (e.g. in comparison to flower producers in Israel or Vietnam) would be lost. African businesses would find it harder, not easier, to prosper since the goods they once sold to UK consumers would likely be displaced with cheaper products emanating from industrialised middle-income states such as China, Vietnam, Israel and Brazil.

What does seem likely, however, is that the UK will simply replicate an existing pattern of EU–Africa ties predicated upon neo-colonial trade and aid linkages. Namely, that the UK will seek to maintain colonial patterns of trade in which Africa sells raw materials and purchases value-added goods from the metropole. Moreover, that the UK will choose to lubricate such asymmetric trade links through the strategic use of aid monies to subvert policymakers in African countries themselves. This situation is oftentimes termed 'neo-colonialism' in the sense that the empirical sovereignty of African states is wholly undermined, and perverted, through the aid machinations of former colonial powers. Kwame

Nkrumah, the first President of an independent Ghana, explained that 'The essence of neo-colonialism is that the state which is subject to it is, in theory, independent and has all the outward trappings of international sovereignty. In reality its economic system and thus its political policy is directed by outside' (Nkrumah, 1965: ix).

In a more contemporary setting, a certain number of scholars including Sirisena (2001), Ndlovu-Gatsheni (2013), Quist-Adade and Dodoo (2015) and Fawole (2018) have convincingly rearticulated Nkrumah's concept of neo-colonialism and have called for its application to contemporary 'development' controversies. Sirisena, for instance, memorably remarks that: 'There is hunger and poverty in the third world because the affluent nations exploit their resources. They exploited the third world some time back under colonialism. Now they exploit them under neocolonialism called market economy and globalization' (Sirisena, 2001: preface). Neo-colonialism, as articulated by Nkrumah, is thereby viewed as a necessary critical concept for analysing contemporary inequalities within North–South relations.

In this vein – and despite the 'pro-poor' discourse of Brexiteer campaigners – there are several grounds upon which to contest their moral economy and to foresee the continuation of a neo-colonial pattern of UK–Africa trade and aid relations. Notably, narratives of benevolent Brexit free trade deals are brought into critical light by the way in which the recent DFID Minister, Priti Patel, alluded to the tying of aid to trade agreements. Patel on several occasions stated that UK aid monies should be used as a leveraging device for the successful conclusion of Brexit trade ties in developing country contexts. A Whitehall associate of Patel remarked that:

> Britain's international aid commitments mean it gets fantastic access to foreign leaders all round the world … We can leverage existing relationships to strike trade deals. The Department for International Development (Dfid) can be used to improve Britain's standing in the world. It will be a completely fresh way of looking at Britain's aid budget. (Swinford and Riley-Smith, 2016)

The use of aid as leverage for trade agreements raises concerns about neo-colonialism. Namely that the trade agreements that Britain pursues will not be beneficial to former colonies, or welcome in African state capitals (hence the need for aid as a 'sweetener'). Instead, the prospect appears likely that the UK will simply mirror the EU's own inequitable EPAs. This is particularly the case since British policy actors (such as Peter Mandelson as EU Trade Commissioner) have played a vital role in the EPAs' content and negotiation. Moreover, in Southern Africa, the UK Chancellor, Philip Hammond and the

UK High Commissioner have indicated to African counterparts that this 'Brexit EPA' option will be the UK's preference:

> Paralleling the UK's trade arrangements with the EU, she [British High Commissioner Judith McGregor] said both sides hoped to effectively transpose the EPA trade arrangements into a bilateral trade deal between the UK and the Southern African countries, also with an agreement to revisit and renegotiate some areas in the future. Presumably, the same will happen with the EU's EPAs with other African regions, though these are less advanced. (Fabricius, 2017)

This 'Brexit EPA' scenario would offer low-tariff access for African producers into British markets on the strict condition that African countries themselves liberalise tariff schedules *vis-à-vis* products emanating from the UK. This would continue a scenario of 'ladder-kicking' whereby African countries remain unable to meaningfully diversify away from colonial patterns of exchange by dint of foreign competition collapsing infant industries (see Chang, 2003).

Brexiteer ministers' apparent focus upon the combination of trade and aid also leaves the distinct impression that what critics in Whitehall daub 'Empire 2.0' will be based upon a neo-colonial attempt to subvert empirical state sovereignty in Africa. Namely, that the ability of African leaders to decide policy, based upon the economic interests of their own business sector, will be undermined by the strategic lure of UK aid monies. Indeed, Nkrumah warned that aid money in these scenarios would be no more than a 'revolving credit, paid by the neo-colonial master, passing through the neo-colonial state and returning to the neo-colonial master in the form of increased profits' (1965: xv). Aid in this sense was not a benevolent gesture or gift. Instead, it was a device for profit-making on behalf of former colonial powers, such as Great Britain and France, perpetuating colonial patterns of production and exchange. The discourse of free trade providing opportunities for job creation and economic prosperity in Africa (qua Liam Fox and Daniel Hannan) remains somewhat dubious should these 'Brexit EPAs' be pursued.

Furthermore, the likelihood of the UK merely replicating the 'reciprocal' free trade framework of the EPAs is cemented by the manner in which the DIT is being influenced by UK business interests (in addition to the aforementioned DFID). In March 2017, for example, the Commonwealth Enterprise and Investment Council – supported by UK mining interests such as Gem Diamonds and manufacturers such as JCB – organised meetings between Liam Fox and African trade counterparts (Chapman, 2017). Such corporate interests, especially manufacturers such as JCB and Rolls Royce, played an important role in promoting reciprocal trade via the EU's EPAs. Tariff liberalisation in African countries is an important goal for such entities, ensuring that they have open markets in which to sell their manufactures. It seems highly unlikely, therefore, that such corporate interests would countenance UK trade arrangements that grant African countries a reprieve from liberalisation commitments. In short, 'Brexit EPAs' seem the most likely scenario since they will secure UK corporations' offensive trade interest in maintaining lucrative markets for their wares. In terms of UK defensive trade interests in agriculture, meanwhile, it does seem unlikely that a Brexit Government led by the Conservative Party would countenance trade agreements that would negatively impact their rural constituencies. This is compounded by the fact that the UK will lose its influence vis-à-vis the reform of the Common Agricultural Policy. If EU member states continue to subsidise their agricultural producers to the detriment of African competition it seems even less likely that the UK should unilaterally depart from such a protectionist mode (irrespective of the free trade narratives of those such as Hannan).

The influential role of UK corporations such as JCB, Rolls Royce and various mining conglomerates also points to the likely entrenchment of neo-colonial forms of Foreign Direct Investment. Companies such as Anglo-Irish firm Tullow Oil have already had their economic interests entrenched in African former colonies via useful interventions from DFID (Langan, 2017: 40). In Ghana for instance, DFID aid monies were supplied to non-governmental bodies for 'consultancy services' regarding the controversial Oil Exploration and Production (E&P) Bill. The Oxford Policy Management group and its roll-out of the DFID-funded Ghana Oil and Gas for Inclusive Growth programme played a key role in securing support from local Ghanaian civil society groups for the E&P Bill. This is despite the fact that it includes a clause which allows the Ghanaian Energy Minister to bypass competitive tendering practices, much to the anger of critical voices within Ghana's Parliament (Lungu, 2016). A continued marriage between UK aid monies under DFID on the one hand, and the UK's offensive trade interests on the other, bodes ill for genuine 'development' opportunities within Africa–UK ties in the Brexit era. Instead, it promises to extend neo-colonial intervention within African (and Commonwealth) countries in the post-Brexit setting.

Perhaps most worrying is that this trade outlook (and the use of aid as leverage) is underpinned by an overarching Brexiteer 'moral economy' in which the UK is seen as the natural saviour of African countries that remain incapable of genuine self-governance. With particular reference to former British colonies within the Commonwealth, there remains a distinct Brexiteer discourse which sees such African countries as little more than pitiable failed states. Boris Johnson, for example, has regularly expressed an imperial romanticism in which the perceived failings of the post-colonial state in Africa are deemed largely to stem from a *lack* of British involvement, as opposed to the legacy of British colonialism. Writing during the Blair premiership, Johnson (2016 [2002]) remarked that:

> we must hope, for the sake of candour and common sense, that he [Blair] does not blame Britain, or colonialism, or the white man [for Africa's current problems]. The continent may be a blot, but it is not a blot upon our conscience. The problem is not that we were once in charge, but that we are not in charge any more ... The best fate for Africa would be if the old colonial powers, or their citizens, scrambled once again in her direction; on the understanding that this time they will not be asked to feel guilty.

This neo-colonial outlook – based upon British political elites' paternalism towards Africa – appears to permeate the current stance of the chief Brexiteers as they seek to implement an independent UK trade policy. Liam Fox (2016), for example, while justifying the need for more 'globalisation' (understood as free trade and liberalisation) has stated that:

> The problem, however, is that while many [African] countries have sufficiently deep financial sectors and sufficiently improved educational systems, many of the institutions and the level of governance still fall below what is required for the poor to benefit fully ... Continued focus on good governance, mediated and encouraged by international aid and assistance programmes, combined with increasing attempts to see a more open and liberal trading environment, are our best hope to see grotesque levels of poverty consigned to history.

Once more the post-colonial state in Africa is viewed as a hopeless entity, mired in corruption and poverty. The UK, meanwhile, is presented as the natural partner for the implementation of a benevolent paternalism. It should be noted, however, that this imperial romanticism is not unique to the Brexiteer ministers themselves. Abrahamsen (2005), in a convincing critique of the Blair Government, notes that British outlooks in that period remained hampered by a post-imperial romanticism (married to a real politik to preserve UK economic and security interests). The Brexiteers' outlook and their 'moral economy' of Africa–UK trade in the post-referendum phase sits in continuity with earlier phases of British foreign and development policies (albeit the imperial romanticism is now taken to new levels amid a push for the so-called 'Empire 2.0'). It is important to stress, however, that African actors are not passive recipients of UK policy preferences, nor of EU policy preferences. It is imperative, therefore, to consider potential avenues for progressive African responses to the UK's instinct for a neo-colonial pattern of trade and aid ties in the post-Brexit period.

UK neo-colonialism encounters African regionalism: whither Brexit EPAs?

African countries, such as those of Southern Africa promised an equivalent UK deal to the current EU EPAs, do not necessarily sit as passive recipients of UK policy preferences. On the contrary, Brexit provides an ideal circumstance in which African former colonies might usefully unite to set the terms of trade with the UK. The question remains, therefore, which avenues would be best pursued to cement African unity in the context of negotiations with the UK former metropole. As witnessed in the case of UK talks with Southern African leaders, there appears to be an immediate preference for (or default to) African RECs such as the Southern African Development Community (SADC). This follows on from the circumstance in which African states currently find themselves vis-à-vis the EU. Namely, the European Commission has sought to conclude EPAs with sub-regions within Africa rather than with the ACP bloc as a whole. Rather than negotiate collectively with the seventy-nine ACP countries, the European Commission thus seeks to conclude the EPAs with sub-regional economic entities such as the Economic Community of West African States and SADC.

It is important to reflect here that there are historical concerns about the pursuit of (sub)regional strategies where African states negotiate as RECs with former colonial powers in Europe. Nkrumah himself warned that regionalism – as opposed to African unity on a pan-continental basis – would leave African nations open to neo-colonial interventions. Nkrumah warned that the 'Balkanisation' of the African continent into its regional entities (Southern Africa, Eastern Africa and so forth) would diminish, not enhance, possibilities for the transformation of neo-colonial patterns of trade and exchange (Langan, 2017: 29). This in fact became the basis of schism between African leaders in the 1960s. The so-called Monrovia Group (committed to a confederal model of African unity) challenged Nkrumah's Casablanca Group (committed to a federal model of African unity) in the immediate years of independence. With the creation of the Organisation for African Unity, as opposed to the Union of African States, which Nkrumah had espoused, the Monrovia Group succeeded in its ambitions to prevent immediate African unification under a federal agency. Adjacent to this decision, RECs (such as the East African Community championed by Julius Nyerere) came to the fore – to the detriment of pan-African institutions (*ibid.*: 29).

In the current context of negotiations with Brexit Britain, therefore, it appears necessary for African leaders to revisit this dilemma of whether to pursue a truly collective front, or to default to the RECs as a means of deciding trade options with the UK. Considering the current state of negotiations with the EU EPAs and the apparent acquiescence of African countries to detrimental tariff dismantling, it would appear that the (sub)regional option does not offer a convincing means of challenging free trade orthodoxies. On the other hand, the ACP group's collective negotiation of the first Lomé Convention in 1975 – hailed by Nyerere as a 'trade union of the poor' – did achieve significant concessions from European negotiators (Whiteman, 2012: 35). In particular, the collective efforts – and unity – of the ACP group in the mid-1970s achieved a non-reciprocal trade regime whereby the EEC recognised the sovereign right of African signatories to protect their nascent industries via high tariff schedules. In addition, the ACP group won the Stabex and Sysmin concessions aimed at stabilising volatile commodity prices in key sectors such as cocoa and minerals (Brown, 2000: 372–4).

It is highly instructive, therefore, that the Ramphal Institute (2017) – linked with the ACP Secretariat – has recently published a comprehensive survey of UK Brexit trade options in the aftermath of the 2016 referendum. The ACP Secretariat itself has made clear its willingness to provide a collective forum for the negotiation of the post-Brexit arrangements with London. In so doing, it seeks to challenge the notion that the ACP grouping is an artificial creation associated with the EEC/EU alone. Instead, the ACP Secretariat envisages the group maintaining its relevance as African states seek to secure market access to UK consumers, while not reducing their own policy space to achieve diversification. Interestingly the report identifies Brexit as a 'threat' to African economic interests in stark juxtaposition to the 'opportunity' presented within the moral economy of Brexiteer narratives:

> The threats that Brexit can pose to ACP economic interests are real and should not be underestimated or ignored. A united Group that pursues a well-informed, comprehensive and effective strategy, will enhance the prospect of achieving its shared objectives and prospering in the post-Brexit era. (Ramphal Institute, 2017: 7)

Moreover, the report states that the ACP group – as opposed to any other body (such as the Commonwealth) – is best placed to act in the interests of all African countries:

> As a group, the ACP is in a much better bargaining position than any of its members or regions, given the total value of UK exports to the countries that are also major suppliers of many important mineral products and commodities and host to substantial UK investment. In addition, such a large group of countries has considerable potential international political authority and influence. It needs to show that its role and significance is more than just an economic cooperation vehicle with the EU but a

valuable and credible international political partner and ally on issues of mutual interest. (*Ibid.*: 13)

In contradistinction to the Brexiteer focus on the Anglophone Commonwealth, the report highlights the need for all African countries to work together regardless of language or Commonwealth status.

This would appear an important point to stress. Namely, that Anglophone African countries would do well to avoid any temptations to rely upon their Commonwealth status to initiate a preferential arrangement compared with Francophone/non-Commonwealth states. This division of Africa into Anglophone and Francophone constituencies would bode ill, both in terms of the likely outcome of trade negotiations with the UK, and in terms of long-term African unity within the auspices of either the ACP bloc or the African Union (AU) itself. Indeed, it would seem important in the circumstance to utilise the ACP bloc as an economic negotiating entity, given its experience of EU African trade policies, while at the same time building greater political cohesion within the corridors of the AU. The combination of economic unity within the ACP bloc, and political unity within the AU, would do well to guard African states against the neo-colonial impulses of Brexiteer government elites in London. Greater resilience within the ACP/AU would also do much to lessen the potential strategic leverage of UK aid monies. Coordination, and self-reliance, within pan-African bodies would mitigate the need for UK aid – while (if necessary) helping to diversify aid revenues beyond the 'traditional' former colonial powers.[2]

In any scenario – whether individual African states negotiate unilateral agreements with Britain; whether RECs play a role similar to their part within the EU EPAs; or whether the ACP bloc rediscovers its collective clout – it remains vital for African elites to manipulate and/or contest Brexiteer discourse. UK decision-makers have publicly promised to pay heed to poverty reduction and development in (Commonwealth) Africa. As discussed, this became an essential plank of justifying Brexit as a whole. The decision to leave the EU ostensibly does not constitute a return to 'Little England' but instead allows opportunities for 'Global Britain' to more readily assist its allies (according to Brexiteer narratives). In this context, it would appear necessary for African elites to achieve a degree of rhetorical entrapment. Namely, to utilise and to repurpose Brexiteer narratives in a way that maximises policy concessions from Her Majesty's Government in London. African leaders, fluent in the Brexit discourse, could aptly embarrass, cajole and prod British negotiators to offer trade scenarios that truly meet the needs of African agriculturalists and manufacturing sectors. Moreover, they could challenge the tying of aid to trade negotiations as an unfriendly and neo-colonial incursion upon their own sovereignty – a paradox given that Brexit has aimed to restore UK Westphalian independence. In short, African leaders – and civil society groups – should mobilise to challenge the UK as it seeks a new trade and aid relationship; and they should certainly give scant credence to the 'pro-poor' development promises of Brexit ministers such as Liam Fox and formerly Boris Johnson. Only by acting in concert, and by manipulating Brexit discourse, can African elites secure a post-Brexit arrangement that comes close to providing a genuine basis for poverty reduction and in breaking the neo-colonial pattern of trade and aid relations.

Conclusions

The UK in the post-referendum phase has committed itself to assisting African (Commonwealth) nations to achieve a fairer trading scenario than heretofore experienced under EU–ACP relations. A central pillar of the Brexit campaign and its discourse was that a decision to leave the EU would open up new opportunities for the UK to help its allies in the former colonies. Moreover, a paternalistic duty of care was expressed in relation to African developing countries as a whole. Given the apparent predatory behaviour of the European Commission in its pursuit of EPAs, Brexiteer campaigners (and now UK government ministers) promise that the UK will not simply replicate disadvantageous patterns of trade and commerce. Instead, 'Global Britain' will put the needs of poorer countries to the fore.

Unfortunately, however, the realities of an independent UK trade policy appear to depart very little from the EPAs currently pursued by the EU in its African relations. As evidenced in terms of recent UK discussions with Southern African countries, the UK's preferred scenario is to achieve 'Brexit EPAs' which merely replicate the reciprocal free trade terms which EU Trade Commissioners (such as Peter Mandelson) have pursued since 2000. Rather than offer an opportunity for non-reciprocal trade arrangements that would secure the right of African states to protect their infant industry, the Brexit trade deals will most likely push UK offensive trade interests to the fore. This is amplified by the declared intention of DFID to use aid as a leveraging device for the conclusion of trade deals conducive to UK commercial interests. Moreover, it is cemented by the influence of UK corporate entities, which have actively sought to harness trade ties between African countries and DIT in a manner which secures their own long-term profitability. A radical or progressive break from the 'neo-colonial' pattern of EU–Africa relations is implausible. Instead the UK – guided by a Brexiteer moral economy infused with imperial romanticism – appears set to lock-in African countries into (neo)colonial forms of trade and production (with little scope for diversification and value addition amidst the import flooding of cheap British goods).

In this circumstance, it appears vital that African countries collectively consider the best forum for contending with the UK's economic interest in maintaining Africa as a source of cheap raw materials and as a proverbial 'dumping ground' for British produce. Already the ACP Secretariat – via the Ramphal Institute – has signalled its willingness to act as a collective mechanism for safeguarding African interests from the 'threat' that Brexit constitutes. Moreover, the ACP bloc warns of the dangers of other bodies (such as the Commonwealth) playing this role and insists that the ACP grouping is relevant beyond EEC/EU affairs. Accordingly, African elites – and civil society groups – would do well to consider the ACP Secretariat's proposed role. Further disintegration of African unity – either on a unilateral country basis or within the RECs – would bode ill for the establishment of progressive trade ties with Brexit Britain. On the other hand, the ACP 'trade union of the poor' (as Nyerere termed the body) might be able to achieve a better arrangement than the EU EPAs. This would be predicated upon the ACP group's ability to strategically manipulate London's pro-poor Brexit discourse and to embarrass UK elites into a position favourable to the controversial EPAs. Global Britain – in this circumstance – could be usefully neutered by the ACP group in terms of UK elites' attempts to entrench neo-colonial forms of trade and aid within Africa.

Notes

1. Indeed, a number of civil society bodies have been vocal in the need to align the UK's trade and development policies to humanitarian norms in a post-Brexit setting. A series of detailed reports by Bond (2017) have notably addressed UK–Africa ties and have set out the challenges facing British charities in achieving development aims in the context of Brexit. The Fairtrade Foundation (2017), meanwhile, has allied with like-minded organisations such as Oxfam, Action Aid, the Trade Justice Movement, CAFOD, Tear Fund, Global Citizen and Traidcraft to campaign for equitable terms within UK–Africa trade deals.
2. It should be noted that there are substantial institutional deficiencies with the AU as it currently stands. In recognition of this, President Kagame (2017) of Rwanda recently issued a detailed report on proposed institutional reforms of the organisation, which include a clearer division of labour between the AU and the RECs. The urgency of such reforms is amplified by the need for effective political coordination among African states in post-Brexit relations.

References

Abrahamsen, R. (2005) 'Blair's Africa: the politics of securitisation and fear', *Alternatives: Global, Local, Political*, 30:1, 55–80.

American Enterprise Institute (2017) 'The future of UK trade policy: remarks from the Right Honorable Liam Fox MP, UK Secretary of State for International Trade', www.aei.org/wp-content/uploads/2017/07/170724-AEI-Liam-Fox-Future-of-UK-Trade-Policy.pdf [accessed 30 August 2017].

BBC News (2000) 'Brown urges rich to drop debt', *BBC News*, 2 December 2000, http://news.bbc.co.uk/1/hi/uk/1050938.stm [accessed 6 November 2017].

Bond (2017) *What Does Leaving the EU Mean for Development Policy?*, 21 July 2017, www.bond.org.uk/news/2017/07/what-does-leaving-the-eu-mean-for-development-policy [accessed 10 November 2017].

Brown, W. (2000) 'Restructuring North–South relations: ACP–EU development cooperation in a liberal international order', *Review of African Political Economy*, 27:85, 367–83.

Centre for Global Development (2016) *After Brexit: New Opportunities for Global Good in the National Interest* (London: Centre for Global Development).

Chang, H.-J. (2003) 'Kicking away the ladder: infant industry promotion in historical perspective', *Oxford Development Studies*, 31:1, 21–32.

Chapman, B. (2017) 'Liam Fox's "Empire 2.0" meeting is backed by corporate interests and will "fleece" Africa say campaigners', *Independent*, 8 March 2017, www.independent.co.uk/news/business/news/liam-fox-empire-trade-meeting-africa-corporate-interests-claims-a7619326.html [accessed 10 November 2017].

Chatham House (2017) *The UK and Africa in the International System: Priorities and Engagement Post-Brexit – Tobias Ellwood MP Parliamentary Under Secretary of State for the UK Foreign and Commonwealth Office and Minister for the Middle East and Africa*, 20 April 2017 (London: Chatham House).

Deb, U. K. (2007) 'Non-tariff barriers in agricultural trade: issues and implications for least developed countries', *ARTNeT Policy Brief*, No. 12, May 2007 (Dakar: ARTNet).

Express (2016) 'EU trade policies are hurting African farmers, says Tory MP', *Express*, 28 April 2016, www.express.co.uk/news/politics/665341/EU-trade-policies-african-farm-tory-james-cleverly-mp [accessed 30 August 2017].

Fabricius, P. (2017) 'Brexit Europe, not Brexit Africa', ISS Today, 9 March 2017, https://issafrica.org/iss-today/brexit-europe-not-brexit-africa [accessed 10 November 2017].

Fairtrade Foundation (2017) *Brexit: Time to Make Trade Fair*, www.fairtrade.org.uk/en/get-involved/current-campaigns/brexit [accessed 10 November 2017].

Farand, C. (2017) 'UK government post-Brexit plans to create Africa free-trade zone are being internally branded "Empire 2.0"', *Independent*, 6 March 2017, www.independent.co.uk/news/uk/home-news/uk-government-africa-free-trade-zone-post-brexit-empire-2-liam-fox-international-commonwealth-a7613526.html [accessed 10 November 2017].

Fawole, W. A. (2018) *The Illusion of the Post-Colonial State: Governance and Security Challenges in Africa* (Lanham, MD: Lexington Books).

Fox, L. (2016) 'Don't blame globalisation for poverty', *Guardian*, 30 September 2016, www.theguardian.com/commentisfree/2016/sep/30/globalisation-poverty-corruption-free-trade-liam-fox [accessed 10 November 2017].

Hurt, S. R. (2016) 'The EU's Economic Partnership Agreements with Africa: "decent work" and the challenge of trade union solidarity', *Third World Thematics*, 1:4, 547–62.

Johnson, B. (2016 [2002]) 'Africa is a mess, but we can't blame colonialism', *The Spectator*, 2 February 2002, https://blogs.spectator.co.uk/2016/07/boris-archive-africa-mess-cant-blame-colonialism/ [accessed 10 November 2017].

Kagame, P. (2017) *The Imperative to Strengthen Our Union: Report on the Recommendations for the Institutional Reform of the African Union* (Kigali: Office of the President of Rwanda).

Langan, M. (2014) 'Decent work and indecent trade agendas: the European Union and ACP countries', *Contemporary Politics*, 20:1, 23–35.

Langan, M. (2016) *The Moral Economy of EU–Africa Association* (London: Routledge).

Langan, M. (2017) *Neo-colonialism and the Poverty of Development in Africa* (London: Palgrave).

Lowe, J. (2016) 'Commonwealth Day: why does it matter to the UK's Brexit camp?', *Newsweek*, 14 March 2016, www.newsweek.com/commonwealth-day-brexit-ukip-eu-436481 [accessed 30 August 2017].

Lungu, N. (2016) 'This Mahama-Dagabu-Buah 2016 E&P bill is a vulture bill for oil companies', *The Voiceless*, 4 July 2016, http://thevoicelessonline.com/6388–2/ [accessed 10 November 2017].

McGreal, C. (2002) 'Blair confronts "scar on world's conscience"', *Guardian*, 7 February 2002, www.theguardian.com/world/2002/feb/07/politics.development [accessed 6 November 2017].

Millar, J. (2017) 'Brexit's Africa boost: UK will benefit from creative new trade deals, says Daniel Hannan', *Express*, 16 July 2017, www.express.co.uk/news/uk/829203/brexit-trade-africa-daniel-hannan-eu-common-agricultural-policy [accessed 30 August 2017].

Monteith, B. (2017) 'Trade the immoral customs union for fruitful deals that benefit the developing world', *City A.M.*, 27 July 2017, www.cityam.com/269211/trade-immoral-customs-union-fruitful-deals-benefit [accessed 30 August 2017].

Murray-Evans, P. (2016) 'Myths of Commonwealth betrayal: UK–Africa trade before and after Brexit', *The Round Table: The Commonwealth Journal of International Affairs*, 105:5, 489–98.

Ndlovu-Gatsheni, S. J. (2013) *Empire, Global Coloniality and African Subjectivity* (Oxford: Berghahn).

Nimenya, N., de Frahan, B. and Ndimira, P.-F. (2009) 'A tariff equivalent of non-tariff barriers on European horticultural and fish imports from African countries', http://iatrc.umn.edu/wp-content/uploads/2009Dec-Nimenya.pdf [accessed 23 February 2018].

Nkrumah, K. (1965) *Neo-colonialism: The Last Stage of Imperialism* (London: Panaf).

Plummer, J. (2015) 'Commonwealth dream looms large in Brexit campaign', *BBC News*, 26 November 2015, www.bbc.co.uk/news/business-34855940 [accessed 30 August 2017].

Price, S. and Nunn, A. (2016) 'Managing neo-liberalisation through the Sustainable Development Agenda: the EU–ACP trade relationship', *Third World Thematics*, 1:4, 454–69.

Quist-Adade, C. and Dodoo, V. (eds) (2015), *Africa's Many Divides and Africa's Future: Pursuing Nkrumah's Vision of Pan-Africanism in an Era of Globalization* (Newcastle: Cambridge Scholars).

Ramphal Institute (2017) *After Brexit: Securing ACP Economic Interests* (London: Ramphal Institute).

Razzaque, M. and Vickers, B. (2016) 'Post-Brexit UK trade policy for international development: issues and ways forward', in M. Mendez-Parra, D. Willem te Velde and L. A. Winters (eds), *The Impact of the UK's Post-Brexit Trade Policy on Development: An Essay Series* (Brighton: UK Trade Policy Observatory).

Sayer, A. (2000) 'Moral economy and political economy', *Studies in Political Economy*, 61, 79–103.

Sayer, A. (2004) 'Moral economy', University of Lancaster, June 2004, www.lancaster.ac.uk/fass/resources/sociology-online-papers/papers/sayer-moral-economy.pdf [accessed 4 January 2019].

Sayer, A. (2007) 'Moral economy as critique', *New Political Economy*, 12:2, 261–70.

Sayer, A. (2015) 'Time for moral economy', *Geoforum*, 65, 291–3.

Sayer, A. (2016) 'Moral economy, unearned income and legalized corruption', in D. Whyte and J. Wiegratz (eds), *Neoliberalism and the Moral Economy of Fraud* (London: Routledge), 44–56.

Siles-Brügge, G. (2014) 'EU trade and development policy beyond the ACP: subordinating developmental to commercial imperatives in the reform of GSP', *Contemporary Politics*, 20:1, 49–62.

Sirisena, M. (2001) *World Bank and Neocolonialism: A Socio-economic, Philosophical and Political Analysis* (Colombo, Sri Lanka: Stamford Lake Publication).

Swinford, S. and Riley-Smith, B. (2016) 'Britain to "leverage" £11bn of foreign aid to build new trade deals after Brexit', *Telegraph*, 30 July 2016, www.telegraph.co.uk/news/2016/07/30/britain-to-leverage-11bn-of-foreign-aid-to-build-new-trade-deals/ [accessed 10 November 2017].

UKIP (2016) 'Britain can trade around the world post-Brexit', 1 May 2016, www.ukip.org/britain_can_trade_around_the_world_post_brexit [accessed 30 August 2017].

Whiteman, K. (2012) 'The rise and fall of Eurafrique: from the Berlin conference of 1884–1885 to the Tripoli EU–Africa summit of 2010', in A. Adebajo and K. Whiteman (eds), *From Eurafrique to Afro-Europa* (London: Hurst and Company).

3
The UK and Africa relations: construction of the African Union's peace and security structures

Kasaija Phillip Apuuli

This chapter discusses the role of the UK in supporting African Union (AU) peace and security structures, particularly the AU's Peace and Security Architecture (APSA), since 2010. The 1997–2010 Labour Government, unlike its immediate predecessors (Conservative governments led by Margaret Thatcher and John Major), gave Africa policy a high profile, and showed enthusiasm for grand initiatives like the New Partnership for Africa's Development, a programme for African regeneration. The Labour Government's African policy style was marked, on the one hand, by Afro-optimism and by a conviction that Britain, as a pivotal power, could make a difference in Africa. It was also, however, characterised by a desire to build the capacity of African states and institutions to help them (and, by extension, the UK) ward off the risks to international stability associated with issues such as ethnic and religious conflict, population and environmental pressures, competition for resources, terrorism and transnational crime (Dodd and Oakes, 1998). It thus 'anticipated continuing and perhaps growing calls for contributions to international peace support and humanitarian operations' (*ibid.*). The AU, in this regard, promoted the notion of 'African solutions for African problems', at the centre of which is APSA. Under the Labour Governments of Tony Blair and Gordon Brown, the UK stepped forward to support African peacekeeping and APSA.

This chapter argues that this UK approach to African security, and APSA, has survived well into the current era of Conservative government. Contemporary UK support for APSA continued to be rooted in two core agendas that lay behind Labour-era assistance. First, that African home-grown initiatives will ensure peace and security of the continent. Secondly, the securitisation of relationships with the continent in the post-9/11 era, where it is argued that conflict and unrest in Africa could spill over and destroy the lives of UK citizens. The chapter argues that UK support to AU peacekeeping activities in countries such as Mali, Somalia and South Sudan under David Cameron and Theresa May, and to APSA structures more generally, can still be analysed effectively through these two Labour-era lenses.

The chapter also underlines, however, the emergence of tensions, contradictions and ambiguities in the UK–AU/APSA relationship since the fall of the Labour Government in May 2010 – as domestic UK pressures have driven Conservative-led governments to recalibrate their relations with the continent. For while the June 2016 Brexit vote has encouraged UK policymakers to strengthen security links with non-European partners (including in Africa), concerns regarding continued illegal migration of persons from Africa to Europe have undermined the UK–Africa relationship. Similarly, the UK's disregard for AU processes in its 2011 involvement in Libya has further damaged the partnership.

The chapter is organised into three sections. The first section places the post-2010 period in context by examining the evolution of UK and Africa peace and security relations up to the year 2010 when the Labour Party lost power to a Conservative–Liberal Democrat Coalition Government. While the first part of this period (1960s through to mid-1990s) was characterised by ambivalence within UK–Organisation of African Unity (OAU) relations, from the time the Labour Party under Tony Blair ascended to power in 1997 up to 2010, UK–AU relations in the area of peace and security can be characterised as hyper-active. The UK came to focus more on the peace and security challenges facing the continent. In this regard, it supported the AU peace and security structures and Africa came to be seen by the UK as a frontline against terrorism. The second section demonstrates the continuities in UK support for African security structures since 2010 through exploring the two core agendas that have underlain it since the Blair era: securitisation and support for 'African solutions to African problems'. The chapter concludes, however, by reflecting on emerging challenges in the UK–Africa security partnership in the wake of Brexit.

UK–O/AU relations

From independence to New Labour (1960s–1997)

Following the independence of most of its colonies in the early 1960s, UK policy towards Africa came to be characterised by 'benign neglect' (Chafer, 2011:

57) and, sometimes, acrimony. The UK maintained no military bases in Africa, and undertook virtually no interventions (except in Kenya during 1963–4). Nevertheless, the country maintained military advisors who worked with the armed forces of many of their former colonies (Salihu, 2017). During the first half of the 1960s up to the late 1970s, two issues affected UK–OAU relations. First, the independence of Rhodesia (later Zimbabwe). The white minority had declared unilateral independence in 1965, whereupon the OAU requested that the UK intervene to reverse this development. When the UK failed to use force to reverse the white minority rule in Rhodesia, the OAU asked its members to sever relations with the minority. Secondly, the apartheid regime in South Africa. Apartheid was inimical to the OAU's essential aspirations of freedom, equality, justice and dignity for the African peoples.[1] Moreover, apartheid policy conflicted with one of the purposes of the OAU, namely eradication of all forms of colonialism from Africa.[2] The Conservative Government headed by Alec Douglas-Home – while critical of apartheid – maintained certain UK arms exports to South Africa for external defence including anti-tank and surface to air missiles (Phythian, 2000). This position was opposed by the OAU.

In the early 1970s, the Conservative Government headed by Edward Heath announced that the UK would resume arms sales to South Africa including those for riot control that were used to enforce apartheid policy, a position that further complicated UK relations with the OAU and the Commonwealth. When unrest intensified in South Africa, the European Economic Community imposed a set of very limited trade and financial sanctions on South Africa in September 1985, and the Commonwealth countries adopted similar measures in October 1985 (Levy, 1999: 6). Prime Minister Margaret Thatcher opposed comprehensive sanctions on South Africa, a stance that angered the OAU.[3] Following the release of Nelson Mandela from prison in 1990, a rapprochement between the UK and OAU ensued, only for relations to sour once again, from the late 1990s onwards, as a result of the UK's policy towards Zimbabwe, which imposed sanctions on Robert Mugabe's Government following the adoption by the latter of the indigenisation policy. The OAU opposed the sanctions regime, with Tanzanian President Benjamin Mkapa describing it as 'neo-colonialism and economic colonialism' (afrol News, 2002).

From Blair to Cameron (1997–2010)

UK–OAU relations remained somewhat static under the Conservative Government of John Major, which had replaced that of Margaret Thatcher in 1990. While Major's Government committed to cancel two-thirds of the official debts of fifteen of its poor African debtors, British aid to Africa continued to decrease (Taylor, 2010: 36). Relations nonetheless took a dramatic turn with the coming to power of the Labour Party under Tony Blair in May 1997. If one philosophy arguably came to embody British foreign policy under Blair's government, it was interventionism (Miller and Smith, 2008: 9). Within a few weeks of coming to power, Foreign Secretary Robin Cook proposed that the new Labour Government would inject 'an ethical dimension' into British foreign policy, most notably by paying greater attention to human rights issues (*ibid.*: 9). This new, interventionist foreign policy was fully set into motion by the 1999 Kosovo crisis and then reinforced by the UK's role in helping to end the civil war in Sierra Leone, the largest unilateral UK military intervention since the 1982 Falklands campaign (Kargbo, 2006: 297). In relation to the Kosovo intervention, which set the stage for the UK's intervention in Sierra Leone, Blair observed thus:

> we are witnessing the beginnings of a new doctrine of international community. By this I mean, the explicit recognition that today more than ever before, we are mutually dependent, that national interest is to a significant extent governed by international collaboration, and that we need a clear and coherent debate as to the direction this doctrine takes us in each field of international endeavour. (Blair, 1999)

He also observed that 'acts of genocide can never be a purely internal matter. When oppression produces massive flows of refugees which unsettle neighbouring countries, then they can properly be described as threats to international peace and security' (*ibid.*).

At the annual Labour Party Conference in October 2001, Prime Minister Blair observed that 'the state of Africa is like a scar on the conscience of the world. But if the world as a community focused on it, we can heal it. And if we do not, it will become deeper and angrier' (Mbakwe, 2004: 20; McGreal, 2002). He further submitted that 'deepening poverty and disillusionment in Africa could provide a fertile breeding ground for a new generation of terrorists' (*ibid.*). While Blair made these observations against the backdrop of the 9/11 terrorist attacks against the USA, they came to form the basis upon which subsequent UK Africa policy was to be built. The UK continued to search for ways to help Africa overcome its peace and security challenges through building and supporting regional institutions, especially the AU. The UK was among a number of Western governments to enthusiastically buy into the notion of 'African solutions to African problems' (Chafer, 2011: 59; Williams, 2011: 190).

The establishment of the AU marked an institutional change, signalling a break from much of the post-independence era by establishing new principles for regional cooperation and integration (Brown, 2012: 1891). The OAU, the predecessor of the AU, was not successful in ending the numerous intractable conflicts that had afflicted the continent for a long time. Thus the AU's institutions, powers and objectives were supposed to amount to a fundamental shift away from the constraints imposed on actions under the OAU Charter. The major change under the AU has been a renewed emphasis on building a continental security regime that is capable of managing and resolving African conflicts (Arthur, 2017: 8). The APSA is a coherent structure which includes norms and mechanisms to effectively and capably deal with the underlying causes of conflict and their non-conventional nature and consequences (*ibid.*: 5).[4]

The totality of the Labour Government's pronouncements on Africa buttressed the UK's position in helping the growth of the AU peace and security structures, including the peacekeeping mission that was launched to deal with the problem of Darfur, Sudan. The crisis in Darfur escalated in February 2003 when rebels of the Sudan Liberation Movement/Army (SLM) attacked local police stations (Mazo, 2009: 73). In counter-insurgency operations, the Sudan Government launched a campaign of 'ethnic cleansing' against civilians of the Fur, Zaghawa and Masalit ethnic groups – the same ethnicities as the rebels – assisted by militias drawn from rival ethnic groups, known as the *Janjaweed*, whom the government supported, armed and trained (Human Rights Watch, 2006). By 2007, over two million people had been displaced, many fleeing across the border to Chad, and the number of killed and wounded has been estimated by the United Nations at somewhere between 200,000 and 500,000 (Mazo, 2009: 73).

The AU Mission in Sudan (AMIS), comprising African military observers, was established at the end of May 2004, and became operational the following month. AMIS was the first all-African peace support mission and was thus viewed as 'a test of the AU's capacity to bring peace and security to the continent' (AU, 2005). When the mission experienced problems of funding and logistics, Blair argued forcefully that 'the West should fund it' (Williams, 2011: 190). The UK's engagement with the Sudan conflict was informed by the role (together with the USA and Norway) it played in the negotiations and signing of the 2005 Comprehensive Peace Agreement between the Government of Sudan and the SLM (Chafer, 2011). Subsequently, the focus of the UK came to rest on Darfur because of the fear that the events there could spark a wider regional crisis. In terms of actual support provided to AMIS, at the May 2005 pledging conference the UK initially pledged and actually contributed in kind £6.6 million (AU, 2005), which included 600 vehicles, diverse equipment and airlift of Nigerian troops (Bachmann, 2011). The contribution was eventually raised to £19 million (Reliefweb, 2005).

Under New Labour, the UK further extended support to several peace and security initiatives in Africa. From 2007–10, it supported the AU Mission in

Somalia (AMISOM) to the tune of £15 million, covering military equipment, logistics and salaries for military personnel (Pirozzi and Miranda, 2010: 41). It has also supported the development of a Rapid Deployment Capability of the African Standby Force (ASF), and the African Peace Support Trainers' Association among others, since the late 2000s (*ibid.*).

The UK also extended support to a number of Regional Economic Communities in Africa as part of this assistance. In this regard, it supported the Economic Community of West African States's (ECOWAS)'s Peace Keeping Centre in Bamako, Mali; and the Kofi Annan International Peacekeeping Training Centre, in Accra, Ghana (*ibid.*). In East Africa, it supported the East African Standby Force (EASF) Headquarters and the International Peace Support Training Centre in Nairobi, Kenya (*ibid.*). In Southern Africa, it has supported the Southern African Development Community's Regional Peacekeeping Training Centre in Harare, Zimbabwe (*ibid.*).

The Labour Government's view of Africa and the role the UK played supporting the various AU peacekeeping missions, as described above, established the basis upon which the Conservative–Liberal Democratic Coalition Government continued to engage with the AU after the 2010 elections.

Post-2010 UK–AU relations

Arising out of the initiatives taken by the Labour Governments between 1997 and 2010, the UK has continued to be supportive of AU peace and security structures. The result of this has been an increase in UK support to the APSA structures, and peacekeeping missions in Somalia and, more recently, South Sudan – where the UK has deployed 400 troops to serve under the United Nations Mission in South Sudan operation (Ray, 2017). The UK has also continued to provide military, logistical, engineering and training expertise to the UN Support Office to AMISOM (British Embassy Mogadishu, 2015). Further, the UK hosted a number of high-profile international meetings on the Somalia situation in February 2012, May 2013 and June 2017.

The main motivation for the UK to extend support to the AU's peace and security structures under Cameron and May has continued to be the notion that Africa is at the forefront of containing insecurity that could easily affect UK populations. In other words, Africa is seen by UK Governments through the prism of security. In the next section, we demonstrate how Africa has continued to be securitised through the Blair, Brown, Cameron and May Governments, and detail the AU peace and security structures that are supposed to ensure that security prevails on the continent.

Securitisation of Africa

The theory of securitisation is best understood as the broadening of the security agenda (Abrahamsen, 2013: 128). Securitisation is the specific speech act of framing an issue as an 'existential threat' that calls for extra-ordinary measures beyond the routines and norms of everyday politics (*ibid.*: 129). In the context of UK–Africa relations, the Labour and post-2010 Conservative-led Governments have increasingly presented African issues within a narrative of security, from climate change to migration and from HIV/AIDS to Ebola (*ibid.*: 130). With regard to Ebola, for example, David Cameron observed that 'the disease has the potential to become a serious global threat with ... security consequences' (Cameron, 2014). The increased prevalence of conflict on the African continent provided the empirical evidence of this claim.

Abrahamsen (2004: 678) has observed that 'although the al-Qaida cells responsible for the terrorist attacks on the USA had no more and probably fewer links to countries in sub-Saharan Africa than to London, Hamburg or Florida, the 9/11 attack was quickly incorporated into policy discourses on Africa'. The attacks were widely interpreted as demonstrating beyond dispute that conflict and unrest in one part of the world could spill over and destroy the lives of thousands on the other side of the globe (*ibid.*). The Blair Government made frequent references, as Abrahamsen argues, to how the terrorist attacks demonstrated the dangers of globalisation and a shrinking world where boundaries have become irrelevant. In this regard, Blair opined that 'today's conflicts rarely stay within national boundaries' (Blair, 2001). It is within this context, that conflicts in Africa were – and continue to be – seen as potential threats to the security of the UK in particular, and the world in general.

In February 2004, Blair announced the setting up of the Commission for Africa, drawing membership from the North and Africa to find solutions to African conflicts.[5] All the Commissioners participated in the endeavour in their personal capacities. The establishment of the Commission came against the backdrop of the lead-up to the UK presidency of both the EU and the G8. Prime Minister Blair promised to use the UK's position to focus on Africa (Plaut, 2004: 705). Blair observed thus:

> Africa is the only continent to have grown poorer in the past 25 years, its share of world trade has halved in the generation, and it received less than 1% of direct foreign investment, 44 million children do not go to school, millions as you know die through famine, or disease, or conflict, and Africa risks being left even further behind. That is why in the context of our G8 Presidency in the year 2005, I have decided with others to form a Commission for Africa to take a fresh look at Africa's past, present

and future. It will be a comprehensive assessment of the situation in Africa and policies towards Africa. What has worked, what has not worked and what more can and should be done. (*Ibid.*: 704)

After a year of work, the Commission released its report in March 2005. Resolving conflicts in Africa was identified as one of the priority areas in which the continent needed to be supported by Western countries. The Commission observed that the developed world has a moral duty – as well as a powerful motive of self-interest – to assist Africa (Commission for Africa, 2005: 11). The responsibility for peace and security lies primarily with African Governments, but the Commission also noted that the actions of developed countries are essential to making this desire a reality (*ibid.*: 150). African regional organisations were singled out to be utilised to prevent and resolve conflict when tensions cannot be managed at national level, through effective early warning, mediation and peacekeeping (*ibid.*: 12).

The Commission also observed that African and developed countries should invest in the prevention of violent conflict in Africa for the following reasons (*ibid.*: 151–3). First, violent conflict causes huge human suffering and denies many Africans their most basic right to life and security. Secondly, violent conflict and insecurity severely undermine development by increasing poverty; reducing growth, trade and investment; and destroying vital infrastructure and 'human capital' through death, injury and displacement. Violent conflict encourages high levels of military expenditure, diverting resources away from development and helps spread malnutrition and infectious diseases, including HIV and AIDS, through breakdown in services, the rapid movement of refugees and internally displaced persons, and the use of rape as a weapon of war. Thirdly, violent conflicts, once sparked, can create intractable and ongoing tensions that are very difficult to resolve. Lastly, reacting to conflict is more expensive for the international community than preventing it.

The Commission's observations further cast Africa in the security light. In February 2006, Foreign Secretary Jack Straw, in a keynote speech in Abuja, Nigeria underlined that 'conflict [and] terrorism' (Vines, 2018: 130) were the key pillars of the UK's engagement with Africa. This view did not change much after the Conservative–Liberal Democrat Coalition Government came to power in 2010. To mitigate the causes of conflict, during his visit to South Africa and Nigeria in July 2011, Cameron launched the Africa Free Trade Initiative aimed at creating 'prosperity partnership' between the UK and Africa based on development, trade and investment (All Parliamentary Group for Trade out of Poverty, 2016). The Coalition Government's Africa Minister James Duddrige noted that it was in the UK's national interest to promote prosperity and security on the African continent (Duddrige, 2015).

The Boko Haram (Nigeria) and al-Shabaab (Somalia) terrorism has attracted the attention of the UK. In the case of Somalia, Foreign Secretary William Hague visited Mogadishu in 2012 to highlight the UK's engagement with the country (Vines, 2018). It has been noted that Cameron prioritised Somalia policy, greatly strengthening UK engagement including the re-opening of the British embassy in Mogadishu in 2013 (*ibid.*). In 2015, the UK doubled its UN peacekeeping contribution by deploying troops to Somalia among others. Dealing with the Al Shabab insurgency topped the UK agenda, leading to the UK organising and hosting international conferences on Somalia in February 2012 and May 2017.

The Boko Haram insurgency in Nigeria and other Lake Chad Basin states escalated at the same time as the Coalition Government came to power in the UK in mid-2010. As a result, the UK deployed over 350 troops to Nigeria in 2016, as an addition to seventy Royal Air Force personnel already training the Nigerian Air Force (House of Commons, 2017). Between April 2015 and January 2017, the UK trained around 22,000 Nigerian military personnel (*ibid.*). In addition, the UK provided life-saving medical supplies to equip 5,000 Nigerian troops in their fight against the Boko Haram insurgency (*ibid.*). According to Defence Secretary Michael Fallon, 'by helping our allies defeat terrorism and international crime [in Africa], UK forces make ... Britain more secure' (*ibid.*).

Lastly, the UK has also been helping in efforts to stabilise the Sahel region of Africa. In this regard, two initiatives have been undertaken. First, the UK has specifically been supplying French air forces deployed in the Sahel (*ibid.*). Secondly, as a long-term strategy to stabilise the West African and Sahel regions, the UK in December 2016 established a British Defence Staff (BDS) for West Africa based in Abuja, Nigeria. The BDS West Africa acts as a regional hub for the UK's defence efforts including engaging with Nigeria and other countries in the Lake Chad Basin focusing on the transnational threats from the Boko Haram insurgency (*ibid.*).

Supporting 'African solutions to African problems': UK support for APSA

As noted, when establishing the AU the institution's founders recognised the fact that conflicts in Africa constitute a major impediment to the socio-economic development of the continent.[6] They also noted that the need to promote peace, security and stability is a pre-requisite for the implementation of the development and integration agenda. The defunct OAU was not successful in ending the numerous intractable conflicts that afflicted the continent.

The UK has played a role in the construction of the various components of the APSA. In this regard, as observed above, it was an early partner in the peacekeeping efforts of the AU in Darfur, Sudan in the context of promoting the notion of African solutions to African problems and has continued to do so in Mali, South Sudan and Somalia since the era of the Blair/Brown Labour Government.

The UK has reshaped its peace and security assistance to Africa to match continental developments (Bachmann, 2011). The assistance is channelled through the Africa Conflict Prevention Pool (ACPP), which connects the efforts into a single departmental strategy of the Department for International Development, the Foreign and Commonwealth Office and the Ministry of Defence. The ACPP maximises the effect of conflict prevention policies of each of the three departments (*ibid.*). The ACPP finances a wide array of activities including the deployment of conflict and Peace Support Operations (PSOs) advisors with the AU, Intergovernmental Authority on Development, ECOWAS and the EASF (*ibid.*).

The UK has been one of the major forces behind the growth of the Kofi Annan International Peace Training Centre in Ghana, where it deployed four staff members, including the Executive Director and the Resource Director, for several years, until it withdrew in 2010 (*ibid.*).

Since 2010, the British Peace Support Team for East Africa (BPST(EA)) based at Kenya's International Peace Support Training Centre in Karen, Nairobi has participated in the training and preparation of the EASF, which is an integral force of the ASF. The EASF comprises Burundi, Comoros, Djibouti, Eritrea, Ethiopia, Kenya, Rwanda, Seychelles, Somalia, Sudan and Uganda. In addition, BPST trainers in South Africa helped to build the Southern African Development Community Standby Force, also an integral force of the ASF (*ibid.*).

Generally, therefore, the UK's conflict and military advisors deployed to Addis Ababa were behind much of the conceptual development of the ASF during the 2010s and have ensured that the different components of the ASF match more closely, with greater coherence between the military, police and civilian components (*ibid.*). In January 2016, the AU Peace and Security Council declared the full operational capability of the ASF (AU, 2016a).

Lastly, the ACPP has directly supported some of the AU PSOs. For example, first it provided pre-deployment training and financed the transportation (for a total of £5.7 million) of 2,600 soldiers from South Africa, Ethiopia and Mozambique to serve under the AU Mission in Burundi that was launched in 2003 (Bachmann, 2011). The ACPP also shouldered the running costs of the second ECOWAS operation in Liberia, providing £400,000 to the Nigerian forces (*ibid.*).

Recent issues affecting the UK–AU relationship

Though Conservative-led Governments' approaches to peace and security in Africa since 2010 have continued to be driven by similar sentiments to those of New Labour, contextual factors have also intervened – altering how both the UK and African actors view one another. This final section explains how a number of recent crises have led to the emergence of tensions and ambiguities in the UK–AU relationship.

The UK's intervention in the Libya crisis, 2011

In February 2011, Libyans mounted protests in a bid to get rid of the Government of Muammar Gaddafi. The protests were inspired by the events that had taken place earlier in Tunisia and Egypt, which resulted in the removal of the Governments of Presidents Ben Ali and Hosni Mubarak respectively. The Libya protests began in the eastern town of Benghazi, and the Government responded by deploying the security forces in a bid to suppress them. The AU called on both parties to seek a peaceful end to the crisis. To buttress its call, first, the AU established a four-point roadmap to guide the process on peaceful resolution of the crisis. Secondly, it established a High Level ad Hoc Committee on Libya (hereinafter High Level Committee), comprising five Heads of state and government together with the Chair of the Commission, to undertake mediation.[7] The roadmap established the following: a call for the immediate cessation of all hostilities; the cooperation of the Libyan authorities competent to facilitate timely delivery of humanitarian assistance to the needy population; the protection of foreign nationals, including the African migrants living in Libya; and the adoption and implementation of the political reforms necessary for eliminating the causes of the crisis (Apuuli, 2017). With regard to the High Level Committee, it was mandated to,

> engage with all the parties in Libya and to continuously assess the evolution of the situation on the ground; facilitate an inclusive dialogue among the Libyan parties on the appropriate reforms; and engage the AU's partners, in particular the Arab League, the Organization of the Islamic Conference, the European Union and the United Nations to facilitate coordination of efforts and seek their support for the early resolution of the crisis. (AU, 2011)

The AU initiatives were, however, sidelined by the adoption of Resolution 1973 by the UN Security Council (UNSC), which authorised the use of force to protect civilians and civilian-populated areas under attack in Libya, including Benghazi.[8] Upon the adoption of Resolution 1973, countries including the UK, first individually and later under the North Atlantic Treaty Organisation (NATO) military umbrella, launched air strikes against Gaddafi's forces. Even before the resolution had been adopted, Prime Minister David Cameron told Parliament on 28 February 2011 that Britain 'must not tolerate this regime using military force against its own people' (International Institute for Strategic Studies, 2011: 1). He added that he had asked 'the Ministry of Defence and the Chief of the Defence Staff to work with our allies on plans for a military no-fly zone' (*ibid.*: 1).

The use of force against the Gaddafi regime resulted in the sidelining of the AU initiatives to resolve the crisis peacefully. In April 2011, Presidents Obama (USA) and Sarkozy (France) and Prime Minister Cameron (UK) authored an open letter in which they stated that 'it is impossible to imagine a future of Libya with Gaddafi in power. Gaddafi must go and go for good' (BBC News, 2011). In the event, Gaddafi was killed on 20 October 2011 after being cornered by rebels following an air strike on his convoy by NATO forces.

The undermining and eventual ignoring of the AU initiatives on Libya by the Western countries frustrated the AU, who resented being marginalised by their self-proclaimed partners in African peace and security. As a result, the AU developed a strong desire to become financially self-sufficient, especially in the area of peace and security (International Crisis Group, 2017: 3). In this regard, in July 2015 AU leaders pledged to fund 25 per cent of the organisation's budget for peace and security by 2020 (*ibid.*). The collection of a 0.2 per cent import levy on all eligible goods imported into the continent is intended partly to be used to fund AU peace and security activities, thus weaning the organisation from Western country (including UK) support (AU, 2016b).

The levy is set to become operational in 2018, and every member state is required to adopt national legislation to implement it. In some countries like Rwanda, the cabinet has already passed a draft law to establish the levy on imported goods (Kagire, 2017). Other countries that are at various stages of enacting legislation to provide for the levy include Chad, Congo-Brazzaville, Ethiopia and Kenya (*ibid.*).

Brexit and illegal immigration

One of the issues that has dogged successive UK governments in the recent past is popular pressure to stem the tide of illegal immigrants that enter the country every year. This has been a particular concern for the Conservative Party – along with its (at times) political competitor the UK Independence Party. In fact, one of the main campaign pivots of the 'Leave EU' advocates during the UK's EU membership referendum in 2016 was immigration. Among the illegal immigrants that have been arriving in the UK are many Africans. In 2015 alone, more than one million refugees and immigrants fleeing war, persecution and poverty in the Middle East and Africa crossed into Europe (International Crisis Group, 2017). As then Home Secretary, Theresa May described the immigration to Europe as 'intolerable' (BBC News, 2015). She opined that 'economic immigrants rescued from the Mediterranean [Sea] trying to reach Europe should be returned home' (*ibid.*). The immigration crisis was one of the catalysts that contributed to the UK's decision to vote to leave the EU. The 'Leave EU' campaign 'stirred up people's concerns about immigration' (Merrick, 2017), leading to its win. The leave campaign advocated 'taking back control' of UK borders (Johnston, 2017) in order to limit immigrants entering the country.

When she became Prime Minister, May pledged £100 million to return Somali refugees to Somalia, and to encourage people escaping war zones not to cross the Mediterranean Sea (Mason, 2016). This money includes £20 million to encourage refugees who fled Somalia to return home from Dadaab camp in Kenya; and £4 million to help support the process of returning the Somali refugees (*ibid.*). May's announcement was met with dismay by humanitarian organisations, with children's charity War Child terming it 'disappointing' (Ridley, 2016). When May called the 8 June 2017 snap election, one of the pivots of the Conservative manifesto was immigration (Conservative Party, 2017: 40). According to the International Crisis Group, generally the EU's (and UK's) positions on immigration have angered the AU member states, who see them as being 'discriminatory [in] approach', especially in the way African illegal immigrants are treated (International Crisis Group, 2017: 9). The forcible return of illegal immigrants from EU countries including the UK has also been a bone of contention. During her tenure as Home Secretary, May advocated for the deportation of failed asylum seekers from mainland Europe, which would ease pressure on UK borders (Hall, 2015). At the Conservative Party Annual Conference in Manchester in October 2015, May announced plans to deport thousands more failed asylum seekers from the UK (*ibid.*). The forcible return of illegal immigrants to their countries of origin has angered some AU member states (International Crisis Group, 2017). While at the EU–AU Summit on immigration held in Valetta, Malta in April 2015 the EU offered £1 billion to African countries 'to take back tens of thousands of illegal migrants', they rejected the offer (Stevens, 2015). The peak of African countries' anger on EU/UK deportation policy manifested when Mali refused to receive two illegal immigrants deported by France (BBC News, 2016).

On 23 June 2016, however, the UK voted in a referendum to leave the EU. Under the announced timetable, the UK would leave the EU at the end of March 2019. This state of affairs further complicates the UK–AU relationship vis-à-vis peace and security. Traditionally, the UK has been the biggest contributor to the European Development Fund (EDF) that has been supporting the AU's peace and security initiatives through the African Peace Facility (APF). Between 2014 and 2016, the UK contributed almost 15 per cent (€4.478 billion) of the budget of the EDF (International Crisis Group, 2017). Through the APF alone, the EU has channelled substantial funding to the AU amounting to over €2 billion since 2004 (EU, 2017). The withdrawal of the UK from the EU will leave a big funding hole for AU peace and security activities, and the future of UK support in this area remains ambiguous.

Leaving the EU nonetheless compels UK policymakers to widen and deepen its security relationships beyond Europe, including in Africa. James Duddrige, a British Conservative MP and a leading advocate of Brexit, has promised that the UK would increase security assistance to Africa after it leaves the EU (Sow and Sy, 2016). To buttress his point, Duddrige has noted that when the EU took a decision at the beginning of 2016 to reduce the budget of AMISOM by 20 per cent, the UK opposed it (*ibid.*). Nevertheless, it has generally been conceded that it seems unlikely that current levels of spending on the AU's peace and security programmes will be maintained after the UK leaves the EU (International Crisis Group, 2017) – with unclear implications for future relationships. Moreover, EU countries, especially the UK and France, have long used the EU's financial instruments to further their own interests in Africa. For example, the Cameron Government put Somalia at the top of its foreign policy agenda, and in this regard hosted an international conference on Somalia in 2012 (Foreign and Commonwealth Office, 2012). Following the conference, Somalia received significant new funding from the APF. However, the UK departure from the EU will likely result in a reallocation of EU support away from the Horn of Africa, in particular Somalia, to the Sahel and West Africa. Suffice to note that France has been leading the efforts to establish new security arrangements in the Sahel region, including the G5 Sahel force charged with combating terrorism in the region, which received €50 million in June 2017 from the APF.[9]

Conclusions

The transformation of the OAU to the AU occurred immediately after the Labour Government came to power in 1997 in the UK. The Labour Government came with a new policy towards Africa, which specifically sought to help Africa overcome its numerous problems especially in the area of peace and security. This was a departure from the Conservative Governments of Heath and Thatcher, whose policy towards Africa was sometimes disinterested and, more often, acrimonious. The Labour Governments of Blair and Brown declared that they would focus on Africa by helping the continent to resolve the many conflicts that afflicted it at the time. The terrorist attacks against the USA on 11 September 2001 further buttressed the UK's argument that instability in Africa could pose a threat to the peace and security of the UK. This has continued to be the main motivation behind UK support of the AU's peace and security structures since 2010. In recent times, however, other factors have intervened, with UK–AU relations hitting a rough patch as a result. Particularly central in this regard have been domestic UK concerns – and government responses to these, with immigration and Brexit being particularly central. In the final analysis, UK–AU relations are in a period of flux due to changing priorities and mechanisms for engagement on both sides. In light of these shifts, the relationships will need to be renegotiated, and whether this will lead to persistence of existing patterns of engagement in new forms, or a significant rethinking of the premises and practices of UK–AU relationships, remains to be seen.

Notes

1 Preamble, Charter of the OAU, 479 U.N.T.S. 39, entered into force 13 September 1963.
2 Article II (1) (d), Charter of the OAU, 479 U.N.T.S. 39, entered into force 13 September 1963.
3 Note that the UK imposed arms and oil embargoes, and sports sanctions on South Africa.
4 The APSA comprises the African Union Commission, the Peace and Security Council, the Continental Early Warning System, the African Standby Force, the Military Staff Committee, the Panel of the Wise, the Peace Fund, the Regional Economic Communities/Regional Mechanisms and Post-Conflict Reconstruction and Development.
5 It comprised seventeen Commissioners, including Blair himself, Tanzanian President Benjamin Mkapa, Ethiopian Prime Minister Meles Zenawi, Economic Commission for Africa chief K. Y. Amoako, UN Under Secretary and Executive Director of Habitat Anna Tibaijuka, the UK's Chancellor Gordon Brown, former Head of the International Monetary Fund Michel Camdessus, former USA Senator Nancy Kassebaum and Sir Bob Geldof. The full list of Commissioners can be found online at: www.commissionforafrica.info/commissioners [accessed 13 August 2017].
6 Preamble, Constitutive Act (2000).

7   The Committee members were Presidents Denis Sassou Nguesso (Republic of Congo), Amadou Toumani Toure (Mali), Mohamed Ould Abdelaziz (Mauritania), Jacob Zuma (South Africa), and Yoweri Museveni (Uganda).
8   See UNSC Resolution 1973 (2011) adopted at its 6498th meeting, S/RES/1973 (2011), 17 March 2011, para. 4.
9   Countries contributing to this are Burkina Faso, Chad, Mali, Mauritania and Niger.

References

Abrahamsen, R. (2004) 'A breeding ground for terrorists? Africa & Britain's "War on Terrorism"', *Review of African Political Economy*, 31:102, 677–84.

Abrahamsen, R. (2013) 'Blair's Africa: the politics of securitization and fear', in R. Abrahamsen (ed.), *Conflict and Security in Africa* (Woodbridge: James Currey), 127–45.

Afrol News (2002) 'Zimbabwe: EU and US sanctions fail to impress Zimbabwe', 20 February 2002, www.afrol.com/News2002/zim011_eu_us_sanctions.htm [accessed 19 December 2017].

All Parliamentary Group for Trade out of Poverty (2016) *Inquiry into the UK's Africa Free Trade Initiative Final Report*, October 2016, www.tralac.org/images/docs/10674/afti-inquiry-final-report-october-2016.pdf [accessed 21 December 2017].

Apuuli, K. P. (2017) 'The African Union's mediation mandate and the Libyan conflict (2011)', *African Security*, 10:3–4, 192–204.

Arthur, P. (2017) 'Promoting security in Africa through Regional Economic Communities (RECs) and the African Union's African Peace and Security Architecture (APSA)', *Insight on Africa*, 9:1, 1–21.

AU (2005) *Overview of the AU's Efforts to Address the Conflict in the Darfur Region of the Sudan*, CONG/PLG/2 (I), 26 May 2005, https://reliefweb.int/report/sudan/overview-aus-efforts-address-conflict-darfur-region-sudan [accessed 2 February 2018].

AU (2011) *Communiqué of the 265th Meeting of the Peace and Security Council*, 10 March 2011, https://au.int/sites/default/files/pressreleases/24209-pr-communique_en_10_march_2011_psd_the_265th_meeting_the_peace_and_security_council.pdf [accessed 2 February 2018].

AU (2016a), Peace and Security Council 570th Meeting, PSC/PR/BR.(DLXX), *Press Statement*, 21 January 2016, www.peaceau.org/uploads/psc-press-statement-570-amani-en.pdf [accessed 10 May 2016].

AU (2016b), *AU Peace Fund – Securing Predictable and Sustainable Financing for Peace in Africa*, August 2016, www.peaceau.org/uploads/auhr-progress-report-final-020916-with-annexes.pdf [accessed 21 December 2017].

Bachmann, O. (2011) *The African Standby Force: External Support to an 'African Solution to African Problems'?*, Research Report 11:67 (Brighton: Institute for Development Studies), www.ids.ac.uk/files/dmfile/Rr67web.pdf [accessed 21 December 2017].

BBC News (2011) 'Libya letter by Obama, Cameron and Sarkozy: full text', *BBC News*, 15 April 2011, www.bbc.com/news/world-africa-13090646 [accessed 23 October 2017].

BBC News (2015) 'Mediterranean migrant crisis: May wants some people returned', *BBC News*, 13 May, www.bbc.com/news/uk-32716735 [accessed 23 December 2017].

BBC News (2016) 'Mali sends back migrants deported by France', *BBC News*, 30 December 2016, www.bbc.com/news/world-africa-38467244 [accessed 25 December 2017].

Blair, T. (1999) 'The Blair doctrine', *PBS News Hour*, 22 April 1999, www.pbs.org/newshour/bb/international-jan-june99-blair doctrine4—23/ [accessed 31 July 2017].

Blair, T. (2001) 'Speech to the Labour Party Conference', *Guardian*, 2 October 2001, www.theguardian.com/politics/2001/oct/02/labourconference.labour6 [accessed 12 August 2017].

British Embassy Mogadishu (2015) 'UK pledges military personnel to support peace and stability in Somalia', 7 October 2015, www.gov.uk/government/news/uk-pledges-military-personnel-to-support-peace-and-stability-in-somalia [accessed 28 August 2017].

Brown, W. (2012) 'A question of agency: Africa in international politics', *Third World Quarterly*, 33:10, 1889–908.

Cameron, D. (2014) *Annual Report on the National Security Strategy and Strategic Defence and Security Review: Written Statement HCWS159*, 18 December 2014, www.parliament.uk/business/publications/written-questions-answers-statements/written-statement/Commons/2014-12-18/HCWS159 [accessed 20 December 2017].

Chafer, T. (2011) 'The AU: a new arena for Anglo-French cooperation in Africa?', *Journal of Modern Africa Studies*, 49:1, 55–82.

Commission for Africa (2005) *Our Common Interest* (London: Commission for Africa).

Conservative Party (2017) *Forward Together: Our Plan for a Stronger Britain and a Prosperous Future* (London: Conservative Party).

Dodd, T. and Oakes, M. (1998) 'The Strategic Defence Review White Paper', House of Commons Library Research Paper 98/91, 15 October 1998, http://researchbriefings.files.parliament.uk/documents/RP98-91/RP98-91.pdf [accessed 23 December 2017].

Duddrige, J. (2015) 'How much does Africa matter? Defining the UK's Africa policy under the Coalition Government', keynote address, UK Africa policy, the prosperity agenda and the 'Golden Thread': Between Idealism and pragmatism, Chatham House, London, 23 March 2015, www.chathamhouse.org/sites/default/files/field/field_document/15%2003%2023%20UK%20Africa%20policy%20-%20Minister%20transcript%20(edited).pdf [accessed 3 January 2019].

EU (2017) 'Towards the fifth Africa–EU Summit: peace and security', 4 May 2017, https://eeas.europa.eu/sites/eeas/files/vc_factsheet_peace_and_security_short_clean_final.pdf [accessed 28 August 2017].

Foreign and Commonwealth Office (2012) *London Conference on Somalia: Communiqué*, 23 February 2012 (London: Foreign and Commonwealth Office).

Hall, M. (2015) 'Goodbye illegals: more than 400,000 failed asylum seekers will be deported in EU plan', *Express*, 8 October 2015, www.express.co.uk/news/politics/610602/Migrants-deported-asylum-seekers-Theresa-May [accessed 23 December 2017].

House of Commons (2017) 'UK relations with West African countries', Westminster Hall, 25 January 2017, http://researchbriefings.files.parliament.uk/documents/CDP-2017-0028/CDP-2017-0028.pdf [accessed 21 December 2017].

Human Rights Watch (2006) *Sudan: Imperatives for Immediate Change – The African Union Mission in Sudan*, 19 January 2006, www.hrw.org/report/2006/01/19/sudan-imperatives-immediate-change/african-union-mission-sudan [accessed 5 August 2017].

International Crisis Group (2017) *Time to Reset African Union–European Union Relations*, Crisis Group Africa Report No. 255, 17 October 2017 (Brussels: International Crisis Group).

International Institute for Strategic Studies (2011) 'Libya: direct military hits, unclear political targets', *Strategic Comments*, 17:3, 1–3.

Johnston, I. (2017) 'Brexit: anti-immigrant prejudice major factor in deciding vote, study finds', *Independent*, 21 June 2017, www.independent.co.uk/news/uk/politics/brexit-racism-immigrant-prejudice-major-factor-leave-vote-win-study-a7801676.html [accessed 25 December 2017].

Kagire, E. (2017) 'Rwanda approves draft bank law on new tax for financing AU operations', *The East African*, 11–17 February 2017.

Kargbo, M. S. (2006) *British Foreign Policy and the Conflict in Sierra Leone 1991–2001* (Bern: International Academic Publishers).

Levy, P. I. (1999) 'Sanctions on South Africa: what did they do?', Yale University, www.econ.yale.edu/growthpdf/cdp796.pdf [accessed 27 July 2017].

Mason, R. (2016) '100 million pound sterling aid budget to be spent controlling immigration from Africa', *Guardian*, 20 September 2016, www.theguardian.com/uk-news/2016/sep/20/100m-uk-aid-budget-returning-north-african-refugees [accessed 23 December 2017].

Mazo, J. (2009) 'Darfur: the first modern climate-change conflict', *Adelphi Papers*, 49:409, 73–86.

Mbakwe, T. (2004) 'Africa Commission takes off', *New African*, June 2004.

McGreal, C. (2002) 'Blair confronts "scar on world's conscience"', *Guardian*, www.theguardian.com/world/2002/feb/07/politics.development [accessed 31 July 2017].

Merrick, R. (2017) 'Brexit leave campaign "stirred up" fears about immigration, says Boris Johnson's deputy', *Independent*, 3 October 2017, www.independent.co.uk/news/uk/politics/boris-johnson-eu-immigration-brexit-leave-campaign-alan-duncan-fears-a7981521.html [accessed 24 December 2017].

Miller, J. L. V. and Smith, B. (2008) *British Foreign Policy since 1997*, Research Paper 08/56, 23 June 2008 (London: House of Commons Library).

Perraudin, F. (2015) 'Theresa May: UK will not participate in EU migrant resettlement proposals', *Guardian*, 13 May 2015, www.theguardian.com/politics/2015/may/13/theresa-may-uk-eu-migrant-resettlement-scheme [accessed 23 December 2017].

Phythian, M. (2000) *The Politics of British Arms Sales Since 1964* (Manchester: Manchester University Press).

Pirozzi, N. and Miranda, V. V. (2010) *Consolidating African and EU Assessments in View of the Implementation of the Partnership on Peace and Security* (Brussels: Istituto Affari Internazionali).

Plaut, M. (2004) 'Blair and Africa: the Africa Commission', *Review of African Political Economy*, 31:102, 704–11.

Ray, J. (2017) 'Britain's contributing 400 troops to South Sudan peacekeeping mission', *ITV*, 7 February 2017, www.itv.com/news/2017–02–07/britains-contribution-to-un-peacekeeping-in-south-sudan/ [accessed 25 August 2017].

Reliefweb (2005) 'Sudan: UK to provide £19 million support to African Union Darfur mission', 13 June 2005, http://reliefweb.int/report/sudan/sudan-uk-provide-%C2%A319-million-support-african-union-darfur-mission [accessed 10 August 2017].

Ridley, L. (2016) 'Theresa May's plan to spend 100 million pound sterling keeping migrants away from UK torn apart by war', *Huffington Post*, 21 September 2016, www.huffingtonpost.co.uk/entry/theresa-may-foreign-aid-migrants-refugees-ethiopia-somalia_uk_57e23f22e4b0db20a6e78c27 [accessed 23 December 2017].

Salihu, N. (2017) 'The colonial legacy of civil military relations and democratic stability in West Africa', *Conflict Trends* 2016/4, ACCORD, 16 February 2017, www.accord.org.za/conflict-trends/colonial-legacy-civil-military-relations-democratic-stability-west-africa/ [accessed 18 December 2017].

Sow, M. and Sy, A. (2016) 'The Brexit: what implications for Africa?', 21 June 2016, www.brookings.edu/blog/africa-in-focus/2016/06/21/the-brexit-what-implications-for-africa/ [accessed 28 August 2017].

Stevens, J. (2015) 'Migrant summit in chaos as African countries refuse to take back Europe's failed asylum seekers', *Daily Mail*, 12 November 2015, www.dailymail.co.uk/news/article-3315183/Migrant-summit-chaos-African-countries-REFUSE-Europe-s-failed-asylum-seekers.html [accessed 24 December 2017].

Taylor, I. (2010) *The International Relations of Sub-Saharan Africa* (New York: Continuum).

Vines, A. (2018) 'To Brexit and beyond: Africa and the United Kingdom', in D. Nagar and C. Mutasa (eds), *Africa and the World: Bilateral and Multilateral International Diplomacy* (London: Palgrave Macmillan), 119–42.

Williams, P. D. (2011) *War and Conflict in Africa* (Cambridge: Polity).

4
The securitisation of UK aid and DFID programmes in Africa: a comparative case study of Cameroon, Central African Republic, Ethiopia, Kenya and Uganda

Ivica Petrikova and Melita Lazell

This chapter explores the securitisation of development aid from the pre-2010 Labour Government to the post-2010 Conservative–Liberal Democrat Coalition. It finds a number of consistencies in the approaches of the two Governments, but also an intensification of the securitisation of development aid, both in discourse and in practice, under the Conservative Coalition.

In December 2017, Foreign Secretary Boris Johnson explicitly committed to using the aid budget to support UK foreign policy aims, including combating terrorist groups in Africa (BBC News, 2017). In the context of the UK reassessing its position on the world stage in light of Brexit, this explicit commitment articulated a way for the UK to project its power and influence abroad and to solidify its self-proclaimed position as the 'world's leading soft power', which includes its commitment to overseas development (Her Majesty's Treasury and Department for International Development, 2015: 9). However, using UK aid to support national security interests can be placed within the broader securitisation-of-development trend, which has seen a pledge to spend 50 per cent of aid on fragile states and, against expectations, the Conservative Government's promise to maintain the 0.7 per cent of Gross National Income aid commitment (Lunn and Booth, 2016: 4; see also Chapters 1 and 6).

The securitisation trend has influenced the policy discourse of many Western donors, including the UK, since the late 1990s. After a brief period following the end of the Cold War, when security concerns were delinked from development and donors reluctant to engage in conflict zones (Suhrke and Buckmaster, 2006: 340), the late 1990s saw a resurgence of securitisation. Hilary Benn, as Secretary of State for International Development in 2005, emphasised that within an interdependent world, conflict and crime cross borders and, as such, no country 'can remain aloof from the effects of insecurity elsewhere' (Department for International Development, 2005a: 3–5). This discursive trend of connecting conflict and fragility in the Global South with domestic security – the 'development–security nexus' – has intensified since the early 2000s, with conflict and weak governance in Africa highlighted as central to UK security concerns (e.g. Department for International Development, 2007: Her Majesty's Treasury and Department for International Development, 2015).

Empirical analysis of aid-provision trends in this regard is still scarce, but does suggest that the UK has, in line with the policy discourse, generally augmented the provision of development aid and prioritised activities deemed to enhance security, broadly defined. What exactly does this aid fund, however, and what are its impacts on the recipient countries? This chapter sheds light on these questions through a comparative analysis of UK aid programmes in five Sub-Saharan African countries – Cameroon, Central African Republic (CAR), Ethiopia, Kenya and Uganda – between 2002 and 2015. Particular attention is paid to the comparison of pre-2010 (Labour Governments) and 2010–15 (Conservative–Liberal Democrat Coalition) periods.

We find that in line with the discourse, aid securitisation as conceptualised here progressed in the five case-study countries gradually between 2002 and 2015. The most notable change from Labour to the Coalition Government in this regard was the preference to channel 'securitised' aid to countries of more strategic importance to the UK. A closer look at three examples of 'securitised' aid projects, implemented by the Conservative-led Department for International Development (DFID), unfortunately demonstrated that such projects were not likely to contribute to one of the key aims of securitised aid provision: the sustainable reduction of conflict and instability in the recipient countries.

The chapter starts with an overview of UK development policy discourse from the late1990s to 2015, demonstrating how it has been framed within the 'security–development nexus' by both Labour and Coalition Governments. We then summarise existing empirical analyses of UK aid securitisation and explain the chapter's methodological approach. Finally, we present and discuss our results and analyse their significance in the concluding remarks.

Securitisation within the policy discourse

Since the early 2000s, academics and development non-governmental organisations (NGOs) have become increasingly concerned that international development has become securitised (Brown and Grävingholt, 2016; Duffield, 2001; McConnon, 2014; Oxfam, 2011). They maintain that conflict and instability in the Global South are conceived as a Western security threat and that development agencies have modified their agendas in response, prioritising national security objectives and increasing funding to the military and security sector (Fisher and Anderson, 2015: 134).

Within UK policy discourse, the securitisation of development is well established. It stretches back to the late 1990s/early 2000s, when globalisation was recognised to pose risks as well as opportunities (Department for International Development, 2000; 2005b). Global challenges, including conflict and instability, were no longer seen as contained by distance or borders, and this notion gained particular momentum in the context of the 'War on Terror' (Straw, 2002).

The securitisation discourse is underpinned by three related beliefs. The first is that underdevelopment and conflict in the Global South are mutually reinforcing (e.g. Department for International Development, 2005a: 3; Her Majesty's Treasury and Department for International Development, 2015: 3–5). The second belief is that instability and conflict in the Global South are potential sources of insecurity for the Global North, including the UK (Department for International Development, 2005a: 3–5; 2012: 2; Greening, 2015a; 2015b). 'There is no doubt', according to the then International Development Secretary, 'that these problems – if left un-tackled – will reach our own doorstep. Anyone who wants to take an insular view of the world only needs to look at the scenes in Calais these last few weeks' (*ibid.*). Conflict and instability overseas were accordingly described as bearing 'clear consequences for UK peace, security, and prosperity' (Her Majesty's Treasury and Department for International Development, 2015: 13). Within this context, 'fragile' and 'conflict-affected' states are particularly conceived as a threat, as they are especially susceptible to criminal and terrorist networks and give rise to transnational refugee flows (Department for International Development, 2005a: 5, 10; 2015b). Embedded within this discourse, then, is a strong assumption that through terrorism, international crime and refugee flows, insecurity and underdevelopment in the South have the potential to erode national security in the UK.

The third belief is that development aid can be used to enhance national security (i.e. the securitisation of development aid) (Her Majesty's Treasury and Department for International Development, 2015: 3; Watt, 2010). Increasing aid to fragile states, for example, is believed to help the UK government counter terrorism: 'We think it's in everyone's interest to encourage stability in areas where conflict and terrorism might otherwise dominate. That's why we think it's important to keep up overseas aid payments, even though money may be tight at home' (Department for International Development, 2015a). Unsurprisingly, given its *raison d'être*, DFID explicitly depicts aid as a powerful tool for reducing conflict in the Global South and creating 'a safer ... world' (Department for International Development, 2012: 1).

According to DFID policy documents, the rationale for providing aid to reduce conflict and instability overseas is twofold – enhanced national security along with a moral imperative (e.g. *ibid.*: 1). This dual justification for aid has been used to explain the UK's commitment to development aid by both Labour and subsequent Conservative/Coalition Governments. However, the balance shifted slightly more towards national security concerns in the post-2010 period. For example, while DFID's key development policy document under Brown's Labour administration stated that 'aid should be used only to tackle poverty, not for narrow self-interest' (Department for International Development, 2009: 6), the key development policy document under the Coalition Government was titled *UK Aid: Tackling Global Challenges in the National Interest* (Her Majesty's Treasury and Department for International Development, 2015).

Nevertheless, beyond understanding how aid provision has been framed to UK and international audiences, it is important to consider the real-world implications of securitisation: what kinds of programme are actually promoted within the discourse, specifically in Africa? Africa is a region of strategic importance to the UK (*ibid.*: 14). Violence, conflict, instability and extremism in the continent are identified as the root causes of unprecedented migration flows to Europe (*ibid.*: 7, 13). According to the policy discourse, reducing conflict and instability in Africa requires two types of development intervention. The first seeks to encourage the development of democratic, inclusive societies which respect human rights. Interventions promoting this 'golden thread of democracy' (*ibid.*: 11) include strengthening civil society and the rule of law, tackling marginalisation and exclusion, and progressing the rights and opportunities of women and girls (Greening, 2015b).

The second type of development programmes presented as reducing conflict are explicit conflict prevention and resolution measures. These include the disarmament of civilians, reforms of the security, police and justice sectors, and civilian peacebuilding activities (Department for International Development, 2003). The discourse is explicit about the increased need for such investments in fragile, conflict-affected states and, overlapping with this group, in states of strategic concern to the UK, for example due to the numbers of refugees received (e.g. Greening, 2015b) and/or the scale of domestic terrorism (e.g. Department for International Development, 2005a).

In summary, since the late 1990s DFID policy documents produced under both Labour- and Conservative-led Governments have strongly reflected aid securitisation – the belief that development aid can and should be used in the national security interest. The main distinction lies in a stronger accompanying moral justification for aid under Labour administrations (Abrahamsen, 2005: 61), with post-2010 Coalition Governments focused more openly on the national security imperative. However, according to the discourse of both administrations, development aid can contribute to that imperative through two types of intervention: first, democratisation programmes and, secondly, explicit conflict prevention measures. Having established this securitisation of development at the level of policy discourse, particularly in relation to Africa, we now turn to examining its effects on actual aid programming.

Has the securitised discourse affected development-aid provision?

The securitisation of development aid differs from earlier manifestations of aid reflecting donor self-interest. Previous studies linked Western donors' aid commitments to bilateral trade (Bueno de Mesquita and Smith, 2009), favourable votes at the United Nations (Alesina and Dollar, 2000) and Security Council seats (Kuziemko and Werker, 2006). The securitisation of development aid holds, in contrast, that conflict and fragility in the Global South exist as a threat to national security.

The literature investigating this topic maintains that the security–development nexus has affected the distribution of development resources, although few studies to date have examined how. For instance, McConnon argued that the 'shift in discourse' coincided with the 'prioritisation of fragile states in aid flows' and 'specific programmes aimed at addressing [donor] security concerns' (2014: 1146). Similarly, Brown and Grävingholt found that 'international aid agencies revised their aid strategies to reflect new security concerns and increased aid to strategic conflict-affected countries' (2016: 1–2). Western donors' security concerns were further accused of skewing global aid spending by Oxfam (2011) and Saferworld (2011).

In our earlier, large-N analysis of UK aid securitisation (Lazell and Petrikova, 2017; Petrikova and Lazell, 2019), we examined UK aid disbursements to the two sectors seen as crucial for reducing the domestic security threat posed by the Global South – 'democratisation' and 'conflict, peace and security' – and found them increasing between 1995 and 2015 both in absolute and relative terms. Furthermore, conflict-affected countries consistently received more Conflict Prevention and Resolution, Peace and Security (CPS) aid from the UK than countries not affected by conflict; however, only strategically important

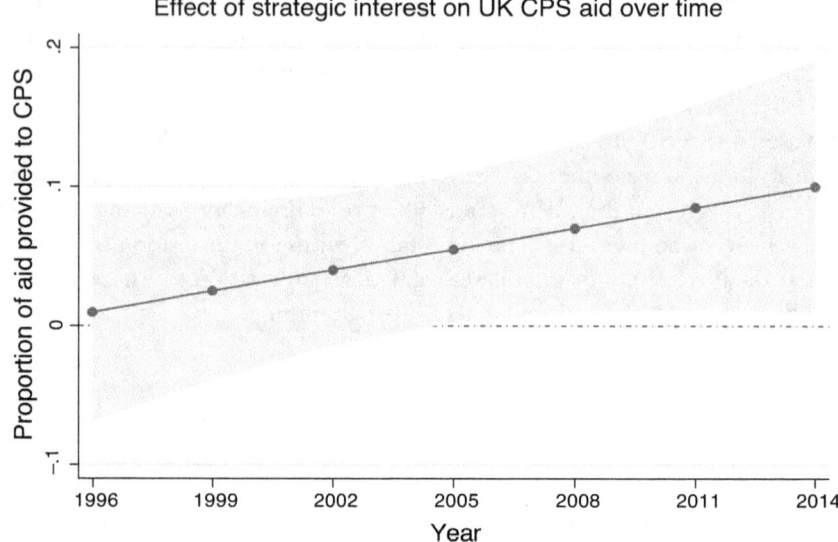

Figure 4.1 The effect of strategic interest on UK provision of conflict prevention and resolution, peace and security (CPS) aid to conflict-affected countries.
Source: from Lazell and Petrikova (2019): dependent variable – proportional provision of UK CPS aid to developing countries; main independent variables – countries' conflict-affectedness and strategic interest to the UK. Data from Creditor Reporting System, Uppsala University Conflict Data Programme (UCDP), United Nations High Commissioner on Refugees database, Stockholm International Peace Research Institute, and Global Terrorism Database.

conflict-affected countries received relatively more democratisation aid as well.[1] This became, as Figure 4.1 demonstrates, particularly notable after 2010, suggesting a potential shift in the pattern of aid disbursement coinciding with the change in government.

To recap, it seems clear from existing research that the securitised policy discourse has affected aid programming on the ground. However, little research to date has addressed the question of aid securitisation's specific impact on the recipient countries. The study presented here makes a step in that direction by examining in greater detail the types of aid programme supported by DFID under the headings of 'democratisation' and 'conflict, peace and security'; considering their impact in five sub-Saharan African countries.

Methodology

Case selection

The African countries examined here – Cameroon, CAR, Ethiopia, Kenya and Uganda – were chosen because they represent a diverse range on the conflict-affectedness and UK strategic interest scales as well as in terms of their former colonisers and dominant languages. At the same time, the countries' geographical proximity enhances the suitability of their comparison.

We used the criteria of conflict-affectedness and UK strategic interest in case selection on the basis of results from our quantitative securitisation study (Lazell and Petrikova, 2019). This indicated, as summarised above, that UK aid securitisation on the ground was apparent in three ways:

1. an increase, both absolute and relative, in the provision of UK aid to democratisation and CPS activities in aid-recipient countries over time;
2. relatively more CPS aid provided to conflict-affected countries;
3. relatively more democratisation aid provided to conflict-affected countries of high strategic interest to the UK than to strategically less important conflict-affected countries.

As Table 4.1 displays, Ethiopia, CAR and Uganda experienced conflict between 2002 and 2015, while Kenya and Cameroon were largely unaffected,[2] with the exception of Kenya's post-2007 election violence. In terms of UK strategic interests, due to the number of refugees received from each country, Western terrorist casualties in that country and the country's arms receipts from the UK, Ethiopia is of the highest strategic interest, followed by Uganda and Kenya, with Cameroon and CAR of significantly lower interest. The strategic interest of

Table 4.1 Key statistics about the five African case-study countries.

	Cameroon	CAR	Ethiopia	Kenya	Uganda
GDP per capita, PPP (2011 USD)	3289	626	1533	2836	1666
Population, total (mill)	22.83	4.55	99.87	47.24	40.14
Conflict intensity (average 2002–15) (min 0, max 1)	0	1	1	0	1
Strategic interest (average 2002–15) (min 0, max 3)	0.012	0.007	0.079	0.028	0.059
UK aid per capita (average 2002–15)	1.32	1.15	3.03	2.85	3.36

Source: World Development Indicators and Uppsala Conflict Data Program.

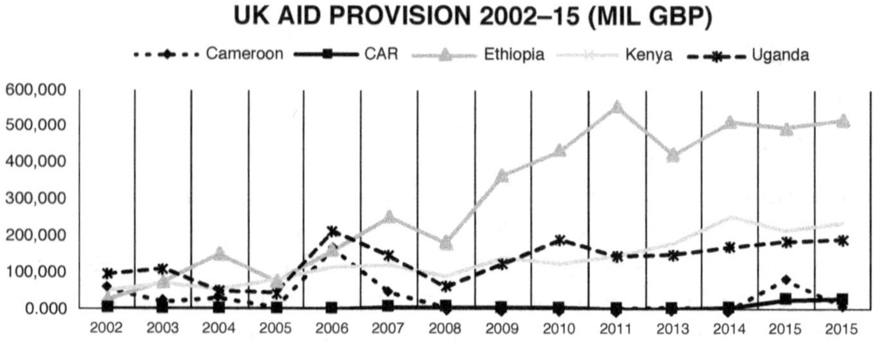

UK AID PROVISION 2002–15 (MIL GBP)

Figure 4.2 UK aid provision to the five case-study countries, 2002–15.
Source: OECD Creditor Reporting System.

each country to the UK, to a large extent, overlaps with the countries' former colonial status, with Kenya and Uganda former UK colonies and Cameroon and CAR former French colonies. Although Ethiopia remained un-colonised for most of its history, it has been a strategic Western ally in the War on Terror since 9/11 (Feyissa, 2011).

The three countries of higher strategic interest to the UK – Ethiopia, Uganda and Kenya – received substantially more UK aid per capita (~3 GBP per person annually) than the two strategically less important countries, CAR and Cameroon (~1 GBP per person annually) in the timeframe examined. Averaging the numbers, however, covers up the reality, evident from Figure 4.2, that in all the case-study countries with the exception of Cameroon, UK aid provision per capita substantially – but quite gradually – increased between 2002 and 2015, in line with the UK's commitment to and eventual attainment of the Organisation for Economic Co-operation and Development (OECD) target of 0.7 per cent GDP aid spending in 2013.[3] Only in Cameroon did total UK aid provision per capita decline, by 83 per cent, between 2002 and 2015. It is also interesting, although perhaps not surprising, that the amount of UK aid provided does not dovetail with the order of the countries' economic deprivation, with the poorest country of the five – CAR – receiving the lowest amount of UK aid per capita.

Theoretical framework, data collection and analytical methods

The first step in the empirical analysis is to inspect whether aid securitisation, as defined above, can be detected in UK aid flows to the five case-study countries. We do this by looking at the absolute and relative aid disbursements to democratisation and conflict, peace and security activities between 2002 and

2015. 2002 is the first year for which data on aid disbursements broken down by sectors and projects are available, while 2015 was the most recent at the time of research. We break up this timeframe into three periods – 2002–5, 2006–10 and 2011–15 – in order to analyse whether any change occurred following the transition from Labour to Conservative-led Governments after 2010.

The data on aid flows come from the OECD Creditor Reporting System (CRS). Aid to democratisation activities is classified by CRS under the code 152: I.5.a and includes support for democratic participation and civil society, legal and judicial development, legislatures and political parties, public administration and finance, elections, anti-corruption, human rights, women's rights and free media. Aid to conflict, peace and security activities, classified by CRS under the code 152: I.5.b, contains aid channelled to security-system management and reform; civilian peacebuilding, and conflict prevention and resolution; participation in international peacekeeping operations; removal of landmines; and work with child soldiers.

The second step in the empirical investigation is to examine the types of activity funded through DFID under the headings of democratisation and CPS and to consider their potential impact. We do this by looking again at the three time-periods – 2002–5, 2006–10 and 2011–15 – to observe whether the Conservative Coalition Government instituted any notable changes to African 'securitised' aid programming. We finish the analysis by inspecting, in greater detail, three democratisation/CPS aid projects implemented by DFID after 2010. The selection of the specific projects emanated from the results of the preceding analysis and hence is discussed later.

Findings

Provision of democratisation and conflict, peace and security aid in total and relative terms

To assess whether UK aid provision to the five case-study countries reflects the general securitisation trend, Table 4.2 shows how much aid the UK provided to democratisation and CPS activities in Cameroon, CAR, Ethiopia, Kenya and Uganda between 2002 and 2015, and the proportion of total UK aid flows to the countries these flows constituted. The two most apparent observations from the table are that:

1. democratisation activities attained significantly more financial support than CPS activities;

Table 4.2 UK provision of aid to democratisation and CPS activities between 2002 and 2015.

	Democratisation aid					
	mill USD			% total aid		
	2002–05	2006–10	2011–15	2002–05	2006–10	2011–15
Cameroon	0.81	0.45	0.08	8.44	18.48	3.98
CAR	0.27	0.00	0.09	50.65	0	0.36
Ethiopia	5.13	11.59	15.29	7.84	5.04	3.18
Kenya	5.17	5.12	12.28	8.19	4.49	6.09
Uganda	8.89	15.69	18.98	14.22	13.08	11.19
	Conflict, peace, and security aid					
	mill USD			% total aid		
	2002–05	2006–10	2011–15	2002–05	2006–10	2011–15
Cameroon	0.00	0.01	0.00	0	0.84	0.44
CAR	0.00	0.00	0.00	0	0	0
Ethiopia	0.19	0.54	2.48	0.74	0.21	0.49
Kenya	0.00	1.92	3.09	0	1.65	1.57
Uganda	0.06	1.47	1.42	0.12	1.26	0.86

Source: OECD Creditor Reporting System.

2. the countries of higher strategic interest to the UK (Ethiopia, Kenya, and Uganda) received significantly more democratisation and CPS aid – as well as total aid, as evident from Figure 4.2 – from the UK than countries of lower strategic interest (Cameroon and CAR). In turn, Cameroon and CAR, former French colonies, obtained significantly more French aid than Kenya and Uganda, former UK colonies.[4] Previous studies found former colonial ties to be a significant, but gradually waning, factor in European aid flows between the 1960s and 2010s across the world (Berthélemy, 2006; McKinlay and Little, 1978; Petrikova, 2016). Our findings show that UK – as well as French – aid provision in Africa continues strongly to reflect colonial divisions.

Looking specifically for securitisation trends discovered in our large-N quantitative study (Lazell and Petrikova, 2019) in this five-country sample yields mixed results. First, we look at whether the UK increased its disbursement of democratisation and CPS aid to the five countries over time. There has indeed been a steady rise in the provision of democratisation and CPS aid in absolute terms, particularly to Ethiopia, Kenya and Uganda, the three strategically more important countries. In relative terms aid disbursement to democratisation and

CPS activities flagged under the Conservative Coalition Government, however, indicating that other aid destinations must have received even larger boosts. There are two exceptions – the provision of democratisation aid to Kenya and of CPS aid to Ethiopia increased between 2006 and 2010 and between 2011 and 2015 also in relative terms.

If the other two elements of aid securitisation observed in the quantitative analysis (*ibid.*) were to hold here as well, conflict-affected countries (CAR, Ethiopia and Uganda) should receive more CPS aid than countries not significantly affected by conflict (Cameroon and Kenya) and strategically important conflict-affected countries (Ethiopia and Uganda) should be greater recipients of democratisation aid than strategically less important countries at conflict (CAR). The latter is indeed true, at least after 2005, with CAR receiving minimal amounts of democratisation aid from the UK compared to Ethiopia and Uganda, in both absolute and relative terms. However, CAR receives no CPS aid from the UK either, which is surprising given the high-intensity conflict underway in the country and also goes some way towards contradicting the first securitisation element described in this paragraph.[5] In a further contradiction, since 2006 Kenya – a country not officially regarded as suffering from conflict despite some insecurity issues – has received proportionally the most UK CPS aid out of the five countries examined, more than conflict-affected Ethiopia and Uganda.

In summary, empirical evidence from the five African countries provides some support for the contention that UK aid has become increasingly securitised over time. However, under the Conservative Coalition Government, this trend is particularly observable in countries of high strategic interest to the UK – Ethiopia, Kenya and Uganda. What impact does this type of securitised aid provision have on the recipients? In order to answer this question, we need to understand what programmes 'democratisation' and 'CPS' aid actually fund. The next section expounds on this topic.

Democratisation and conflict, peace and security activities funded by different UK administrations

To appreciate what the increase in securitised aid flows means for the aid recipients, we look at democratisation and CPS activities that the UK financed in the five African countries. Table 4.3 lists the five highest-funded types of DFID democratisation aid programmes during the periods 2002–5, 2006–10 and 2011–15. Overall, investments in 'public sector policy and administrative management' and in 'democratic participation and civil society' were most popular. The first category includes initiatives aimed at strengthening the countries' governments – for example, helping with the formulation of poverty reduction

Table 4.3 Five highest-funded democratisation activities.

	2002–5	2006–10	2011–15
Cameroon	Democratic participation & civil society (2.48)	Democratic participation & civil society (1.23)	Human rights (0.10)
	Elections (0.33)	Public sector policy & administrative management (0.65)	Anticorruption (0.09)
	Human rights (0.30)	Human rights (0.12)	Women's rights (0.06)
	Legal & judicial development (0.12)	Free media (0.08)	Free media (0.05)
	Public sector policy & administrative management (0.03)	Legal & judicial development (0.07)	Elections (0.04)
CAR	Public sector policy & administrative management (1.07)		Women's rights (0.44)
Ethiopia	Public sector policy & administrative management (26.30)	Public sector policy & administrative management (43.47)	Public sector policy & administrative management (25.20)
	Democratic participation & civil society (4.12)	Public finance management (7.10)	Democratic participation & civil society (24.40)
	Public finance management (1.73)	Democratic participation & civil society (4.13)	Women's rights (20.22)
	Legal & judicial development (0.26)	Elections (2.74)	Legal & judicial development (4.19)
	Free media (0.12)	Human rights (0.44)	Public finance management (2.05)
Kenya	Public sector policy & administrative management (10.90)	Democratic participation & civil society (10.52)	Elections (19.03)
	Democratic participation & civil society (5.12)	Public finance management (5.23)	Democratic participation & civil society (13.67)
	Legal & judicial development (4.15)	Public sector policy & administrative management (4.95)	Public sector policy & administrative management (10.31)
	Human rights (0.43)	Elections (2.13)	Decentralisation (8.77)
	Free media (0.10)	Human rights (0.91)	Free media (3.67)

Uganda	Public sector policy & administrative management (14.56)	Public sector policy & administrative management (33.60)	Decentralisation (24.38)
	Public finance management (8.43)	Public finance management (17.17)	Women's rights (19.99)
	Democratic participation & civil society (5.92)	Democratic participation & civil society (11.83)	Elections (14.91)
	Legal & judicial development (4.62)	Elections (8.06)	Public finance management (12.48)
	Elections (0.91)	Women's rights (3.13)	Public sector policy & administrative management (10.21)

Source: OECD Creditor Reporting System. The costs in $ million are listed in brackets.

strategies or planning health sector reforms – while the second primarily comprises schemes funding civil society organisations. 'Public finance management', where DFID advises aid-recipient governments how to spend public funds, was another popular target of UK democratisation aid.

Nevertheless, all of these programmes – public sector policy and administrative management, democratic participation and civil society, and public finance management – became relatively less popular under the Conservative Coalition Government. In turn, from 2011 onwards DFID began to channel more aid into development projects supporting elections, decentralisation, anti-corruption, human rights and women's rights. As an illustration, while for 2002–5 'women's rights' were not among the top five highest-funded democratisation programmes in any of the five countries, in the period 2011–15 they were among the top three in four out of the five countries (Table 4.3). Some of this development may be ascribed to changes in accounting strategy; analysis of individual aid projects suggested that programmes focused on enhancing women's political participation were more likely to be labelled 'democratic participation and civil society' before 2010 but 'women's rights' after 2010 – perhaps in an effort to seem better aligned with the OECD's recommendations to invest more aid in gender issues (Organisation for Economic Co-operation and Development, 2010). Even controlling for this accounting change, however, the Coalition-directed DFID clearly augmented its investments in development initiatives aimed at strengthening the rights of women and youth.

As with aid securitisation in general, the trends discussed above are less applicable to the two strategically insignificant (to the UK) countries in the sample – CAR and Cameroon. Between 2002 and 2015, the UK supported only two democratisation programmes in CAR, both multilateral and implemented through the African Union. In Cameroon, there was a significant decline in the provision of UK democratisation aid over time. This reduction was even more pronounced than the decline in total UK aid provision to the country after 2010 (see Figure 4.2) – for illustration, the highest-funded UK democratisation activity in Cameroon received almost $2.5 million from 2002–5 but only $0.1 million from 2011–15.

Table 4.4 displays the four highest-funded CPS programmes in the five countries examined and again supports the finding of Conservative aid securitisation primarily in countries of strategic interest to the UK. Both Cameroon and Kenya, which did not suffer from conflict between 2002 and 2015, started receiving CPS funding under the last Labour Government; whereas in strategically important Kenya this form of aid funding increased substantially under the Conservative Coalition Government, in strategically less important Cameroon

Table 4.4 Four highest-funded conflict, peace and security activities.

	2002–5	2006–10	2011–15
Cameroon		Civilian peacebuilding (0.05)	Civilian peacebuilding (0.02)
CAR			
Ethiopia	International peacekeeping (0.75) Removal of land mines (0.13)	Civilian peacebuilding (1.75) Security system management (0.48) International peacekeeping (0.32) Removal of land mines (0.13)	Security system management (8.58) Civilian peacebuilding (3.18) International peacekeeping (0.62) Reintegration (0.02)
Kenya		Civilian peace-building (4.54) International peacekeeping (4.42) Security system management (0.63)	Security system management (9.95) Civilian peacebuilding (4.93) International peacekeeping (0.56)
Uganda	Removal of land mines (0.17) International peacekeeping (0.08)	Civilian peacebuilding (5.95) Security system management (1.23) Removal of land mines (0.15) International peacekeeping (0.03)	Civilian peacebuilding (7.11) Security system management (0.01)

Source: OECD Creditor Reporting System. The costs in $ million are listed in brackets.

it declined. CAR, as pointed out above, received no UK aid for conflict, peace and security activities between 2002 and 2015 despite continuous conflict in the country.

The most common form of CPS aid disbursed was into 'civilian peace-building', which includes development projects aimed at encouraging reconciliation between hostile social groups and providing peace and counter-radicalisation education. Over time, however, there was an increase in the provision of aid to security sector reforms, which comprise projects intent on strengthening recipient countries' judicial systems, education of key civilian and military staff, and police reforms. While DFID (2013: 3) describes its work in security sector reforms as 'ground-breaking', the Independent Commission for Aid Impact (ICAI) (2015: 1) found little evidence that '[DFID's] work [in this area led to] … wider improvements in security and justice outcomes for the poor'. Strengthening the police forces in countries like Ethiopia, where police are routinely deployed to incur violence against civilians (Human Rights Watch, 2017), could further have unintended negative effects on civilian human rights.

To sum up this overview of DFID's democratisation and CPS programmes under different administrations between 2002 and 2015, Conservative-led DFID focused in its provision of 'securitised aid' more on strategically important countries than Labour-led DFID but did not bring about a dramatic change in development programming. Under the 'democratisation' banner, it increased investment particularly in human rights and women's rights, but 'public policy reform and administrative management' and 'democratic participation and civil society' received the bulk of democratisation funding in all time-periods examined. Similarly, 'security sector reform' attained greater support under the Conservative Coalition but 'civilian peace-building' remained an important part of CPS aid throughout 2002–15. We now move on to investigate the impact of the 'securitised' activities on recipients, with the next section examining three specific DFID projects implemented in three of the five case-study countries.

Three examples of 'securitised' development projects

A detailed look at some of the projects categorised under the types of activity receiving more funding as part of the securitisation trend, presented in this section, can help us understand the possible effects of aid securitisation on recipients. We chose these projects from a project database[6] holding DFID post aid-project documentation since 2011 under the International Aid Transparency

Initiative. Prior to choosing the three projects, we made an initial assessment of all democratisation and CPS projects implemented in Cameroon, CAR, Ethiopia, Kenya and Uganda, and made two broad observations. First, many projects did not manage to fully achieve their objectives because of weak commitment – as observed by DFID – on the part of the partners (ministries, civil servants, local NGOs), often due to high staff turnovers or divergent priorities. Secondly, despite this, DFID appeared generous in self-evaluating most of its projects as successful.

In the specific case selection, we were guided by the desire to explore two democratisation projects and one CPS project, reflecting the greater amount of aid flows to the former sector. Further, as aid securitisation under the Conservative-led Government manifested primarily in countries of higher strategic importance to the UK, we chose to examine projects implemented in Ethiopia, Kenya and Uganda rather than in Cameroon or CAR. Finally, we wanted to examine both the traditionally more popular democratisation/CPS activities (public sector policy and administrative management, democratic participation and civil society, civilian peace-building) and those that became more popular under the Conservative Coalition Government (including women's rights, anti-corruption, elections and security sector reform). The three projects selected – a women's rights project in Ethiopia, a security sector reform project in Kenya and a democratic-participation project in Uganda – fulfil all these criteria.[7]

Women's rights project: Girl Effect Ethiopia (duration: November 2011– September 2015; cost: £9.8 million + £2.8 million from Nike Foundation)

This project, implemented by DFID in collaboration with Nike Foundation, aimed to strengthen girls' rights and change the perception of girls in Ethiopian society, in order to reduce societal tolerance for violence against women and child marriages and increase girls' graduation rates. These goals were to be achieved through the creation of a multi-media platform, Yegna, which targets Ethiopians with educational music, drama and talk shows.[8] Both DFID and Girl Effect (formerly Girl Hub) evaluated the project's impact very positively. For example, Girl Effect maintained that 59 per cent of girls who were exposed to Yegna would report their parents to authorities for beating them, as opposed to 31 per cent of non-exposed girls. Similarly, 84 per cent of girls exposed to Yegna planned to wait until eighteen years old to marry, as opposed to 74 per cent of non-exposed girls (Department for International Development, 2016a: 9). The ICAI (2012) raised some warnings about Girl Effect, specifically the unclear pathways between the project's activities and intended outcomes.

Nevertheless, the ICAI review was published at the very beginning of the project's implementation in Ethiopia and many of its recommendations were addressed during the project's later execution (Department for International Development, 2016a).

In 2014, DFID pledged an additional £12 million in funding for Girl Effect from 2015–18. However, this second round of funding was withdrawn in January 2017, after a negative press campaign led by the *Daily Mail* (Malone, 2017). The newspaper labelled the Yegna singers 'Ethiopian Spice Girls' and claimed that the project was the 'undisputed crown' of the 'most wasteful, ludicrous, and patronising projects to "save" Africa' (*ibid.*). In response to the allegations, Girl Effect argued that unlike traditional development projects focused on treating the symptoms of poverty, their approach was one of addressing the cause, by challenging entrenched negative social norms involving girls.[9] Nevertheless, DFID, unable to firmly connect the project's aims and activities to national security interests, ultimately conceded that there were 'more effective ways of invest[ing] UK aid and … deliver[ing] even better … value for taxpayers' money' (Slawson, 2017).

Security sector reform project: improving community security in Kenya (duration: September 2014–March 2018; cost: £14 million)

This DFID-funded project aspired to strengthen safety and security in Kenya by making safety and security services more effective, accountable and responsive (Department for International Development, 2016b). The project focused on three inter-related types of violence – inter-communal, criminal, and against women and girls. To justify the need for the project, DFID invoked the link between reducing insecurity in Kenya and improving security in the UK, in addition to describing the goodness-of-fit between British High Commission Nairobi's objectives and the project's activities (Department for International Development, 2014a). Discussion of a fit between the project's goals and any larger national strategy of the Kenyan Government was conspicuously not mentioned.

The specific strategies that the project employed to achieve its objectives included logistical and legal support to thirty-two police stations across eight selected Kenyan counties (e.g. training police officers, establishing new protocols, strengthening ties between the police stations and community), awareness-raising about the role of police forces in communities, and the organisation of civilian peacebuilding exercises. In its most recent annual review published in October 2016, DFID rated most of the project's activities as successfully achieving the project's specified targets. However, neither the project's initial business case (*ibid.*) nor the annual reviews (Department for International Development, 2015b; Department for International Development 2016b) made it clear how the project's actions planned to realistically reduce insecurity at the national Kenyan level. This finding chimes with the conclusions of the ICAI's evaluation of DFID's investment in recipient countries' security and justice sector, which found aid to security sector reforms to frequently suffer from unclear objectives (2015: 1). ICAI also criticised DFID's preference for contracting international for-profit consulting firms as implementers of security sector reforms, resulting often in overly technical approaches (*ibid.*: 18). This reproach may also be applicable to the Kenyan project, implemented by an international for-profit firm, Coffey International.

These findings have clear implications for the UK's self-declared rationale for providing development aid. Security sector reforms are explicitly supposed to strengthen UK national security by mitigating instability and insecurity in the Global South. If the projects are unable to meet their objectives or have unintended consequences, the contribution they make to UK national security is far from clear.

Democratic participation project: deepening democracy in Uganda (duration: March 2012–December 2016; cost: £12.6 million)

The intended outcome of this DFID project in Uganda was to improve 'accountable, responsive, rights-based governance through [encouraging] effective citizen participation coupled with stronger institutions' (Department for International Development, 2017: 2). In order to achieve this outcome, the project attempted to:

1. strengthen the capacity of citizens, political leaders and selected institutions to understand and play their designated democratic roles;
2. encourage public debate on issues of public interest;
3. enhance the integrity of and citizen participation in the electoral process (*ibid.*).

As a rationale for the project, DFID cited the desire for democracy among Ugandan citizens and the simultaneous disappointment with its present functioning, which, to paraphrase, left DFID with no choice but to invest in democracy-building in Uganda (Department for International Development, 2014b: 1, 11–13). This 'need to intervene' was reinforced by DFID's perceived failure of the UN Development Programme to properly implement democracy-building programmes in Uganda (*ibid.*: 11). Again, the alignment of the Ugandan deepening-democracy programme with any national governmental strategy was not discussed.

In the final annual review, DFID concluded that the project had achieved its goals satisfactorily. However, it is not clear whether questions of attribution were resolved or even properly considered. For example, one of the project's targets was to 'increase the level of [citizen] confidence in claiming their civic and human rights' among 75 per cent of the population (Department for International Development, 2017: 3). This was deemed to have been achieved, despite no relevant quantitative data or analysis of the role that the project played in increasing such confidence among citizens. Further, DFID itself questioned the sustainability of the project's results due to its short duration and its failure to establish relationships with the Ugandan Government (the project mostly worked with Ugandan civil society).

Discussion and concluding remarks

This chapter began by illustrating how, since the late 1990s, UK development policy discourse has become securitised, increasingly emphasising the role that development aid can play in strengthening UK national security. This was the case during both the Blair and Brown Labour Governments and increased further after 2010 under the Conservatives, who have used it to justify raising aid spending amid austerity. The empirical part of the study examined whether this securitised discourse influenced aid programming in five African countries – Cameroon, CAR, Ethiopia, Kenya and Uganda – and how securitised aid programmes may have affected their recipients.

The study found some evidence of aid securitisation in these five countries, by demonstrating that aid flows to the two sectors described as crucial to ensuring security in the Global South – democratisation and conflict, peace and security – increased over time and not only in countries affected by conflict. The most notable change between Labour and Conservative Coalition Governments in this regard is the higher preference of the latter to channel 'securitised' aid particularly to countries of strategic importance to the UK (Ethiopia, Kenya and Uganda). These findings are largely in line with results from our earlier large-N study (Lazell and Petrikova, 2019).

In an attempt to better understand the potential impacts of the 'securitised' aid on its recipients, we looked more closely at specific democratisation/CPS activities funded by DFID in the five African countries in three time-periods – 2002–5, 2006–10 and 2011–15. Across the whole timeframe, the most popular democratisation projects were those aiming to reform policy sectors, encourage democratic participation and civil society, and advise on the management of public finances. The most popular CPS projects focused on civilian peacebuilding. Nevertheless, under the Conservative Coalition Government, DFID began to invest more democratisation funds in projects promoting human rights, women's rights, anti-corruption and competitive elections, and more CPS funds in security sector reforms.

Regarding security sector reforms, the UK considers itself a world-leading donor and expert in the sector. However, the ICAI (2015) found the aid programmes to be problematic, with vague objectives and unclear connections between individual activities and broader aims. The ICAI further criticised DFID's security sector reforms for often being implemented by too-technical for-profit organisations (*ibid.*). The police-reform project in Kenya examined more closely in this study appears to have suffered from all of these issues. Furthermore, security sector reforms instituted without 'national ownership', as was the case here, generally do not attain significant improvements (e.g. ICAI, 2015; Muehlmann, 2008; Nathan, 2007). The project's impact on Kenyan security is therefore unlikely to be either substantially positive or sustainable.

Further, we looked at two democratisation projects in more detail – one aimed at encouraging democratic participation in Uganda and one at strengthening women's rights, an area proportionately more funded under the Conservative Coalition Government, in Ethiopia. The democracy project in Uganda seems to have suffered from similar issues as many unsuccessful democracy programmes in the past; for example, it treated the issues of political participation and democratic quality as technical rather than political and engaged with civil society but not with the government (Uvin, 2004). Based on our brief examination of other DFID-funded democratisation and CPS projects in the case-study countries, this appears to have been a common rather than a solitary occurrence. Additionally, the initiatives for many of the projects – including the Kenyan and Ugandan ones examined here – were external to the aid-recipient countries and consequently DFID struggled to obtain sufficient commitment and collaboration from local partners. The projects' results were hence, as even DFID admitted, often unsustainable.

The Girl Effect was something of an exception in this regard as it was requested by DFID Ethiopia – internally – and used a relatively innovative approach to strengthening women's rights. However, after the project had been disparaged by right-wing media in the UK, the Conservative Government cut off its funding.[10] One of the chief underlying reasons for this move was the inability of the administration, heavily reliant on the securitised discourse in its advocacy of aid provision, to connect the women's rights project more directly with improved security outcomes in the UK.

In conclusion, this chapter has demonstrated through a case study of five African countries that UK securitisation of development aid, which began in the late 1990s, has continued and further intensified under Conservative-led Governments since 2010. A closer examination of the 'securitised' aid activities unfortunately suggested that they were generally unlikely to sustainably reduce the likelihood of conflict and instability in the recipient countries, thus undermining one of the current chief rationales for UK development aid provision.

Notes

1. Strategic importance was estimated on the basis of the number of refugees the UK received; the number of arms the UK exported; the number of terrorist-attack casualties against OECD/EU citizens sustained (Lazell and Petrikova, 2019: 8–9).
2. This is unfortunately no longer the case at the time of writing: www.irinnews.org/news/2017/11/09/refugees-warn-looming-civil-war-cameroon [accessed 14 June 2018].
3. https://data.oecd.org/oda/net-oda.htm [accessed 19 February 2018].
4. https://stats.oecd.org/Index.aspx?DataSetCode=CRS1[accessed 19 February 2018].
5. See www.theguardian.com/global-development/2017/dec/18/the-future-is-very-dark-central-african-republics-relentless-cycle-of-suffering [accessed 19 February 2018].
6. https://devtracker.dfid.gov.uk/ [accessed 2 February 2018].
7. Alternative permutations of projects could have been examined, such as a civilian peacebuilding project in Uganda and an elections project in Kenya – but would have yielded broadly similar conclusions.
8. See www.girleffect.org/what-we-do/yegna/ [accessed 19 February 2018].
9. See www.girleffect.org/what-girls-need/articles/july16/august-launch/a-statement-from-girl-effect-about-yegna-and-our-work-with-dfid/ [accessed 19 February 2018].
10. The International Development Committee subsequently criticised DFID for giving in to the media pressure (Select Committee on International Development, 2017: 4).

References

Abrahamsen, R. (2005) 'Blair's Africa: the politics of securitization and fear', *Alternatives: Global, Local, Political*, 30:1, 55–80.

Alesina, A. and Dollar, D. (2000) 'Who gives foreign aid to whom and why?', *Journal of Economic Growth*, 5:1, 33–63.

BBC News (2017) 'Foreign aid to be shifted to support UK policy, Johnson says', *BBC News*, 31 December 2017, www.bbc.co.uk/news/uk-42528712 [accessed 19 February 2018].

Berthélemy, J. (2006) 'Bilateral donors' interest vs. recipients' development motives in aid allocation: do all donors behave the same?', *Review of Development Economics*, 10:2, 179–94.

Brown, S. and Grävingholt, J. (2016) 'Security, development and the securitization of foreign aid', in S. Brown and J. Grävingholt (eds), *The Securitization of Foreign Aid* (London: Palgrave Macmillan), 1–17.

Bueno de Mesquita, B. and Smith, A. (2009) 'A political economy of aid', *International Organization*, 63:2, 309–40.

Department for International Development (2000) *Eliminating World Poverty: Making Globalization Work for the Poor*, White Paper on International Development (London: Department for International Development).

Department for International Development (2003) *Security Sector Reform*, Policy Brief (London: Department for International Development).

Department for International Development (2005a) 'Fighting poverty to build a safer world: a strategy for security and development', http://webarchive.nationalarchives.gov.uk/+/http:/www.dfid.gov.uk/pubs/files/securityforase.pdf [accessed 19 February 2018].

Department for International Development (2005b) *Why We Need to Work More Effectively in Fragile States* (London: Department for International Development).

Department for International Development (2007) 'Governance, development and democratic politics: DFID's work in building more effective states', http://webarchive.nationalarchives.gov.uk/+/http:/www.dfid.gov.uk/pubs/files/governance.pdf [accessed 19 February 2018].

Department for International Development (2009) 'Eliminating world poverty: Building our common future', www.gov.uk/government/uploads/system/uploads/attachment_data/file/229029/7656.pdf [accessed 19 February 2018].

Department for International Development (2012) *Operational Plan 2012–2015* (London: Department for International Development).

Department for International Development (2013) 'Policy approach to rule of law', www.gov.uk/government/uploads/system/uploads/attachment_data/file/306396/policy-approach-rule-of-law.pdf [accessed 19 February 2018].

Department for International Development (2014a) 'DFID Kenya – improving community security programme: business case and summary', https://devtracker.dfid.gov.uk/projects/GB-1-202509/documents [accessed 19 February 2018].

Department for International Development (2014b) 'Democratic governance facility: deepening democracy programme: business case and justification summary', https://devtracker.dfid.gov.uk/projects/GB-1-202802/documents [accessed 19 February 2018].

Department for International Development (2015a) '2010 to 2015 government policy: overseas aid effectiveness', www.gov.uk/government/publications/2010-to-2015-government-policy-overseas-aid-effectiveness/2010-to-2015-government-policy-overseas-aid-effectiveness [accessed 19 February 2018].

Department for International Development (2015b) 'DFID Kenya – improving community security programme, annual review', https://devtracker.dfid.gov.uk/projects/GB-1–202509/documents [accessed 19 February 2018].

Department for International Development (2016a) 'Girl Hub Ethiopia – project completion review', https://devtracker.dfid.gov.uk/projects/GB-1–202913/documents [accessed 19 February 2018].

Department for International Development (2016b) 'DFID Kenya – improving community security programme, annual review', https://devtracker.dfid.gov.uk/projects/GB-1–202509/documents [accessed 19 February 2018].

Department for International Development (2017) 'Democratic governance facility: deepening democracy programme, annual review', https://devtracker.dfid.gov.uk/projects/GB-1–202802/documents [accessed 19 February 2018].

Duffield, M. (2001) *Global Governance and the New Wars: The Merging of Development and Security* (London: Zed Books).

Feyissa, D. (2011) 'Aid negotiation: the uneasy "partnership" between EPRDF and the donors', *Journal of Eastern African Studies*, 5:4, 788–817.

Fisher, J. and Anderson, D. (2015) 'Authoritarianism and the securitization of development in Africa', *International Affairs*, 91:1, 131–51.

Greening, J. (2015a) 'UK aid in 2015: the progress so far and the priorities ahead', 8 March 2015, Speech given to the Institute of Development Studies, University of Sussex, Brighton, www.gov.uk/government/speeches/uk-aid-in-2015-the-progress-so-far-and-the-priorities-ahead [accessed 2 February 2018].

Greening, J. (2015b) 'Changing world, changing aid: where international development needs to go next', 2 July 2015, Speech given to the Overseas Development Institute, London, www.gov.uk/government/speeches/changing-world-changing-aid-where-international-development-needs-to-go-next [accessed 2 February 2018].

Her Majesty's Treasury and Department for International Development (2015) *UK Aid: Tackling Global Challenges in the National Interest* (London: Her Majesty's Treasury).

Human Rights Watch (2017) 'Ethiopia: events of 2016', www.hrw.org/world-report/2017/country-chapters/ethiopia [accessed 19 February 2018].

Independent Commission for Aid Impact (2012) 'Girl Hub: a DFID and Nike Foundation initiative', https://icai.independent.gov.uk/wp-content/uploads/ICAI-Girl-Hub-Final-Report_P1–51.pdf [accessed 19 February 2018].

Independent Commission for Aid Impact (2015) 'Review of UK development assistance for security and justice', https://icai.independent.gov.uk/wp-content/uploads/ICAI-Report-UK-Development-Assistance-for-Security-and-Justice..pdf [accessed 19 February 2018].

Kuziemko, I. and Werker, E. (2006) 'How much is a seat on the Security Council worth? Foreign aid and bribery at the United Nations', *Journal of Political Economy*, 114:5, 905–30.

Lazell, M. and Petrikova, I. (2019) 'Is development aid securitised? Evidence from a cross-country examination of sector aid commitments', *Development Policy Review*. OnlineFirst. 10.IIII/dpr.12426.

Lunn, J. and Booth, L. (2016) 'The 0.7% aid target: June 2016 update', House of Commons Briefing Paper, 3714, www.researchbriefings.files.parliament.uk/documents/SN03714/SN03714.pdf [accessed 19 February 2018].

Malone, A. (2017) 'Question that ended daftest foreign aid fiasco of them all: did listening to a girl band REALLY stop 40,000 young Ethiopian girls getting married too early?', *Daily Mail*, 10 January 2017, www.dailymail.co.uk/news/article-4111498/Question-ended-daftest-foreign-aid-fiasco-Did-listening-girl-band-REALLY-stop-40–000-young-Ethiopian-girls-getting-married-early.html [accessed 19 February 2018].

McConnon, E. (2014) 'Security for all, development for some? The incorporation of security in UK's development policy', *Journal of International Development*, 26:8, 1127–48.

McKinlay, R. and Little, R. (1978) 'A foreign-policy model of the distribution of British bilateral aid, 1960–70', *British Journal of Political Science*, 8:3, 313–31.

Muehlmann, T. (2008) 'Police restructuring in Bosnia-Herzegovina: problems of internationally-led security sector reform', *Journal of Intervention and Statebuilding*, 2:1, 1–22.

Nathan, L. (2007) *No Ownership, No Commitment: A Guide to Local Ownership of Security Sector Reform* (Birmingham: University of Birmingham).

Organisation for Economic Co-operation and Development (2010) 'Investing in women and girls: the breakthrough strategy for achieving all the MDGs', www.oecd.org/dac/gender-development/45704694.pdf [accessed 19 February 2018].

Oxfam (2011) *Whose Aid Is It Anyway? Politicising Aid in Conflict and Crisis* (Oxford: Oxfam).

Petrikova, I. (2016) 'Promoting "good behaviour" through aid: do "new" donors differ from the "old" ones?', *Journal of International Relations and Development*, 19:1, 153–92.

Petrikova, I. and Lazell, M. (2017) 'Multilateral aid provision in the era of the development–security nexus: examining the discourse and practice', *Conflict, Security & Development*, 17:6, 492–516.

Saferworld (2011) 'The securitisation of aid? Reclaiming security to meet the poor people's needs', www.saferworld.org.uk/Securitisation%20briefing%20pages.pdf [accessed 2 February 2018].

Select Committee on International Development (2017) *UK Aid: Allocation of Resources*, International Development Committee, Seventh Report, https://publications.parliament.uk/pa/cm201617/cmselect/cmintdev/100/100.pdf [accessed 19 February 2018].

Slawson, N. (2017) 'Ethiopian music scheme loses UK aid funding after press criticism', *Guardian*, 7 January 2017, www.theguardian.com/politics/2017/jan/07/ethiopian-music-scheme-yegna-loses-uk-aid-funding-after-press-criticism [accessed 19 February 2018].

Straw, J. (2002) 'Africa matters', *Independent on Sunday*, 3 February 2002.

Suhrke, A. and Buckmaster, J. (2006) 'Aid, growth and peace: a comparative analysis', *Conflict, Security & Development*, 6:3, 337–63.

Uvin, P. (2004) *Human Rights and Development* (Sterling, VA: Kumarian Press).
Watt, N. (2010) 'Protests as UK security put at heart of government's aid policy', *Guardian*, 29 August 2010, www.theguardian.com/politics/2010/aug/29/protests-uk-security-aid-policy [accessed 19 February 2018].

5
The UK and peacekeeping operations on the African continent

David Curran

Seeking to identify how the UK has engaged, and continues to engage, with United Nations (UN) peacekeeping operations on the African continent is a difficult proposition. The UK has been involved on multiple levels, and in multiple different guises when considering different peacekeeping operations. At times, the UK has obstructed the UN's evolution in this area, and at other times the UK has actively supported the development of peacekeeping operations on the continent. With the deployment in 2016 and 2017 of up to four hundred troops to South Sudan, and seventy to Somalia, effectively doubling the UK's existing contribution to all UN operations, it is useful to reflect on this relationship, and to attempt to identify themes that can be seen in UK engagement.

This chapter, therefore, seeks to chart how the UK has engaged with UN peacekeeping on the African continent, using a broadly chronological approach. The chapter argues that while it is difficult to identify a single overarching policy towards UN operations on the African continent, there are identifiable trends which have influenced how policymakers have treated the topic. Most notable is that throughout the UK's history of engagement with peacekeeping on the African continent, there has been varying degrees of scepticism as to the motivations, politics and practicalities of UN missions. The second main trend is that the UK's interactions that effect African-based peacekeeping operations have generally been undertaken on a political level, be it in the chamber of the UN Security Council (UNSC), through the UN secretariat, or through financial and bilateral contributions.

The chapter proceeds as follows. First, the chapter will analyse the UK's interaction with UN peacekeeping in its earlier iterations, looking in particular at missions in Egypt and the Congo (now Democratic Republic of the Congo). This period saw the UN's rise come at the same time as the colonial wain of the UK on the continent. The chapter will then examine peacekeeping during the post-Cold War years. During the 1990s, the UK had little engagement with operations on the African continent, yet developed a peacekeeping doctrine that would shape *all* peacekeeping operations – whether in Africa or beyond. The third part of the chapter examines the period 2000–15, during which time the UK moved away significantly from UN operations but supported their development in other ways. Finally, the chapter will conclude with an examination of how the UK has re-engaged with peacekeeping on the African continent, through looking at the pledges made under the post-2015 Conservative Government.

The Cold War: decolonisation, suspicion and limited interest

Two operations during the Cold War period best outline the UK's approach to peacekeeping in this period: the UN Emergency Force (UNEF I), deployed in the Suez in 1956, and the UN Mission to the Congo (ONUC), deployed in 1964.[1] In both of these cases, UK actions highlighted a mix of two factors. First, a desire to manage the context in a colonial manner, and secondly suspicion of the UN's motives.

The colonial wain

Primarily, UK interactions with UN peacekeeping on the African continent during the Cold War were affected by the UK's colonial relationship with countries on the continent. It was, ironically, the UK's desire to invade the Suez Canal in Egypt (along with France and Israel) on 31 October 1956 which led to UNEF I, the UN's first armed peacekeeping mission (Ramsbotham and Woodhouse, 1999: 252). The UK action was designed to use the force of arms to open access to the Suez Canal, which had recently been nationalised by newly elected Egyptian President, Gamal Abdel Nasser. Even after the peacekeeping operation was authorised by the UN, UK policymakers argued substantially for a role in the Suez, by proposing that UNEF I comprise British and French soldiers. Instead, UN Secretary-General, Dag Hammarskjöld prohibited UK and French forces joining UNEF, opting instead for peacekeepers from small, neutral countries (Briscoe, 2003: 47). Even prominent members of the Commonwealth were excluded, including a contingent from New Zealand, on the grounds that it was too 'pro-British' (New Zealand had supported the British invasion); so was a Pakistani force. A Canadian battalion was put into reserve because it was feared that Egyptians would mistake them for British soldiers (Harbottle, 1971: 15). The Suez invasion had wider implications for the UK's politics, most notably leading to the resignation of the Conservative Prime Minister, Anthony Eden. In terms of the UK/UN relationship, the scene was set for a strained relationship between the UK and UN during this period, whereby states which were embracing independence from former colonisers such as the UK were being supported by the organisation.

This strained relationship was obvious throughout the UK's diplomatic approach to the next significant UN operation on the African continent, ONUC. ONUC was created as a result of a request from the newly elected Congolese leadership for UN intervention to quell an attempted secession of the mineral-rich Katanga province, a secession supported politically and physically by the Belgian Government (which deployed military and administrative personnel to the province). As a result, UN Secretary-General Dag Hammerskjöld, acting under Article 99 of the UN Charter,[2] called the UNSC to intervene in the Congo to halt external aggression (Briscoe, 2003: 102). The UK was not to have military engagement in this conflict but took a high degree of diplomatic interest in ONUC's progress.

Solidarity with other colonial powers was certainly a driver of this diplomatic approach. Initially, the UK was part of a small group opposed to Hammarkjöld's desire to have the UN intervene in Congo to put a halt to external aggression. Instead, Britain supported the Belgian Government's deployment of soldiers and administrators to support Katangan secession.[3] Policymakers saw Katanga as an 'island of stability' in the country (James, 1996: 121) and argued that Belgium's intervention was performing a valuable task and it should not be asked to withdraw on 'the off chance that the United Nations would be able to establish [law and order] all over the country' (*ibid.*: 356–7). Mixed with this solidarity was concern for UK territories bordering the Congo, in particular concern over a spillover into the British dependent territories that bordered the state (and in particular Northern Rhodesia) (Briscoe, 2003: 102). Yet, at the same time, UK diplomats in New York were aware of their position among other states within the UN, and the costs of being perceived as a colonial power among the broader UN membership (James, 1996: 123). This would lead to a mixed voting record on resolutions pertaining to ONUC. For instance, at the beginning of the conflict the UK abstained on UNSC Resolution 143, which established the operation – arguing that there was no clarity in the process of ONUC entering the conflict and Belgian withdrawal. Yet, eight days later, the UK voted for a similar resolution (Resolution 145) calling for Belgian withdrawal, which authorised the Secretary-General to take 'any necessary action' to implement Resolution 143 (Foreign and Commonwealth Office, 1994: 188).

Suspicion of the UN

Linked strongly to the UK's belief that as a colonial power it – and its fellow states – had the ability (and the right) to manage conflict on the continent was a significant amount of scepticism that the UN was an organisation capable of carrying out this task. In the case of UNEF I, the UK's intransigent policy towards the UN's attempts to create the mission saw its diplomats veto successive UNSC resolutions that called for Israeli withdrawal from the invaded territories and the establishment of a peacekeeping force (Ramsbotham and Woodhouse, 1999: 262). Instead, Britain and France argued they could do the job themselves. As a result, UNEF I was created through the General Assembly, under the Uniting for Peace Resolution, first through the US-sponsored Resolution 997 (calling for an immediate ceasefire, reopening of the canal and demanding a withdrawal of forces) which was passed with sixty-five votes to five, with Britain voting against the resolution (Briscoe, 2003: 46).

In the case of ONUC, the UK was sceptical about the UN's ability to restore the authority of the Congolese state in light of the attempted secession of Katanga. There was significant unease among UK policymakers on the force posture of ONUC, in particular the authorisation of 'all necessary measures' to maintain the territorial integrity of the Congo, to expel foreign fighters from Katanga and to ensure the UN's freedom of movement in the country. This unease led to UK diplomats arguing against increased use of force in UNSC debates and abstaining on resolutions authorising robust actions. Yet these actions also served to give the perception that the UK supported Katangan secession (James, 1996: 123). In some ways, this scepticism was well grounded. UN peacekeeping operations were barely in their first decade, yet were being mandated in the Congo to intervene in an internal conflict with a range of local and international conflict parties. Moreover, ONUC was a massive undertaking, making it the largest UN peacekeeping mission of its generation. At its height, almost 20,000 troops served under the ONUC flag. It was also a greatly complex conflict, which brought UN peacekeeping mechanisms into an internal conflict for the first time. ONUC led to major disagreements in the UNSC and created one of the gravest political and financial crises that the UN has encountered (UN, 1985: 215).

Scepticism of the UN's abilities was also linked to the role of the Soviet Union in the organisation. By default, any UN mission was to have Soviet influence due to its permanent seat on the UNSC. This had led to more overt concern from the UK mission concerning another mission, the United Nations Peacekeeping Force in Cyprus, which the UK had felt should be dealt with by the North Atlantic Treaty Organisation (NATO) as opposed to the UN. However, in the case of ONUC the Soviet Union had influence within the UN's policymaking:

its diplomats had branded the Belgian Government as aggressors in the conflict. Moreover, there was concern from UK policymakers over more direct influence on a bilateral level between the Soviet and Congolese Governments (James, 1961: 356–7).

These two competing demands broadly served to confuse the UK's approach to UN peacekeeping in Africa during the Cold War. As a result, the UK was often isolated in the organisation. Briscoe sums this up well in the UNEF I context by stating that the UK's approach meant it had 'been caught attempting to resolve an international disagreement by force of arms, a discredited approach which the United Nations had been established to replace. UNEF appeared as the modern, and morally superior, alternative to the outdated method of dispute settlement which had been attempted by two declining imperial powers' (2003: 47).

Yet, in other ways, the very exposure of the principles and processes of the UN in African conflict had given UK policymakers in London cause to rethink their relationship with the body. In light of ONUC, Foreign Secretary Lord Home, made constructive recommendations for future peacekeeping operations, including 'unambiguous' directives from the UNSC, a requirement for non-partisan actions by the UN, and a need for the UN chain of command to 'convey orders which are made with precision and carried out from the Secretary General down to the lowest officer on the ground' (*ibid.*: 109).

Moreover, 1964 saw the publication of *Britain and the United Nations: Proposals for Peacekeeping including a Commonwealth Force* by the Bow Group, an influential centre-right think-tank. It argued that the UN should not be mistrusted in the light of the episode in the Congo. If anything, it should be credited, for ensuring that the conflict did not worsen and generate into a new battlefield for superpower rivalry. The paper claimed that the UN should not be seen as a 'reckless learner-driver who must at all cost be denied access to a faster vehicle', instead arguing that 'it is, on the contrary, a driver whose vehicle is all brakes and no engine, whose salient feature is defective to perform some of the bigger tasks entrusted to it' (Hanning, 1964: 2). From this, the report found that the military aspect of ONUC was the main reason for failure in the Congo, with the Secretary-General left with contingents with differing levels of competence for a peacekeeping mission. The paper thus argued for a set peacekeeping doctrine across contingents. Importantly, and bringing the discussion back to the colonial dimension, it identified that a 'Commonwealth Force' be created, trained by the UK, to be the bedrock of such missions.

The post-Cold War period

Beyond Suez, Congo and Cyprus, UK engagement with peacekeeping operations during the Cold War was minimal. At the time of the fall of the Berlin Wall, the UK had very little in terms of policy and doctrinal guidance towards the activity. However, the UN was to become a significant actor in a range of conflicts, not least on the African continent, with missions of varying size and function created in Angola, Western Sahara, Somalia, Mozambique, Liberia, Uganda and Rwanda between 1989 and 1993 (UN, 2013). We can split the UK's approach to peacekeeping, during the period of 1989–2000, into two. For much of the 1990s there was a focus on European peacekeeping, yet towards the end of the decade there was a turn towards peacekeeping in Africa with engagement in Sierra Leone.

A focus on Europe

As stated above, the increasing number of peacekeeping interventions in Africa did not necessarily mean that the level to which the UK was involved in missions rose concurrently. In fact, the UK had a light footprint on missions in Africa. This was primarily because the UK's main involvement in UN peacekeeping as a whole was as a major troop contributor to the UN Protection Force (UNPROFOR) in the former Yugoslavia. This investment in a European-based operation arguably led the UK to move focus away from significantly investing in missions on the African continent.

The lack of UK engagement on the African continent fed into more catastrophic results. In the case of the UN Assistance Mission for Rwanda (UNAMIR), the disparity in Western support for the operation and that of UNPROFOR was not lost on those invested in UNAMIR, not least the Force Commander, Romeo Dallaire. He noted how even in the early days of the mission, large Western contributors would argue that in the case of Rwanda they were 'peacekeepinged out' and unable to offer support to UNAMIR, yet would be more prepared to offer support to larger missions in the Balkans (Dallaire, 2004: 89). As the genocide unfolded in Rwanda from April 1994, and with the UK committing no troops to the UNAMIR operation, Britain's representative on the UNSC, David Hannay, argued against reinforcing the UN mission, making the case that 'peacekeeping was not appropriate for civil war and where fighting factions were unwilling to cooperate' (Melvern and Williams, 2004: 10). Although the UK was to provide a field hospital to the UNAMIR II operation in the latter months of 1994, the damage had already been done.

Doctrinal development and Sierra Leone

Like many of the major contributors to peacekeeping in the first half of the 1990s, the UK was part of the general retreat from UN peacekeeping that took place between 1995 and 1999 (Bellamy and Williams, 2010). Nevertheless, as a result of the UK's own experience in Bosnia, and the wider UN calamities in Somalia and Rwanda, significant development in peacekeeping doctrine occurred within the UK, resulting in the development of the 'Peace Support Operation' (PSO) doctrine.

Throughout the 1990s the UK sought to reflect its experiences in peacekeeping operations with doctrinal development. The PSO doctrine was drawn largely from experiences in Bosnia, first by building on ideas of consent promotion seen in the 1994 doctrine 'Wider Peacekeeping' (Ministry of Defence, 1995). Additionally, and more pertinently to peacekeeping on the African continent, the PSO doctrine drew on broader challenges that the UN faced in employing force in its missions. Although UNPROFOR was the primary source of evidence which informed PSO thinking on use of force, it was missions in Somalia (where the use of robust force led to a loss of consent from local groups towards the United Nations Operation in Somalia II mission) and Rwanda (where peacekeepers were targeted as part of the génocidaires' strategy) where lessons about how robust force can be used in the peacekeeping context were learned (Curran and Williams, 2017; Wilkinson, 2000).

As a result of these doctrinal debates, the PSO doctrine sought to match consent promotion activities (the carrot) with the employment of robust peacekeeping (the stick). It therefore advocated that future peacekeeping operations have the flexibility to be '[s]ufficiently flexible, robust and combat-capable to deal with a wide range of scenarios, including operating in a non-permissive environment', with the intention that the mission 'transitions to a less militarised operation which would have greater levels of consent from belligerent groups' (ibid.: 1).

This doctrinal evolution was to have important effects on all UN missions throughout the 2000s, including those deployed on the African continent, and therefore is significant in the context of how the UK relates to African peacekeeping operations. The idea that peacekeeping operations would be operationally designed to allow greater levels of robust force was adopted in the UN's own conceptualisation of peacekeeping, with the 2000 *Report of the Panel on UN Peace Operations* (more commonly known as the Brahimi Report) proposing that UN peacekeepers use force in an impartial manner against what it termed 'spoilers' to a peace process (UN, 2000: 9). Since the Brahimi Report, 'robust peacekeeping' has become increasingly normalised in UN operations (Hunt, 2017), particularly in missions on the African continent.

It was with UK engagement with the United Nations Assistance Mission in Sierra Leone (UNAMSIL) that the UK would test this new approach to peacekeeping. UK military deployment alongside UNAMSIL was suggested as a working example of the 'ethical foreign policy' that characterised the early years of Tony Blair's Labour Government (Williams, 2005). The UK deployment, under Operation Palliser, came predominantly as a reaction to a significantly deteriorating security situation in the state during the summer of 2000, where the UN mission found itself under attack by the rebel Revolutionary United Front (RUF) (Olonisakin, 2005). It had already suffered from a number of challenges ranging from how to uphold a weak peace agreement (that the UK had helped to formulate (Short, 2004: 99)) and how to use force when faced with increasingly confident rebels committing atrocities against civilians. The crisis reached its peak when rebels kidnapped some 500 UNAMSIL peacekeepers, sparking a major crisis (Conflict, Security and Development Group, 2003: 75). It was this breakdown in the UN mission and the resulting instability, as well as the desire to support President Kabbah's Government, that were the primary drivers of UK military intervention (Williams, 2001: 153–4).

Under Operation Palliser, a robust, unilateral combat-capable force was deployed primarily to evacuate UK citizens (Conflict, Security and Development Group, 2003: 77). Although the force was not within the UN's chain of command, it assisted UNAMSIL in securing the capital, Freetown. The force secured the airport for the UN forces, and used robust force against rebel militias to release UK soldiers taken hostage in August 2000. Furthermore, the UK force created a secure zone in and around Freetown, which gave the UNAMSIL operation a stable area from which to deploy and expand. Through this action, the UK force was able to conduct 'operations across the complete spectrum of PSO and partial enforcement operations' (Wilkinson, 2000: 2), and it was able to evolve from an evacuation force, to stabilisation force, to combat search and rescue force, to a training body for the national armed forces (Conflict, Security and Development Group, 2003: 73).

The deployment was credited with tipping the psychological balance of the war in favour of the Sierra Leone Government and persuading the rebels the war was unwinnable, especially after a major battle that occurred during the rescue of British hostages in September 2000 (Dorman, 2009). Furthermore, as Keen argues, the UK's stance made many RUF fighters believe that cooperating with the UN was a more favourable option than fighting British troops, in a sort of 'good cop, bad cop' scenario (2005: 272–3).

From 2000 to 2015: developing peacekeeping from backstage

UK engagement in Sierra Leone also raised questions over motives for engagement with peacekeeping on the African continent, and arguably set the scene for the pattern of UK engagement in peacekeeping operations for the next ten to fifteen years. However, the UK was to draw down its overall commitment to putting boots on the ground in UN peacekeeping operations, meaning a considerably light footprint for those operations on the African continent. Behind this, there were three main drivers, which arguably still resonate to the present day. The first of these has been scepticism over UN-led military responses to violent conflict; secondly, the decreasing strategic necessity to be involved directly in UN missions; thirdly, the notion that engagement in peacekeeping need not be purely undertaken with putting boots on the ground.

Scepticism of UN arrangements

Engagement with UNAMSIL did little to dispel the sense of doubt borne out of the UNPROFOR experience over the ability of the UN to adequately respond to violent conflict. The UK's unwillingness to become involved in UNAMSIL directly was in large part down to the considerable scepticism within the Ministry of Defence over UN competence and its command and control mechanisms (Dorman, 2009: 88). Indeed, one study of the UK operation concluded that 'the British government system was incapable of fully identifying what it wanted its armed forces to do and it was effectively left to the commander on the ground ... to decide policy' (ibid.: 68). The MoD argued that in order to effect a major change in UNAMSIL's fortunes, Britain would have to become a major contributor to the mission and perhaps take on the force commander role, which was a non-starter politically (ibid.: 88; Williams, 2013: 110). Secondly, in the case of Sierra Leone there was little need to identify UK actions as being wholly or partially in response to developing UN capacities for peacekeeping. As the UK intervention developed, policymakers emphasised the need to rescue UK citizens in peril, rather than make the case for strengthening the UN mission. The announcement of the decision to send a 'spearhead force' to Sierra Leone came one day before the British High Commissioner for Sierra Leone instigated the evacuation of UK nationals and the start of the operation (Williams, 2001: 161). Throughout the period 2000–15, both of these characteristics have been notable, and have mitigated against decisions to become significantly involved in operations.

The decreasing strategic need for engagement

Complementing the sceptical approach is the perception in Whitehall that peacekeeping operations were deployed in areas of little strategic value to the UK. The majority of UN peacekeeping operations – eight out of the ten largest – are deployed in Sub-Saharan Africa. Importantly, this part of the world has been identified as not being viewed as a major strategic concern for the UK (Curran, 2015a: 7; Curran and Williams, 2016: 11). This trend was noted not long after New Labour's ethical foreign policy commitments in the early 2000s, with commentators suggesting that the difficulty of justifying additional 'out of area operations' forced the Government to ensure that future operations would be 'operationally feasible and have broad international support', but must also show clear net benefits to the UK (Dorman, 2004: 246).

The ambivalence over engaging in African conflicts extended to UK engagement in the EU Battlegroup structure. In 2008, the UK refused to deploy its troops as an EU battlegroup to support the UN's Mission in the Democratic Republic of Congo (MONUC) to defend the town of Goma in the east of the country. The UK refused despite a number of strong reasons which would have supported deployment. First, the EU was formally asked by UN Secretary-General Ban Ki-moon – through a letter to Javier Solana – to provide forces to support the UN's MONUC deployment; secondly, certain EU member states were enthusiastic about deployment under the Battlegroup concept; and most importantly, the UK was the lead state of one of the EU battlegroups that was supposed to be on call at that time (Curran, 2015b; Gowan, 2010). As Balossi-Restelli suggested, such a deployment faced significant opposition within the UK military, which claimed that an EU deployment would have placed 'serious strain' on the UK military that was already stretched in Iraq and Afghanistan (2011: 171).

Engagement from backstage

With this in mind, the UK has sought to develop peacekeeping as a whole – and operations in Africa – in broader ways. Much of this can be seen in UK activities at a strategic level at New York, and in particular through political and financial backing for operations.

On the UNSC, the UK has been one of the most active P5 members of the Council (along with France) at proposing resolutions, debates and shaping the agenda on issues pertaining to peacekeeping (Tardy and Zaum, 2015: 121). Additionally, the UK is the designated 'pen holder' – the member of the UNSC which takes the lead in drafting resolutions – on several relevant issues, including, Libya, Sierra Leone, Somalia and Darfur, as well as the thematic areas of 'peacekeeping operations',[4] protection of civilians in armed conflict and UNSC Resolution 1325 (on Women, Peace and Security) (UN Security Council, 2013). Britain's status as pen holder and chair of the Protection of Civilians Informal Working Group has also provided a 'useful forum to discuss protection language' in the process of mandate formulation in arguably the most important area in contemporary UN peacekeeping (Foreign and Commonwealth Office, 2012; UN Security Council, 2015). The UK mission in New York has also used its seat on the UNSC to support the Report of the High-Level Independent Panel on UN Peace Operations and recently reiterated three priority areas of reform: 'better protection of civilians; better planning of missions and more targeted and focused mandating; and a more strategic approach to force generation' (Foreign and Commonwealth Office, 2015).

The political contributions in New York are backed up by financial contributions. Until 2016, the UK was the fifth-highest provider of assessed contributions to UN peacekeeping (behind the USA, Japan, Germany and France), providing 6.68 per cent of the UN's annual peacekeeping bill.[5] The UK also makes a notable contribution to the UN's regular budget, which funds the UN's special political missions. It is the fifth-highest contributor, providing 5.179 per cent of the annual total, which in 2014–15 was approximately $5.5 billion. The UK thus currently provides around $850 million (about £590 million) in assessed contributions to UN peace operations annually and has also made additional voluntary contributions (either in cash or in kind) to support UN peacekeeping, and is a leading donor to the UN's Peacebuilding Fund.

It is with these developments in New York that the UK has gained significant traction in shaping the development of peacekeeping operations. The extent to which this is a suitable substitute for actually deploying forces is open to debate. The peacekeeping system is arguably stretched between those who mandate and pay for peacekeeping operations and those who deploy troops into missions. This has been outlined in the UN's recent High-Level Report on Peace Operations, which states that the lack of effective 'triangular cooperation' between the secretariat, UNSC and Troop Contributing Countries (TCCs) 'has generated frustration on all sides, and has impacted mandate implementation' (UN, 2015: 49).

In addition to the strategic-level debates, and as a way of offering some kind of engagement on the ground, the UK throughout the 2000s engaged (and still engages to some extent) in a range of bilateral initiatives, particularly on the African continent. These would include capacity-building initiatives used to support states' abilities to engage in peacekeeping operations. These include the deployment of specialists as part of various regional and bilateral capacity-building programmes, including in Kenya (British Peace Support Team for East Africa and British Army Training Unit Kenya), South Africa (British Peace Support Team South Africa) and Sierra Leone. At times, Britain has provided strategic airlift for UN missions in Mali and South Sudan, and has supported several EU training missions, including in Somalia and Mali. In the case of Mali, the UK sent a forty-strong training team to work alongside personnel from the Irish Defence Forces in training infantry and artillery skills to the Malian Army (Ministry of Defence, 2013). As worthy as this may be, this form of engagement was criticised in some quarters as being a model of 'outsourcing' conflict management on the African continent, where African personnel are trained and equipped to 'bear the burden' of complex operations (Gowan and Whitney, 2015: 3).

2015 onwards: a re-engagement?

It was under the premiership of Prime Minister Cameron that the UK began to look towards deploying as part of a UN mission in Africa in a more favourable light. In September 2014, UK Permanent Representative to the UN, Sir Mark Lyall Grant, linked the draw-down of operations in Afghanistan with a possible upturn in UN deployments more broadly (Foreign and Commonwealth Office, 2014). This came shortly after General Sir Nicholas Houghton, Chief of the Defence Staff, concluded that the UK must 'be far more pro-active in our investment in UN Operations' because 'such operations come pre-funded and with the benefit of an extant legal mandate which confer legitimacy' (Royal United Services Institute, 2013).

With the positive signals coming from the diplomatic and defence communities, in September 2015 Cameron pledged to deploy up to seventy personnel to the UN Support Office in Somalia (UNSOS) and 250–300 personnel to the UN Mission in South Sudan (UNMISS) at a peacekeeping summit co-organised by UN Secretary-General and President Obama (Prime Minister's Office and Ministry of Defence, 2015). This was formalised in the November 2015 Strategic Defence and Security Review which pledged to 'double the number of military personnel' that the UK contributes to UN missions (Prime Minister's Office, 2015: 60), as well as funding from the UK's Conflict Security and Stability Fund of up to £15 million (Green, 2017). In June 2016, the first UK troops began to arrive in South Sudan and they were split into 'two engineer squadron groups, with associated support elements' (Ministry of Defence, 2016a). The following September, the UK pledged to increase this by up to 100 troops (Ministry of Defence, 2016b). In Somalia, UK forces have been commended by the UN for their deployment, and their activities in training the African Union Mission in Somalia and the Somali National Army (UN Support Office in Somalia, 2016).

With these deployments, the UK is arguably beginning to embrace African peacekeeping operations. Yet the stated motivations for such engagement indicate that UK policymakers are more interested in providing national security for the UK than significantly improving the UN's ability to conduct missions. When pledging to commit British peacekeepers to Somalia and South Sudan in September 2015, Prime Minister Cameron made little mention of the importance of UN peace operations and instead couched the pledge in terms of advancing UK national interests. 'What happens in Somalia', Cameron said, 'if it's a good outcome, it's good for Britain, it means less terrorism, less migration, less piracy; ditto South Sudan' (Mason, 2015). Moreover, Defence Secretary Michael Fallon, stated in 2016 that 'it's part of our effort to tackle the instability that leads to mass migration and terrorism. It will help keep Britain safe while improving lives abroad' (Ministry of Defence, 2016b). Terrorism also plays a significant role in the UK Government's justification for the deployment of up to seventy troops to UNSOS, with Fallon stating 'we are determined to tackle terrorism wherever it appears and this deployment demonstrates our commitment to help stabilise Somalia' (Ministry of Defence, 2016c). Arguably, one could suggest that this disinterest with UN operations in Africa – at least at a ministerial level – is not surprising given the history of UK engagement with UN missions on the African continent.

Conclusions

In looking at UK policy towards peacekeeping in Africa, this chapter has offered two broad observations. First, the UK has had difficulty in accepting the UN's role as an effective manager and resolver of conflict on the African continent. This may have begun as outright scepticism, but up until the commitment to UNMISS it has manifested itself in a reluctance to fully engage within missions with significant troop numbers. Arguably a vicious circle exists, whereby the UK will not deploy in large numbers with a UN peacekeeping operation due to concerns over the ability of such operations to fully carry out their functions, yet such missions may only improve as a result of the UK (and other Western states) deploying in large enough numbers. At present, a middle way has been identified regarding physical deployment of forces where UK assets (such as engineering, training, field hospital) are used in missions to develop capacities, where possible, but without significant challenges.

This relates to the second observation, which is that the UK's primary form of engagement has been undertaken away from where the missions are deployed. UK policymakers have sought to influence policy on a strategic level, through doctrine, funding and politics, as opposed to influencing operations through deploying significant numbers of troops. On the one hand, this form of engagement has been effective. The UK has been able to make significant interventions in international fora in order to develop strategic approaches to peacekeeping activity, which has benefited missions at a tactical level. Nevertheless, the strategic-level engagement has its limitations, and has been critiqued by larger TCCs and observers, who note that the UK (like other Western states) has limited tactical engagement with UN operations.

At the international level, the UK's approach to peacekeeping on the African continent can be viewed as being driven more by attempting to keep up to date with shifting geopolitical alignment than long-term investment in African peace and security. The shifting sands of post-colonial engagement set the early tone of UK engagement, as did scepticism of communist influence through the UN. An important factor has also been the UK's relationship with the United States, a relationship that has influenced broader security and defence policy in Whitehall. Arguably, the UK's current rise in providing troop numbers to UN peacekeeping can be explained through the requirement to demonstrate commitment to the UN peacekeeping summits, which were initially led by the US administration under Barack Obama. There are other geopolitical challenges associated with peacekeeping on the African continent. Foremost of these is how the UK reacts to increased activity on the continent from other members of the UNSC, most notably France and China (Dempsey, 2015).

It is also important not to underestimate geographic proximity in this way of thinking. The UK focused on peacekeeping in the Balkans throughout the 1990s, in part due to the proximity of the conflict to Europe, at the cost of peacekeeping on the African continent. Recent UK Government assessments (Prime Minister's Office, 2015) note that there is not a strategic necessity to focus on Sub-Saharan Africa, an area where the majority of the most problematic UN interventions exist. However, were a new UN peacekeeping operation to be deployed in Libya – as some have argued (McGreal, 2015) – there could be a strong chance that the UK may have to engage in some way with this mission.

That peacekeeping is not significant enough to shape the 'national interest' has an effect on how it is treated on a domestic level. On how domestic politics shape this engagement, the question has traditionally been not so much about which party is in power, but more a question over the priorities of the ministers in charge of relevant national ministries (MoD, Foreign and Commonwealth Office and Department for International Development). Peacekeeping has not traditionally been a party political issue, with both Labour, Conservative and Coalition Governments treating engagement with UN peacekeeping in largely the same way. The UK engaged in Bosnia under a Conservative Government, intervened in Sierra Leone under Tony Blair's Labour Government, and announced deployment to South Sudan and Somalia under both Governments headed by Conservative David Cameron. In the 2017 UK general election, possibly the largest divergence was noted, with the Labour Party manifesto explicitly proposing that a possible Labour Government would 'commit to effective UN peacekeeping, including support for a UN Emergency Peace Service' (Labour Party, 2017). The Conservative Party manifesto only mentioned peacekeeping in relation to NATO operations, indicating that the strategic priority for the current Government is to tie any peacekeeping commitment to activities closer to the UK (Conservative Party, 2017).

The 2016 decision of the UK to leave the EU also provides more questions than answers. On the one hand, the UK Government has highlighted the importance of the Commonwealth in participating in the 'rules based international system' (Foreign and Commonwealth Office, 2018). Although the idea has been criticised for a lack of clarity (Select Committee on Foreign Affairs, 2018: 12), it could open new doors to potential defence cooperation with African countries. On the other hand, the UK is removing itself from a regional bloc which has demonstrated a commitment to supporting (albeit through limited missions) peace support missions in Africa. In the two White Papers that have been published to outline government policy on peace operations in the post-Brexit context, the only mention of the activity is a pledge to have a tailored partnership with the EU on 'foreign policy, defence and development', which includes 'arrangements to enable cooperation on crisis management operations, including using civilian and military assets and capabilities to promote global peace and stability, where it is mutually beneficial' (Department for Exiting the European Union, 2018: 63). Elsewhere there is little in the way of concrete policy proposals for continued peacekeeping contributions to Africa. The relatively limited discussion on the role of the UK in the UN in the Government's White Paper on exiting the EU highlights that there has been little thought of this in current policymaking circles.

It is also worth reiterating the point that this chapter has looked at a number of forms of intervention in UN operations – diplomatic intervention in the UN, military intervention in particular missions, financial and political intervention in New York, and bilateral intervention in selected countries. This goes to paint a very mixed picture of UK approaches to African peacekeeping operations, where although there is a great deal of positive work going on in one place, there is a degree of scepticism in another. In many ways, this is a reflection of the UK's wider approach to the UN, where issues of trust, enthusiasm and the extent to which the UK can positively engage are often open to question.

Notes

1. This is initially derived from the French interpretation of the mission, Opération des Nations Unies au Congo.
2. Under which the Secretary-General may bring to the attention of the Security Council any matter which, in his or her opinion, may threaten the maintenance of international peace and security.
3. For more information on the role of the UK in the Congo Crisis, see James (1996) and James (1994).
4. In this capacity, Britain works with the chair of the Peacekeeping Operations Working Group (in 2014/15 this was Rwanda) in drafting resolutions on this topic. It has been observed that the pen holders 'trump' the chairs of the working groups.
5. In 2016, the UK assessed rate dropped to 5.8 per cent, placing it sixth, behind the US, China, Japan, Germany and France.

References

Balossi-Restelli, L. M. (2011) 'Fit for what? Towards explaining battlegroup inaction', *European Security*, 20:2, 155–84.

Bellamy, A. J. and Williams, P. D. (2010) *Understanding Peacekeeping*, 2nd edn (Cambridge: Polity).

Briscoe, N. (2003) *Britain and United Nations Peacekeeping 1948–1967* (Basingstoke: Palgrave Macmillan).

Conflict, Security and Development Group (2003) *A Review of Peace Operations: A Case for Change* (London: King's College London Conflict, Security and Development Group).

Conservative Party (2017) *Forward Together: Our Plan for a Stronger Britain and a Prosperous Future* (London: Conservative Party).

Curran, D. (2015a) 'The EU and the Third Pillar', in D. Fiott and J. Koops (eds), *The Responsibility to Protect and the Third Pillar: Legitimacy and Operationalization* (Basingstoke: Palgrave), 146–70.

Curran, D. (2015b) *The UK and United Nations Peace Operations: Identifying a Way Forward* (London: United Nations Association).

Curran, D. and Williams, P. D. (2016) 'The United Kingdom and United Nations peace operations', *International Peacekeeping*, 23:5, 630–51.

Curran, D. and Williams, P. D. (2017) 'The United Kingdom and UN peacekeeping', in C. de Coning, C. Aoi and J. Karlsrud (eds), *UN Peacekeeping Doctrine in a New Era: Adapting to Stabilisation, Protection and New Threats* (Abingdon: Routledge), 68–89.

Dallaire, Lt Gen. R. (2004) *Shake Hands with the Devil: The Failure of Humanity in Rwanda* (London: Arrow Books).

Dempsey, J. (2015) 'Judy asks: is the UK–U.S. special relationship over?', Carnegie Europe, 22 April 2015, carnegieeurope.eu/strategiceurope/?fa=59867 [accessed 2 February 2018].

Department for Exiting the European Union (2018) *The United Kingdom's Exit From and New Partnership With the European Union White Paper* (London: Her Majesty's Stationery Office).

Dorman, A. (2004) 'The United Kingdom', in L. Elliot and G. Cheeseman (eds), *Forces for Good: Cosmopolitan Militaries in the Twenty-first Century* (Manchester: Manchester University Press), 237–49.

Dorman, A. (2009) *Blair's Successful War: British Military Intervention in Sierra Leone* (Farnham: Ashgate).

Foreign and Commonwealth Office (1994) *Summary of United Nations Security Council Resolutions 1946–1993*, Foreign Policy Document Number 150 (London: Foreign and Commonwealth Office).

Foreign and Commonwealth Office (2012) *UK National Strategy on the Protection of Civilians in Armed Conflict* (London: Foreign and Commonwealth Office).

Foreign and Commonwealth Office (2014) 'Statement by UK Permanent Representative, Sir Mark Lyall Grant, on Strengthening United Nations Peace Operations', New York, 26 September 2014.

Foreign and Commonwealth Office (2015) 'Statement by UK Ambassador, Matthew Rycroft, to the UN at the General Assembly Debate on the High-Level Independent Panel on Peace Operations', 15 October 2015, www.gov.uk/government/speeches/together-we-can-and-must-make-un-peace-operations-the-best-that-they-can-be [accessed 5 December 2017].

Foreign and Commonwealth Office (2018), 'Global Britain and the 2018 Commonwealth Summit: Government Response to the Committee's Seventh Report', https://publications.parliament.uk/pa/cm201719/cmselect/cmfaff/1427/142702.htm [accessed 8 August 2018].

Gowan, R. (2010) 'From rapid reaction to delayed inaction? Congo, the UN and the EU', *International Peacekeeping*, 18:5, 593–611.

Gowan, R. and Witney, N. (2015) *Why Europe must Stop Outsourcing its Security* (London: European Council on Foreign Relations).

Green, D. (2017) 'Conflict, Stability and Security Fund 2016 to 2017 and settlement for 2017 to 2018: written ministerial statement', www.gov.uk/government/speeches/conflict-stability-and-security-fund-2016-to-2017-and-settlement-for-2017-to-2018-written-ministerial-statement [accessed 5 December 2017].

Hanning, H. (1964) *Britain and the United Nations: Proposals for Peacekeeping including a Commonwealth Force* (London: Bow Publications).

Harbottle, M. (1971) *The Blue Berets: The Story of the United Nations Peacekeeping Forces* (London: Leo Cooper).

Hunt, C. (2017) 'All necessary means to what ends? The unintended consequences of the "robust turn" in UN peace operations', *International Peacekeeping*, 24:1, 108–31.

James, A. (1961) *The Politics of Peacekeeping* (London: Chatto and Windus).
James, A. (1994) 'The Congo controversies', *International Peacekeeping*, 1:1, 44–58.
James, A. (1996) *Britain and the Congo Crisis 1960–1963* (Basingstoke: Macmillan).
Keen, D. (2005) *Conflict and Collusion in Sierra Leone* (New York: Palgrave).
Labour Party (2017) *For the Many Not the Few: The Labour Party Manifesto 2017*, https://labour.org.uk/manifesto/ [accessed 5 December 2017].
Mason, R. (2015) 'UK to deploy troops to help keep peace in Somalia and South Sudan', *Guardian*, 27 September 2015, www.theguardian.com/politics/2015/sep/27/uk-to-deploy-troops-to-help-keep-peace-in-somalia-and-south-sudan [accessed 5 December 2017].
McGreal, C. (2015) 'Countries to pledge troops to bolster UN peacekeepers after intense US pressure', *Guardian*, 27 September 2015, www.theguardian.com/world/2015/sep/27/un-peacekeeping-obama-countries-pledge-troops-counterterror [accessed 5 December 2017].
Melvern, L. and Williams, P. (2004) 'Britannia waived the rules: the Major government and the 1994 Rwandan Genocide', *African Affairs*, 103:410, 1–22.
Ministry of Defence (1995) *Army Field Manual Wider Peacekeeping* (London: Her Majesty's Stationery Office).
Ministry of Defence (2013) 'British troops support Mali training mission', www.gov.uk/government/news/british-troops-support-mali-training-mission [accessed 5 December 2017].
Ministry of Defence (2016a) 'UK peacekeepers arrive in South Sudan', www.gov.uk/government/news/uk-peacekeepers-arrive-in-south-sudan [accessed 5 December 2017].
Ministry of Defence (2016b) 'UK bolsters support to peacekeeping in South Sudan', www.gov.uk/government/news/uk-bolsters-support-to-peacekeeping-in-south-sudan [accessed 5 December 2017].
Ministry of Defence (2016c) 'UK Armed Forces deployments tackle security threats in Africa', www.gov.uk/government/news/uk-armed-forces-deployments-tackle-security-threats-in-africa [accessed 5 December 2017].
Olonisakin, F. (2005) *Peacekeeping in Sierra Leone* (Boulder, CO: Lynne Rienner).
Prime Minister's Office (2015) *National Security Strategy and Strategic Defence and Security Review 2015: A Secure and Prosperous United Kingdom* (London: Her Majesty's Stationery Office).
Prime Minister's Office and Ministry of Defence (2015) 'PM pledges UK troops to support stability in Somalia and South Sudan', www.gov.uk/government/news/pm-pledges-uk-troops-to-support-stability-in-somalia-and-south-sudan [accessed 5 December 2017].
Ramsbotham, O. and Woodhouse, T. (1999) *Encyclopaedia of Peacekeeping Operations* (Goleta, CA: ABC-CLIO).
Royal United Services Institute (2013) 'Annual Chief of the Defence Staff lecture 2013: lecture by General Sir Nicholas Houghton GCB CBE ADC Gen, Chief of the Defence Staff, UK Ministry of Defence', https://rusi.org/event/annual-chief-defence-staff-lecture-2013 [accessed 5 December 2017].

Select Committee on Foreign Affairs (2018) *Global Britain and the 2018 Commonwealth Summit*, International Development Committee, Seventh Report, https://publications.parliament.uk/pa/cm201719/cmselect/cmfaff/831/831.pdf [accessed 8 August 2018].

Short, C. (2004) *An Honorable Deception? New Labour, Iraq, and the Misuse of Power* (London: Free Press).

Tardy, T. and Zaum, D. (2015) 'France and the United Kingdom at the UN Security Council', in D. Malone, S. Einsiedel and B. S. Ugarte (eds), *The UN Security Council* (Boulder, CO: Lynne Rienner), 121–38.

UN (1985) *The Blue Helmets: A Review of United Nations Peacekeeping* (New York: United Nations).

UN (2000) *The Report of the Panel on United Nations Peace Operations (UN doc. A/55/305-S/2000/809)* (New York: United Nations).

UN (2013) 'List of peacekeeping operations 1948–2013', www.un.org/en/peacekeeping/documents/operationslist.pdf [accessed 5 December 2017].

UN (2015) *Uniting Our Strengths for Peace – Politics, Partnerships, and People: Report of the High-Level Independent Panel on United Nations Peace Operations* (New York: United Nations).

UN Security Council (2013) *February 2013 Monthly Forecast*, New York: UN Security Council.

UN Security Council (2015) *Cross-Cutting Report: Protection of Civilians in Armed Conflict*, New York: UN Security Council.

United Nations Support Office in Somalia (2016) 'United Nations commends United Kingdom for contribution to peace process in Somalia', https://unsos.unmissions.org/united-nations-commends-united-kingdom-contribution-peace-process-somalia [accessed 5 December 2017].

Wilkinson, P. (2000) *Peace Support Under Fire: Lessons From Sierra Leone* (Brussels: International Security Information Service).

Williams, P. D. (2001) 'Fighting for Freetown: British military intervention in Sierra Leone', *Contemporary Security Policy*, 22:3, 140–68.

Williams, P. D. (2005) *British Foreign Policy under New Labour, 1997–2005* (Basingstoke: Palgrave Macmillan).

Williams, P. D. (2013) 'The United Kingdom', in A. J. Bellamy and P. D. Williams (eds), *Providing Peacekeepers* (Oxford: Oxford University Press), 93–115.

Part II

Africa and UK actors:
parties, publics and civil society

6

Rehabilitating the 'nasty party'? The Conservative Party and Africa from opposition to government

Danielle Beswick*

From 2005, under David Cameron's leadership, a core group of Conservatives embarked upon a campaign to rebrand the Party in the minds of voters. In the arena of international policy, a Conservative commitment to work towards international development spending targets and to maintain a separate Department for International Development (DFID) marked significant shifts in the Conservative approach. Despite these substantial changes in policy, there is relatively little analysis of the role of international development in rebranding, repositioning and redefining the Party. Even less attention has been paid to the particular role that Africa plays in these processes. This is in sharp contrast to extensive research on Africa's place in relation to the self-identification and projected images of Labour Governments and leaders. This chapter begins to address this gap. It draws on Party documents, speeches and media reports, as well as thirty interviews carried out by the author and a research assistant during 2017 with Conservative Party members who have participated in Party-organised overseas development volunteering projects, including MPs, MEPs, Councillors, members of the House of Lords, Party staff and activists. It aims to identify how Africa has featured in a narrative of change in relation to the Conservative Party. In doing so it traces the ways Africa has been used in defining a new Conservative identity, projected both domestically and on an international stage, as part of an attempt to signal credibility as a governing Party in a turbulent international context.

The first section briefly outlines how scholars have sought to explain engagement with Africa, both in terms of policy and as an imagined space imbued with particular qualities and meanings, by Labour and Conservative leaders since

1997. This will argue that analysis of Conservative engagement with Africa, in opposition and government, is a neglected topic and one that requires further investigation. It is also important to acknowledge that it can be difficult to separate Africa policies from wider international development policies, and the chapter therefore occasionally looks to wider development policy in analysing Conservative engagement with Africa. This is justified by the central role Africa has played in UK development policy over the past two decades, as a major recipient of UK development assistance and as a recurring feature in the rhetoric of UK politicians.

The subsequent sections review engagement with Africa under five Conservative Party leaders since 1997. Identifying key moments of engagement with Africa under successive Party leaders in opposition, Coalition and Conservative Government, these will demonstrate that Africa policy has been used to support a narrative of compassionate Conservatism and Party modernisation, signalling a break with previous Conservative administrations and positions. It will also, however, suggest that despite instances of highly visible interactions with Africa, particularly under Cameron's leadership, the continent's profile has been tempered under Conservative-led Government in favour of wider narratives of global development and a resurgent focus on the Commonwealth. The chapter concludes by suggesting this is partly an effort to distance the Conservative approach from those of Blair and Brown, often portrayed as missionary in character and, particularly in Blair's case, as indicative of a 'personal saviour' attitude (Taylor, 2012: 450). However, it is also important to acknowledge the role of African activism and agency in shaping UK–Africa relations, and the impact of the 2016 EU membership referendum result on UK international policy. The chapter will conclude by suggesting that Africa policy provides a useful insight into the Conservative Party's domestic and international concerns at different junctures and, as an indicator of changing Party identity, this aspect of UK policy would benefit from further research.

Explaining Labour and Conservative engagement with Africa

There has been considerable research into Labour's engagement with Africa during the premierships of Tony Blair (1997–2007) and Gordon Brown (2007–10). Though the detail of the arguments varies, these analyses share two core claims. The first is that the rise of Africa on UK policy and public agendas reflected the personal agendas and ambitions of these two leaders. The second shared element is that this employed idealised and apolitical images of Africa, and UK engagement with the continent, in order to project a positive image of

Britain and its engagement with the world. The works of Julia Gallagher (2011), Ian Taylor (2005; 2012), Paul Williams (2010) and Rita Abrahamsen (2005) are illustrative of these analyses. In comparison to the detailed systematic analyses of Labour engagement with Africa since 1997, little attempt has been made to trace and understand Conservative Party engagement with Africa during the same period. The accounts which do exist tend to focus on international development more broadly, or the Commonwealth, rather than Africa specifically. These tend to reduce change to merely a cynical strategy of 'detoxification', or more generously characterise it as part of a process of Party modernisation (Heppell and Lightfoot, 2012; Heppell et al., 2017). More recent analysis by Mawdsley (2017) has sought to explain the rise of 'national interest' narratives in Conservative international development policy from 2010, and while this is a welcome addition to these debates it largely excludes the period in opposition, during which these policies were crafted and tested within the Party.

This limited scholarly consideration of the drivers of Conservative Party engagement with Africa specifically is both problematic and surprising, particularly given the commitment of the 2010–15 Conservative-led Coalition, and Conservative Governments under Cameron (2015–16) and his successor Theresa May (since 2016), to maintaining an independent development ministry and to pursuing, and later meeting, a 0.7 per cent of Gross National Income (GNI) aid spending target. The subsequent sections of this chapter review Africa policy and engagement under five Conservative leaders. The analysis is focused primarily on Cameron's tenure, reflecting the fact that his leadership saw some of the most high-profile engagements with Africa.

It is important, however, to recognise that Cameron's engagement with Africa did not emerge in a vacuum. Interviewed in 2017, former Shadow International Development Secretary (May 2005–May 2010) and International Development Secretary (May 2010–September 2012) Andrew Mitchell highlighted the importance of former Conservative Party leader Michael Howard's engagement with development, describing this as a key factor in persuading some cynical Party members to 'go along with' Cameron's efforts in this area despite their scepticism.[1] We will therefore briefly review notable engagements with Africa during the leadership periods of William Hague (1997–2001) and Iain Duncan Smith (2001–3), which contrast with later leaders, and also Howard (2003–5), who signalled the first significant shifts in Conservative Party thinking on development challenges broadly and UK–Africa relations specifically. We will then focus on Africa visits and policy shifts announced by Cameron's Party during his time in opposition (2005–10), as leader of a Coalition Government (2010–15) and heading a Conservative administration (2015–16), before providing brief reflections on May's administration and current trends. This will demonstrate that Africa has been a growing area of interest and concern for the Conservative Party leadership since the electoral defeat to Labour in 1997. It will also show, however, that the framing of Africa and of UK–Africa relations has shifted over time, with Africa moving from an afterthought under Hague and Duncan Smith to become a signifier of Party modernisation and continuing UK global ambition under Cameron, with the latter trend further exacerbated under May.

Africa as an afterthought: William Hague 1997–2001 and Iain Duncan Smith 2001–3

Following the landslide Labour victory in the 1997 general election, the priority for the Party under Hague was to reconnect with voters. Domestic political themes, including traditional Conservative leitmotifs of tax and immigration, dominated Hague's public statements (Kelly, 2001). In this context, it is perhaps unsurprising that there was little emphasis on Africa. There was little pressure for Hague and his team to formulate substantive policy positions on issues relating to Africa, particularly because, as Porteous (2005: 289–90) notes, Blair's focus on Africa was markedly less during his first term in office than in his second. Where Africa did appear in speeches and statements by Hague, this was largely reactive, in response to government policy rather than signalling any attempt to develop a distinctive Conservative approach to Africa or to international development. The Party supported the deployment of British troops to Sierra Leone in 2000, the most direct UK foreign policy engagement in Africa at the time (Coll, 2010). The 2001 Conservative Party manifesto made no mention of Africa, though it did engage with development more widely, committing to work towards the 0.7 per cent of GNI aid spending target, signalling an intention to engage more with the Commonwealth, and stating that the Party would seek to reform global trade (Conservative Party, 2001). Hague's limited focus on Africa specifically, in favour of a conviction that the Commonwealth needed to regain a more prominent place in UK international relations, would later be reflected during his tenure as Foreign Secretary under Cameron.

Under Iain Duncan Smith, Africa remained marginal in Conservative foreign policy statements. The notable exception to this was in relation to Zimbabwe. The most high-profile public pronouncement related to Africa was a call from Duncan Smith and his Shadow Foreign Secretary Michael Ancram to tie Western aid to Africa to the removal from power of President Robert Mugabe. This was dismissed by Labour and by many development charities as unjustifiable, with Oxfam and Save the Children arguing that help for famine-affected Southern Africa should not be made 'hostage to the unfolding situation in Zimbabwe'

(Morris, 2002). In a letter to Blair, Duncan Smith called for the boycotting of Mugabe's address to the World Summit on Sustainable Development in Johannesburg, South Africa, arguing: 'You could not possibly share a platform with someone who seeks to humiliate our country and place British citizens at great risk' (Guardian, 2002). This may not, however, have had the effect intended. Porteous (2005: 291) notes that in spite of domestic pressure from the UK public to take proactive action against the Mugabe regime, reflected in the Conservative response to the Zimbabwe situation, the UK had limited leverage with which to force change. Furthermore, by provoking British anger Mugabe was able to cast himself as a 'hero', standing up to neo-colonial pressures. The vocal Conservative engagement on this issue may have conversely helped to reinforce Mugabe's position rather than threaten it (*ibid.*: 290–1).

On wider development policy, Duncan Smith signalled less commitment than Hague to raising UK aid spending towards the 0.7 per cent target, stating in the House of Commons that the party supported 'the goal of increasing the average EU contribution to 0.39 per cent by 2006' (Hansard, 2002). Under these two leaders, although each had sought to persuade voters that the Conservative Party remained outward-facing, domestic focus remained dominant and Labour enjoyed a relatively free hand in its development policy and in relations with Africa. What focus there was on Africa was limited and reactive, responding to crises rather than seeking to set out any new agenda or alternative approach to challenge that of Labour.

The beginnings of a Conservative approach to Africa: Michael Howard, 2003–5

Under Michael Howard, the profile of both international development and of Africa grew significantly. We begin to see the establishment of themes which recur under Cameron and eventually find their way into government policy, including the articulation of a distinctive Conservative approach to international development and a renewed UK engagement with supporting peacekeeping in Africa.

At the 2004 Party Conference in Bournemouth, the focus on Zimbabwe observed under Hague and Duncan Smith re-emerged, with Shadow Foreign Secretary Ancram declaring that one of the first actions of a Conservative Government would be to seek a UN Security Council resolution to send monitors and observers into Zimbabwe, enforced by British troops if necessary (Tempest, 2004). This was part of an attempt to differentiate the Conservative approach to Africa from that of Labour. Shadow International Development

Secretary Alan Duncan criticised Blair, saying 'his trip to Africa lets him pose, but if he won't call the horror in Darfur in Sudan by its right name – genocide – how can we expect effective action that will save lives?' (*ibid.*). This characterisation of Labour, and Blair particularly, as being image-obsessed was positioned in contrast to the Conservatives, who called publicly for decisive action and British leadership in African crises.

A second key event which highlights changing Conservative engagement with development was the Boxing Day Tsunami in December 2004, which prompted an outpouring of sympathy and unprecedented UK public donations to a joint charity appeal. Reflecting on this tragedy, Howard took the opportunity to highlight the generosity of British people, a theme that was particularly prevalent in his addresses to Christian audiences (Howard, 2005a). He linked disaster response to values he identified with conservatism – charity, and compassion for those in need. In early 2005, Howard gave a speech titled 'The Conservative approach to international development' in which he highlighted the values necessary to tackle world poverty, values which he linked directly to the Conservative Party: 'Trusting free enterprise; upholding the rule of law; accepting our moral duty to help those less fortunate' (Howard, 2005b). Making connections to traditional Conservative-claimed themes of free trade and promoting opportunity, he proposed a Trade Advocacy Fund to provide legal training and representation for developing states in trade disputes. This was part of a call to make 'fair trade freer and free trade fairer', speaking to a key theme of the Make Poverty History campaign, which Howard supported and which had galvanised public interest in Africa and development. A Conservative MP interviewed during 2017 noted that this was one of the points at which they began to receive letters and direct questions from constituents asking 'what the Conservatives proposed to do about the world's poor'.[2]

In the same speech, Howard committed to increasing UK aid by 20 per cent by 2008, and working towards meeting the UN target of spending 0.7 per cent of GNI on overseas development (*ibid.*). This matched Labour's commitments. He did, however, also signal divergence from Labour approaches, highlighting a need for greater UK control over aid channelled through the EU, and an intention to prioritise tackling of waste and corruption. Though there was significant focus on international development globally, Howard also made a specific effort to ensure Africa retained UK attention. His speech at the Tabernacle Christian Centre in April 2005 noted 'we have thought a lot about Asia recently, but we must never forget Africa' (Howard, 2005a). Repeating themes from the January speech, he highlighted the need to improve trade systems and restated the Conservative pledge to match Labour aid commitments. Both were mentioned again in Howard's questions to the Prime Minister in Parliament in June, as he pushed Blair on whether the UK was doing enough to challenge farm subsidies by the US and EU, which disadvantaged producers in many African states (Hansard, 2005). Under Howard, engagement with Africa through development was presented primarily as a moral responsibility, fighting for 'what we know is right' (Howard, 2005a), a choice rather than an obligation, and an issue of fairness. Self-interest and national interest made comparatively little appearance in these formal statements and speeches, though this was to change under Cameron's leadership, and Howard began to explicitly link Africa policy with Conservative values, beginning to outline an alternative to the approaches of the Blair administrations.

An emerging Africa strategy: Cameron in opposition, 2005–10

Cameron's election as party leader came as a surprise to many. A relatively new MP who had held only one shadow cabinet post – and for only seven months – before becoming leader, he made a virtue of his ability to appeal to a new generation of voters. His campaign slogan, 'change to win', summed up his message to the Conservative Party: to effectively challenge Labour would require real change, not simply cosmetic reform. Immediately following his election as leader, Cameron began to lay claim to issues and causes traditionally associated with Labour and the Liberal Democrats, including international development and climate change (Carter and Clements, 2015; Heppell and Lightfoot, 2012). Two international visits to African states during his time as opposition leader provide a useful window into his determination to challenge prior Conservative policies and to pursue a new Conservative re-engagement with Africa, despite the potential political costs.

In August 2006, Cameron visited war-torn Darfur with his Shadow International Development Secretary Andrew Mitchell, and made an unannounced trip to South Africa to meet the former President and iconic leader of the anti-apartheid movement, Nelson Mandela. In doing so he sought to demonstrate his credentials as a potential international statesman, but also took the opportunity to position engagement with Africa as part of Conservative Party modernisation, saying: 'Engaging in the challenges facing Africa is a key part of modern Conservatism' (Brogan, 2006). The left-leaning *Guardian* newspaper suggested that this was an 'audacious bid to seize the issue of African aid and development from Gordon Brown' (Temko, 2006), a sentiment echoed by an article in the right-leaning *Daily Mail* (Brogan, 2006). Cameron's praise for Mandela provided a sharp contrast with the views expressed by one of his other political idols, Margaret Thatcher. He criticised the Thatcher Government's failure to back sanctions against apartheid South Africa and spoke regretfully of its characterisation of Mandela as a terrorist (*ibid.*). The new stance on apartheid provoked fury from some on the right wing of the Party, with one questioning 'whether David Cameron is a Conservative' (Borger, 2013) and another describing his comments as 'ignorant' (Temko, 2006).

During a second trip to Africa, Cameron again courted controversy. In July 2007 he chose Rwanda, where Conservative Party members were undertaking short-term development projects during the summer, to launch the Party's Policy Group Report on Global Poverty. These overseas social action (volunteering) projects are described by their founders and proponents as crucial in exposing Conservatives to the myriad ways that governments, communities and civil society seek to address challenges of poverty, in the UK and overseas (Kite, 2007).[3] This inaugural trip coincided with severe flooding in Cameron's Witney constituency. A report in the *Daily Mail* describes the moment when Cameron launched the Party's development declaration in the Rwandan Parliament:

> hardly anyone had turned up for his keynote speech, and spin doctors were panicking about embarrassing TV footage of empty seats. Then the lights went out. As a symbol of Cameron's fortunes, the scene ... could hardly have been more apt. Back home ... there was anger that he was 4,000 miles away pontificating about global poverty. (Ashcroft and Oakeshott, 2015)

Recalling this episode, Mitchell – a primary advocate and long-term organiser of Party-supported overseas development projects – has spoken of his concern as to the headlines that would result back in the UK, and the impact this might have on the future of the projects.[4] Combining this with poor by-election results for the Party, Cameron faced significant disquiet, with members of the backbench 1922 Committee hinting to journalists that they might imminently raise a vote of no confidence in his leadership. Despite these challenges, Cameron, flanked by Mitchell, maintained his commitment to a new and highly public Conservative engagement with Africa. The 2009 Conservative Green Paper on International Development, *One World Conservatism*, also demonstrates this. It places significant emphasis on Africa, mentioning it over fifty times, and many of the statistics and individual quotes from citizens of developing states in the report that are used to demonstrate the scale of the challenge of human development are drawn from sub-Saharan Africa (Noxolo, 2012).

During his time as opposition leader we clearly see Cameron's strong personal commitment to both UK engagement with Africa and to a leadership role for the UK in international development. Narratives of Africa and visits to Africa were used during this period by Cameron's team to support a new image of the Conservative Party – compassionate, globally minded. They were also used to lay claim to traditionally Labour-dominated policy territory on development, environment and Africa. This allowed Cameron's team to emphasise their pragmatism, recognising shared aims and goals in common with other political parties. As noted earlier, this was not only a feature of Cameron's leadership; Howard had made the same commitments previously. Cameron's visits to Africa and the speeches he made during them signalled a break with the Party's past, but at the same time sought to emphasise the extent to which engaging with Africa and Africans, including but not only through development assistance, was compatible with Conservative values. This links back to narratives established under Howard, highlighting values of charity, entrepreneurship and support for individuals to help themselves improve their lives. As indicated by the media coverage of his Africa trips, Cameron's placing of Africa front and centre, without apology or excuse, in his effort to change the Party and win voters, was not risk-free (see Mawdsley, 2017). It also suggested that this would be a key arena for UK foreign policy under any future Conservative Government. A key test of this would of course be how UK Africa policy fared if the Conservatives took power in 2010.

Continued Africa focus in government: Cameron's Coalition

The failure of the Conservatives to win an absolute majority in the 2010 elections was a blow to Cameron's credibility within the Party. Nevertheless, through Coalition with the Liberal Democrats he was able to form a Government that lasted a full parliamentary term. The Coalition configuration makes it difficult to attribute the continued extensive UK–Africa engagement during this period to any single party. The Liberal Democrats, keen to demonstrate the impact of their influence on the new administration, sought to claim the enshrining of the 0.7 per cent of GNI development assistance target in UK law as their victory. However, many high-profile Conservative ministers also publicly supported the initiative and the Party did not use mechanisms at its disposal – for example through the Party whip – to seek to derail the bill during its passage through Parliament.

There are other signs of the embedding of UK–Africa engagement in government policy, driven by Conservative politicians headed by Cameron, Mitchell and Chancellor of the Exchequer George Osborne. Cameron's tour of Africa in 2011 provides a high-profile illustration of this. His decision to go ahead with the trip, despite the 'phone-hacking' scandal that had erupted in the UK, drew significant criticism. As allegations emerged of News International journalists illegally accessing voice messages on private mobile phones belonging to celebrities, members of the royal family and teenage murder victim Milly Dowler, Cameron's absence was attacked by both Conservative and opposition politicians. Journalists later reflected that Cameron seemed to have a gift for being out of the country – specifically in Africa – at just the wrong moment, referencing his 2007 trip to Rwanda as a case in point (Ashcroft and Oakeshott, 2015; Watt, 2011). Nevertheless, though the 2011 tour was cut from four days to two, with visits to Rwanda and newly independent South Sudan dropped from the agenda, Cameron still visited South Africa and Nigeria, accompanied by a major UK business delegation. He and Mitchell foregrounded two main pillars of UK commitment to Africa: aid, and the promotion of economic growth and markets in Africa. Cameron made a high-profile speech in Lagos, Nigeria, which clearly set out his response to those sceptical of his commitments to UK aid to and trade with Africa. The Lagos speech expressed concern for humanitarian crises in East Africa, before stating: 'But today I've come here to Lagos ... because there's another story unfolding on this continent ... This can be Africa's moment ... there are unprecedented opportunities to trade and grow, raise living standards and lift billions from poverty' (Cameron, 2011).

It is no coincidence that the two stopping points on this abbreviated visit were the economic powerhouses of the continent, and Cameron's speech specifically referenced the growing role of China in Africa. Commenting on the decision to go ahead with the trip, the *Daily Mail* reported that Cameron recognised that there was a new 'scramble for Africa', and that sustained engagement was necessary to counter the influence of China and other rising powers (Groves, 2011). This is a clear illustration of the ways in which development was increasingly repositioned under Cameron in order to emphasise the benefits to the UK, supporting UK national interest (see Mawdsley, 2017).

This visit provided the most explicit and direct articulation of Cameron's response to critics of UK aid and UK engagement with Africa, particularly those within his own Party and the media. He sought to challenge negative stereotypes of Africa and Africans, highlighting business opportunities and African ownership of development strategies (Groves, 2011). He also sought again to differentiate the approach of his Government from that of its Labour predecessors, stating that he was not here to 'hector or to lecture' Africans and noting his pride in 'my generation', free of the 'shadow' of neo-colonialism, who had campaigned against debt and in favour of action on poverty (Cameron, 2011). Cameron emphasised the break with the past – 'we see Africa in a new way, a different way' (*ibid.*). The changing relationship with Zimbabwe provides a useful illustration of this, with Cameron's Government favouring engagement with Mugabe and respect for Zimbabwe's sovereignty. This was in sharp contrast to both the statements of Duncan Smith and Howard before him, and the Labour policy of supporting sanctions against the Zimbabwean Government.

If the period in opposition had been about establishing Africa as an arena for projection of Conservative Party identity – caring, compassionate, globally minded – then the Coalition period can be regarded as one of consolidation and reframing. It saw the reinforcement of commitments, along with a very public rebuffing of those who had perhaps anticipated that a Conservative-led administration would let Africa quietly disappear from view. Though they had the power at their disposal to drop commitments to aid and to quietly disengage from Africa, Cameron's Conservatives did neither. This cannot be credibly attributed purely to the influence of the Liberal Democrats (Hall-Matthews, 2011). Instead, it reflects clear continuities from the Conservative period in opposition, particularly under Cameron and Howard.

In the domestic arena, under the Coalition, as earlier in opposition, we see Africa used as a backdrop against which to present the Conservative Party in a positive, compassionate light. A case in point is the Conservative Party's use of its allocated television airtime in the lead-up to the 2011 Party Conference to make an appeal for public support to deal with a crisis in East Africa. Featuring a host of cabinet ministers and the Prime Minister, the broadcast sought to position the UK role in humanitarian relief as above the everyday competition between political parties for the support of voters, saying explicitly: 'some things are more important than politics' (Robinson and Wintour, 2011). The way Africa was referenced in speeches, however, also became increasingly imbued with narratives of national self-interest and security during this period (Mawdsley, 2017), particularly when discussing why those sceptical of aid to Africa should reconsider their position. In the 2011 Lagos speech Cameron told his audience: 'There is another point to make to the aid sceptics: when states are broken, conflicts rife, it's not just the people of those countries that suffer – we suffer back at home from a surge in illegal immigration, asylum seeking and even terrorism' (Cameron, 2011).

The portrayals of Africa had become more complex and nuanced, with the Conservatives' transition from opposition to government making superficial and one-dimensional renderings of the continent harder to maintain. In government, the Party needed to demonstrate the differences between its approach to Africa and to development from that of Labour, particularly if it was to diffuse tensions within the Party and with voters and the right-leaning press over aid spending (Heppell et al., 2017; Mawdsley, 2017). Its strategy for addressing this dilemma strongly mirrored the dual justification for engagement with the continent made by the Commission for Africa in 2005 and under the Labour Governments of Blair and Brown: moral duty and enlightened self-interest.

Cameron's personal commitment to engagement with Africa was highly visible following Nelson Mandela's death in 2013. Cameron's 'lavish tribute' for the former South African leader again highlighted the break from positions held by previous Conservative Party leaders (Borger, 2013). His was the official position of the Government and the Party; the flag over Downing Street flew at half-mast in tribute, and Foreign Secretary William Hague described Mandela as 'one of the greatest moral and political leaders of our time' (Hague, 2013). Cameron's willingness to publicly own and champion his commitment to development more widely was also recognised on an international stage: in 2012 he was appointed co-chair of the panel exploring successors to the Millennium Development Goals, alongside Presidents Ellen Johnson-Sirleaf of Liberia and Susilo Bambang Yudhoyono of Indonesia. A former senior Party member, interviewed by the author in 2017, recollected Cameron's determination to secure this role and the intense lobbying undertaken to achieve it.[5] Similarly, after Justine Greening replaced Mitchell as Secretary of State in 2011, Mawdsley notes that the UK 'manoeuvred hard' for her to be named as co-chair, and representative for 'established donors', on the Global Partnership for Effective Development Cooperation (2017: 227).

These roles provided opportunities to shape international development, emphasising values that resonated with those associated with the Conservative Party. These included entrepreneurship, engaging with the private sector and supporting self-reliance. In the UK policy sphere, Bilateral and Multilateral Aid Reviews in 2011 allowed the administration to highlight their departure from Labour on UK aid. Though they may have pledged to support the 0.7 per cent of GNI aid spending target, they were keen to show that they had different views on how it should be spent. This was rooted largely in an attack on aid under Labour as being wasteful, offering poor value for money and lacking in transparency. The reviews saw bilateral aid programmes cut from forty-three to twenty-seven, with Mitchell emphasising the need to concentrate UK efforts where they could do the most good and where the UK had greatest national interest. African states made up twenty-two of forty-three bilateral programmes prior to the review and seventeen of twenty-seven following it. This represents an increase in Africa's share of UK bilateral programmes (in absolute numbers, rather than size/value) from 51 per cent to 62 per cent. The establishment of an Independent Commission for Aid Impact also served to imply the failures of formal scrutiny of aid spending under Labour, and was intended to underscore Mitchell's pledge to ensure that UK aid was transparent, accountable and represented the best possible value for UK taxpayer money.[6]

These changes, taken together, demonstrate that although the Conservatives had pledged to meet spending targets for UK aid, and ring-fenced the development budget, this would not simply lead to a continuation of Labour policies. This signalling of a distinctive Conservative approach to development was important for the Party approaching the 2015 general election, with many Conservative Party members and MPs uncomfortable with the similarities between Cameron's policies and those of New Labour.[7] For example, a commentary from Conservative think-tank the Bow Group in 2013 criticised the continuities between Blair and Cameron, citing Cameron's claim while in opposition to be the 'heir to Blair'. The continued existence of DFID and its large – protected – budget were held up as a key example of this Labour influence and an indicator of a drift away from Conservative preferences. The Group argued that the Party must 'return to surety of conservatism – it must come now, or come too late' (Bow Group, 2013).

Africa embedded: Conservative Governments from Cameron to May

The Conservative election victory in 2015 marked the start of the first Conservative majority Government in nineteen years. Though the commitment to spend 0.7 per cent of GNI on aid had been enshrined in law, the new administration provided an opportunity for the Conservative Party to set out revised positions on aid and to rethink relations with Africa as part of a wider consideration of the UK's place in the world (see Mawdsley, 2017). Cameron's tenure lasted only fourteen months, with much of the second half of this dominated by campaigning on the EU membership referendum, which would lead to his resignation in July 2016. Nevertheless, during this short time we see significant new engagements with Africa. In September 2015, Cameron announced that 300 soldiers would be sent to South Sudan and seventy to Somalia to support peacekeeping efforts. This was linked by Cameron directly to wider UK national interests, with the PM suggesting that 'bringing stability to both countries could help to ease the migration crisis that is seeing hundreds of thousands of migrants cross the Mediterranean to reach Europe' (Riley-Smith, 2015).

Following Cameron's resignation, Priti Patel, an aid sceptic, was appointed by Theresa May to the post of International Development Secretary. This raised concerns within the development community about the continued commitment to aid targets and prioritising poverty reduction, as well as about the future of an independent DFID: Patel had previously spoken in favour of restructuring UK aid to place more emphasis on trade and foreign policy links (Mawdsley, 2017). In the aftermath of the vote to leave the EU, it initially seemed that Africa had slipped down the UK policy agenda. This was evidenced by the complaints raised by many African ambassadors and high commissioners to the UK at an event hosted by Chatham House in 2016, that they were seeing few visits from UK ministers and secretaries of state. There was also disquiet at the combining of ministerial portfolios for the Middle East and Africa under May's reshuffle, with African representatives arguing this was detrimental to the UK's relations with Africa. During this time, Mitchell remained an outspoken advocate for aid, making the case for considering aid to be in the UK national interest on the Conservative Home website, which although independent of the Party enjoys close links with senior members (Mitchell, 2016), and in a series of events at the annual Party Conference in Birmingham. He highlighted the increasing amount of aid spent by departments other than DFID, praising the multiplier effect that this could have on development results but also warning of the need to ensure scrutiny and value for money across these other departments to maintain the integrity of UK aid and public support (*ibid.*). Patel's speech at the Party Conference reiterated the connection Cameron had made between UK aid and humanitarian assistance overseas, and 'reducing the pressures of mass migration' (Patel, 2016). It also highlighted Britain's leadership role in development, citing the Ebola response as a case where 'it fell to the UK, the USA and others to grip the situation' (*ibid.*).

The second bilateral aid review, delayed and later finalised by Patel following her appointment, signalled an intention to focus on Africa's 'arc of instability', and the promotion of private sector investment (Department for International Development, 2016). Patel was consistent in her argument, similar to that of Howard, that Conservative values are necessary for effective development, emphasising employment, encouraging markets and trade (Mawdsley, 2017). In sharp contrast, Foreign Secretary Boris Johnson referred to Africa as 'that country' during his Conference speech (Harris, 2016), and has been linked with a campaign to reallocate part of the UK aid budget to defence, a move which many fear would lead to a reallocation of funds away from the poorest states and people, particularly in Sub-Saharan Africa. This campaign is perhaps unsurprising given the budget cuts faced by the Foreign and Commonwealth Office (see Chapter 1), as well as concerns that the UK may fail to honour its commitment as a North Atlantic Treaty Organisation member to spend 2 per cent of GNI on defence. DFID spending, which accounts for most but not all aid spending, grew by 24 per cent between 2010–11 and 2016–17, at a time when the average government department (excluding defence, health and education) recorded a cut of 28 per cent (Krutikova and Warwick, 2017: 2).

There were, as noted earlier, few high-level visits to Africa under May. This situation might have been expected to continue after the reduction in the Conservative majority following the general election in 2017, but instead there have been signs of a growing engagement with Africa. This is reflected in high-profile visits during the summer 2017 parliamentary recess by Patel and Johnson, to Somalia and Nigeria, as well as the appointment of a Minister for Africa (Rory Stewart), who also visited Somalia during 2017. Although it is still too early in the May administration to draw any firm conclusions, these visits and personnel changes raise the possibility that Africa's profile may again be rising as the UK seeks new partnerships, based on historical links, partly in response to fears of a diminishing global role post-Brexit (Mawdsley, 2017; Chapter 1).

Conclusions

From this review of Conservative Party engagement with Africa, through opposition, Coalition and then Conservative-led government, and under five different Party leaders, there are clearly some recurring themes that emerge. These suggest that Conservative Africa policies are not purely a cosmetic exercise, nor are they easily explicable as *ad hoc* or opportunistic. Instead, we see a degree of continuity in engagement with Africa, which fulfilled a number of key purposes for the Party: allowing the projection of an image of compassionate Conservatism, demonstrating a break with past iterations of the Party; demonstrating a break with Labour policies on development, and the potential to pursue development in ways more aligned with Conservative Party values; and demonstrating a positive vision for UK global engagement, as a development leader and outward-facing, despite the result of the referendum on EU membership. Engagement with Africa has supported Conservative Party claims to be globally minded and compassionate, while mindful of Britain's national interest, and to be a party which has changed, seeking to lay claim to an area of UK policy that had been dominated by the Labour Party.

In providing the first analysis of contemporary Conservative Party engagement with Africa, the chapter has posited that this engagement serves particular purposes for the Party, both domestically and internationally. It has also demonstrated a degree of continuity across the approaches of not only different leaders, but also across election outcomes, which suggests this engagement is purposeful and strategic. It is possible to argue that this is the result of pragmatic recognition within the Party leadership that, since Labour's 1997 victory, the world has changed and the Party must change too. Nevertheless, this is an area of Conservative policy which brings political risks, with considerable domestic opposition to aid spending targets and ring-fencing (Mawdsley, 2017), as well as signalling a break with the past that some 'traditional' Conservatives consider to be at odds with Party values (Heppell *et al.*, 2017). Against this backdrop, and given the role which international development has come to play in UK international policies and domestic political debate, it is important to understand the underpinning drivers of continued UK–Africa engagement. This chapter has set out potential avenues for further inquiry. An improved understanding of these phenomena is crucial if we are to better explain the drivers and directions of UK–Africa relations. This is an important task in light of uncertainty and upheaval in UK domestic politics, as well as the international arena, which are likely to continue over the coming years.

Notes

* The research and discussions informing this chapter were undertaken as part of an ESRC Seminar Series on 'UK Africa Policy After Labour' (ES/L000725/1, 2013–17). Interviews cited here were conducted with funding from the University of Birmingham Research Engagement and Collaboration Hub. I am grateful to Dr Mattias Hjort for assistance with the REACH-funded Conservative development volunteering project.
1 Author interview with Rt Hon. Andrew Mitchell MP, former Secretary of State for International Development (2010–12) and founder of Project Umubano, Sutton Coldfield, 21 April 2017; Stephen Crabb MP, former organiser of Project Umubano, London, 17 July 2017.
2 Author interview with Stephen Crabb MP, former organiser of Project Umubano, London, 21 July 2017.
3 Author interviews, including with: Rt Hon. Andrew Mitchell MP, Sutton Coldfield, 21 April 2017; Stephen Crabb MP, London, 17 July 2017; Rt Hon. Sir Desmond Swayne MP, former Minister of State for International Development (2014–16), telephone interview, 25 April 2017; and Pauline Latham MP, member of the House of Commons International Development Select Committee (2010–15, 2015–17, 2017–ongoing), Derby, 14 July 2017.
4 Author interview with Rt Hon. Andrew Mitchell MP, Sutton Coldfield, 21 April 2017.
5 Author telephone interview with Conservative former government minister (anonymity requested), June 2017.
6 Author interview with Rt Hon. Andrew Mitchell MP, Sutton Coldfield, 21 April 2017.
7 Author interview with Conservative MP (anonymity requested), July 2017.

References

Abrahamsen, R. (2005) 'Blair's Africa: the politics of securitization and fear', *Alternatives: Global, Local, Political*, 30:1, 55–80.

Ashcroft, M. and Oakeshott, I. (2015) 'Toxic issue of foreign aid and an astonishing remark by the Chancellor: how David Cameron's Africa trip to make case for overseas spending divided Tory MPs', *Daily Mail*, 24 September 2015.

Borger, J. (2013) 'The Conservative party's uncomfortable relationship with Nelson Mandela', *Guardian*, 6 December 2013.

Bow Group (2013) 'Blair's Britain, by the Conservative Party', 28 February 2013, www.bowgroup.org/policy/blairs-britain-conservative-party [accessed 25 September 2017].

Brogan, B. (2006) 'Cameron's surprise date with Mandela', *Daily Mail*, 24 August 2006.

Cameron, D. (2011) 'PM's speech on aid, trade and democracy', delivered by UK Prime Minister David Cameron in Lagos, Nigeria, 19 July 2011, www.gov.uk/government/speeches/pms-speech-on-aid-trade-and-democracy [accessed 20 December 2018].

Carter, N. and Clements, B. (2015) 'From "greenest government ever" to "get rid of all the green crap": David Cameron, the Conservatives and the environment', *British Politics*, 10:2, 204–25.

Coll, S. (2010) 'Think tank: William Hague', *The New Yorker*, 14 May 2010, www.newyorker.com/online/blogs/stevecoll/2010/05/william-hague.html [accessed 28 December 2017].

Conservative Party (2001) 'Time for common sense', general election manifesto 2001, www.conservativemanifesto.com/2001/2001-conservative-manifesto.shtml [accessed 28 December 2017].

Department for International Development (2016) *Rising to the Challenge of Ending Poverty: The Bilateral Development Review 2016* (London: Department for International Development).

Gallagher, J. (2011) *Britain and Africa under Blair: In Pursuit of the Good State* (Manchester: Manchester University Press).

Groves, J. (2011) 'Cameron warns Africans over the "Chinese invasion"', *Daily Mail*, 20 July 2011.

Guardian (2002) 'Beckett: Zimbabwe issue must not hijack summit', *Guardian*, 23 August 2002, www.theguardian.com/politics/2002/aug/23/foreignpolicy.uk [accessed 28 December 2017].

Hague, W. (2013) 'Foreign Secretary statement on the death of Nelson Mandela', 5 December 2013.

Hall-Matthews, D. (2011) 'Liberal Democrat influence on Coalition international development policy', *Area*, 43:4, 511–12.

Hansard (2002) House of Commons Hansard Debates for 18 March 2002, column 23.

Hansard (2005) House of Commons Hansard Debates for 8 June 2005, pt 3, column 1235.

Harris, S. A. (2016) 'Boris Johnson describes Africa as "that country" during Conservative Party conference speech', *Huffington Post*, 3 October 2016.

Heppell, T. and Lightfoot, S. (2012) '"We will not balance the books on the backs of the poorest people in the world": understanding Conservative Party strategy on international aid', *Political Quarterly*, 83:1, 130–8.

Heppell, T., Crines, A. and Jeffery, D. (2017) 'The UK government and the 0.7% international aid target: opinion among Conservative parliamentarians', *British Journal of Politics and International Relations*, 19:4, 895–909.

Howard, M. (2005a) 'Make Poverty History', Speech by leader of HM Opposition Rt Hon. Michael Howard MP, delivered at Tabernacle Christian Centre, London, 24 April 2005.

Howard, M. (2005b) 'The Conservative approach to international development', Speech by leader of HM Opposition Rt Hon. Michael Howard MP, delivered at Conservative Campaign headquarters, London, 11 January 2005.

Kelly, R. (2001) 'Conservatism under Hague: the fatal dilemma', *Political Quarterly*, 72:2, 197–203.

Kite, M. (2007) 'Project Africa: Tories' drive to re-brand party', *Telegraph*, 18 March 2007.

Krutikova, S. and Warwick, R. (2017) 'The changing landscape of UK aid', Briefing Note BN204, Institute for Fiscal Studies.

Mawdsley, E. (2017) 'National interests and the paradox of foreign aid under austerity: Conservative governments and the domestic politics of international development since 2010', *Geographical Journal*, 183:3, 223–32.

Mitchell, A. (2016) 'Aid and development: there is a great deal more to be done', Conservative Home, 27 September 2016, www.conservativehome.com/platform/2016/09/andrew-mitchell-aid-and-development-there-is-a-great-deal-more-to-be-done.html [accessed 20 December 2018].

Morris, N. (2002) 'Charities angry at Tory plan to use aid as a weapon to topple Mugabe', *Independent*, 23 August 2002.

Noxolo, P. (2012) 'One world, big society: a discursive analysis of the Conservative green paper for international development', *Geographical Journal*, 178:1, 31–41.

Patel, P. (2016) 'Building a global development system for the 21st century', Speech delivered by Rt Hon. Priti Patel MP, Secretary of State for International Development, at Conservative Party Conference, Birmingham, 2 October 2016, http://cfid.org.uk/watch-priti-patels-speech-at-conservative-party-conference/ [accessed 20 December 2018].

Porteous, T. (2005) 'British government policy in Sub-Saharan Africa under New Labour', *International Affairs*, 81:2, 281–97.

Riley-Smith, B. (2015) 'David Cameron: UK troops to go to Africa to help counter extremists', *Telegraph*, 27 September 2015.

Robinson, J. and Wintour, P. (2011) 'Tories ditch political broadcast in favour of charity appeal', *Guardian*, 3 October 2011.

Taylor, I. (2005) '"Advice is judged by results, not by intentions": why Gordon Brown is wrong about Africa', *International Affairs*, 81:1, 299–310.

Taylor, I. (2012) 'Spinderella on safari: British policies towards Africa under New Labour', *Global Governance*, 18:4, 449–60.

Temko, T. (2006) 'Cameron: we got it wrong on apartheid', *Guardian*, 27 August 2006.

Tempest, M. (2004) 'Tories back intervention in Africa', *Guardian*, 6 October 2004.

Watt, N. (2011) 'Why David Cameron pressed ahead with Africa trip as hacking storm rages', *Guardian*, 19 July 2011.

Williams, P. D. (2010) 'Britain and Africa in the twenty-first century', in J. Mangala (ed.), *Africa and the New World Era: From Humanitarianism to a Strategic View* (Basingstoke: Palgrave Macmillan), 37–52.

7
Labour, international development and Africa: policy rethinking in opposition

William Brown

Labour's Africa policy under the Governments of Tony Blair (1997–2007) and Gordon Brown (2007–10) was remarkable both for its prominence and its ambition. Few UK Governments in recent times have made Africa such a focus of foreign and development policy. Not only did the UK respond actively to crises as they arose, whether in Sierra Leone or Zimbabwe, but the Labour Government came to promote a long-term and high-profile programme of support for African development. Indeed, Labour made so much of the running on international development that not only did David Cameron feel compelled to back Labour's pledges on aid spending but his first Secretary of State for International Development, Andrew Mitchell, claimed that international development policy had moved beyond party politics (Glennie, 2012). Labour's policy effort in government was not without its problems and tensions, and has been the subject of a substantial literature.[1] However, in opposition, and in a markedly different domestic and international climate, Labour had to rethink its approach.

How Labour's policy evolved in the years of opposition has not been explored in any depth in the academic literature. This chapter charts the discussions and changes that sought to remould Labour's international development policy as the Party moved away from the Blair–Brown era. The focus is mainly on the broader subject of international development policy, as it is in those terms, rather than 'Africa policy' more specifically, that the issue has largely been handled. Nevertheless, Labour's policy development in this area addresses topics that are central to any future Africa policy, should the party return to government, and Africa has remained 'front and centre' in Labour's thinking on international development policy.² This chapter draws on Labour Party documentation, the limited contemporary media and online commentary its policy discussions generated, speeches and some author-conducted open interviews with key figures in Labour's international development team.³

The chapter begins by outlining some of the background to Labour's policy development, covering, first, the issues Labour's shadow international development team faced on entering opposition and, secondly, the key policy processes over the period 2010–17. It then assesses the tensions and ongoing challenges facing the Party over international development policy. The chapter argues that while there has been a conscious attempt to move beyond the Blair–Brown approach to international development, it has done so in a far less benign external environment than it had faced in the decade from 1997. Attempting to use both the Sustainable Development Goals (SDGs) and a commitment to place human rights and social justice at the heart of development policy, the Party has been partially successful in finding an effective left-of-centre approach to development. Constraints on this rethinking, including external and internal change, the turnover of Shadow Secretaries of State and issues to do with the Party's policy process, mean that some key tensions remain to be resolved.

Into opposition: context and process

Labour's thirteen years in office transformed Britain's international development landscape and brought Africa to the centre of policy. After many years in which development cooperation had languished at the margins of government, while aid budgets were reduced, the years between 1997 and 2010 saw massive changes: the creation of a new department (the Department for International Development (DFID)) with cabinet-level representation, a schedule to reach the long-standing commitment to reach the 0.7 per cent of Gross National Income (GNI) aid target, and significant and sustained diplomatic efforts to boost international commitments to development in Africa. Yet, as the Party entered what was to prove a prolonged period of opposition, policy on international development faced a number of challenges.

Context

Foremost among these was the altered environment for development cooperation, both nationally and internationally, a context that arguably became progressively more hostile as the period in opposition progressed. Entering opposition, the Party faced a world 'changed beyond recognition' (Glennie,

2011). Indeed, almost every factor that had enabled Labour to achieve so much in international development and in its policy on Africa – a growing international and domestic economy, a public dialogue domestically and internationally that was generally favourable towards addressing poverty and debt crises, and a supportive coterie of big non-governmental organisations (NGOs) – was absent or under threat. Moreover, as Kirsty McNeill (one-time advisor to Gordon Brown) and Andrew Small argued, big tectonic shifts in the developing world, which Labour only partially grappled with while in government – the rise of middle-income countries, a transformed geopolitical environment in Africa and a new 'geography of development' – meant that 'many of the operating assumptions of the period [were] redundant' (McNeill and Small, 2014). In 2013, McNeill and Small wrote, 'even 2010 feels like a foreign country' (McNeill and Small, 2013).

Secondly, there were also tensions within Labour's previous approach to international development that would require some rethinking. The rise of large developing countries and accelerated growth in Africa, coupled with a need to design a global post-2015 development agenda, meant that the old approaches to development were in question. There was a need both to address the Western-centrism of UK policy (despite the contribution of African agency in some of the more high-profile summits (Landsberg, 2011)) and the missionary zeal around 'doing good' in Africa which continued to characterise some aspects of UK policy (Gallagher, 2013). Indeed, it was perhaps for this reason that it was relatively unproblematic for Conservative leader David Cameron to adopt and adapt into his 'golden thread', much of Labour's essentially liberal political and economic programme of change *for* Africa (Brown, 2006; 2016).

Thirdly, Labour faced an ongoing tactical problem of how to respond to the changed Tory position on Africa and the policies of the Coalition Government, outlined in detail in Chapter 6. Secretary of State for International Development, Andrew Mitchell went as far as to claim that 'there is not a Conservative, Liberal Democrat or Labour development policy, but a British one' (Glennie, 2012). Given that day-to-day criticism of government policy is part of the opposition's task, it presented Labour with the problem of how to sustain and strengthen the bi-partisanship on aid while also holding the Government to account.[4] Over time, as we shall see, policy space began to open up between Labour and the Government, although that arguably generated new problems for the opposition.

Labour's policy process

For Labour, as with the Conservatives, influences on policy and the policy process itself differ considerably between time in government and periods of opposition. In office, Labour's policy was closely coordinated through Number 10, with party leaders Blair and Brown exerting influence over most areas. In addition, when in government, the civil service, government political advisors and the departments of state, and the need to respond quickly to real-world events, all give a different character to the policy process. In opposition, policy is a more internal party process, though external actors and world events can and do exert some influence.

A key difficulty in Labour's rethinking on international development is that there are multiple sources of policy. Between 2010 and 2017, Labour's policies emerged from three main locations: the leader and the *ad hoc* policy reviews launched by Ed Miliband and the shadow cabinet; initiatives of the Shadow Secretaries of State (in this case for International Development); and the work of the Party's formal policymaking machinery centred on the National Policy Forum (NPF) and annual conference.

While the election of a new party leader often signals changes in policy, Ed Miliband's leadership election victory itself had limited impact on international development policy, prompting one commentator to ask whether Labour 'still cares about international development' (Haddad, 2010). The Iraq war aside, international issues had not played a major role in Miliband's leadership contest, with attention more focused on domestic issues, austerity and how to reposition Labour. Although Miliband launched a large number of *ad hoc* policy reviews, including one led by Harriet Harman on international development in 2011, the latter produced few concrete results and her successor as Shadow Secretary of State, Ivan Lewis, reorganised and internalised the review of policy within the shadow team.[5]

In the absence of a strong impetus from the leadership, the second area of policy work – the statements and initiatives undertaken by the Shadow Secretaries of State for International Development – proved to be more significant in this issue area. Their influence on policy broadly fell into two kinds: major speeches and statements on policy areas, developing and refining Labour's stance on a range of issues; and day-to-day shorter-term interventions, often in response to, and critical of, government policy. However, Labour had seven incumbents in this role between 2010 and 2017, which presented considerable challenges to sustained policy development.[6] While there is evidence of cumulative policy development, as various policy ideas and pledges were sustained or recycled by successors in the role, at the level of overarching strategy the record is more fragmented.

Though Harriet Harman established what became a consistent focus on achieving and writing into law the 0.7 per cent of GNI aid target (Harman, 2011b), the most concerted early period of policy development came under her successor,

Ivan Lewis. Lewis set out to build an agenda to develop a broader progressive vision of international development that 'built on but was not hidebound' by New Labour's legacy.[7] Developed through a series of consultations with NGOs, business and academics, a key focus of this work was outlining Labour's view of a post-2015, post-Millennium Development Goals, development agenda. Lewis's position centred on ten targets,[8] all of which featured to some extent in subsequent Party statements on international development, though often not in so coherent a manner. Lewis's work also concretised an approach to international development that was rights-based and universalistic, somewhat in contrast to the special programmes of funding (particularly and specifically for Africa) of the Blair and Brown era. Lewis also adapted some of Miliband's domestic 'responsible capitalism' language, to put forward a more critical take on the global political economy, in contrast to the Blair-era promotion of liberalisation and integrating Africa into international markets. Lewis also promoted policy commitments on labour standards, anti-corruption and good governance pronouncements that addressed western governments and corporations as well as African states.[9]

Some of these themes were further developed by Lewis's successors. The renewed focus on inequality was recast by Jim Murphy as a need for international development policy to address inequalities of power: 'the economic power to prosper … the social power of opportunity … and the political power to demand change and use a ballot box to effect it' (Murphy, 2014; see also Cartmail, 2014). However, Murphy was not in post long enough to develop the ideas much further. Similarly, in turning the various strands of policy development into a series of concrete manifesto commitments, Murphy's successor, Mary Creagh drew on, but again reorganised, previous work. In three key speeches, in late 2014 and early 2015, Creagh focused in turn on tackling conflict-affected and fragile states; tackling inequality (with a particular focus on achieving universal health coverage and the role of the private sector); and responsible capitalism (focusing on workers' rights, ethical and sustainable supply chains, and the payment of taxes) (Creagh, 2015a; 2015b).[10] Creagh's approach also showed a new focus on the 'meso' level operating between the global organisations and the multiple micro-level initiatives – the missing link between 'giant global organisations and the mother in DRC or South Sudan who turns up at a clinic to find no vaccines, no healthcare workers' (Creagh, 2015a). To a significant degree, the policy as set down in the 2015 manifesto largely reflected these three themes.

After the 2015 election defeat, policy development was slow to regain momentum. The turmoil that engulfed the Party, with the election of Jeremy Corbyn as leader, affected Creagh's successor, Dianne Abbott, a close ally of

Corbyn. Abbott held the post for only nine months, though she made a series of criticisms of the Tory Government's 'privatisation and securitisation' of aid (e.g. Abbott, 2016). Her successor in June 2016, Kate Osamor, faced a 'crash course in crisis management', despite having had only a year's experience as an MP (Casalicchio, 2016). This included not only the conflict within the Parliamentary Labour Party and the ongoing refugee crisis associated with the war in Syria, but also the prospect of radical changes in DFID policy, as arch-aid critic Priti Patel took the helm as Secretary of State. Up to 2017 much of Osamor's time was taken with fire-fighting the Government's aid policy, defending the 0.7 per cent of GNI aid target and in critiquing what she saw as an overly business-focused approach to aid spending (Osamor, 2016a; 2016b; 2017a). However, in a major speech at Chatham House, 'Development aid in turbulent political times', Osamor sought to 'put human rights and social justice at the heart of British Foreign policy' and emphasised earlier Labour themes of corporate responsibility, workers' rights, and transparency and fairness in tax regulation (Osamor, 2017b). These ideas were taken further in a keynote address to the Overseas Development Institute in London in November 2017, which pledged to add a second strategic aim of reducing inequality to DFID's goal of poverty reduction (Osamor, 2017c). The move represented the beginnings of another attempt to reframe the guiding purpose of policy, although it also drew on existing pledges.

The third area of policy development was the Party's formal internal party process centred on the NPF. This rolling programme of policymaking was revamped under Blair's leadership and, though relatively marginalised when the Party was in office, arguably had a more prominent role in opposition. The work of the NPF is split into different policy commissions, and for international development the policy commission on international issues was the key arena of discussion (titled 'Britain in the world' up to 2012, renamed 'Britain's global role' following the 2012 reform of the NPF and the 'International' policy commission after 2015).

To a considerable extent, the discussions of the NPF commission's work on international development closely followed the initiatives of the shadow team, at times reflecting close consultation between the two. The NPF commission in 2013 adopted Lewis's focus on the post-2015 global agenda (National Policy Forum, 2013: 140) and in 2014 reiterated Jim Murphy's inequalities of power in development (National Policy Forum, 2014: 202). The NPF's cycle of work, known as 'Agenda 2015', produced a 'final' report agreed at annual conference in 2014. This, after further consultations with Shadow Secretary of State Mary Creagh, was the basis for the 2015 general election manifesto.

The NPF established a similar process in 2016 called 'Agenda 2020' leading up to what was then the expected date of the next general election. Prime

Minister Theresa May's snap general election in 2017 short-circuited this process. Though the NPF, and its new 'International' policy commission, had begun consultation processes in autumn 2016 and spring 2017 (National Policy Forum, 2016b; 2017a) the election required a speedy and *ad hoc* formation of 2017 manifesto commitments under the Party's 'Article 5' provisions following a separate Party-wide manifesto consultation (Labour Party, 2017).[11]

Given the controversies in the Party after the election of Jeremy Corbyn, there is perhaps less policy difference between the 2015 and 2017 pledges on international development than might have been expected. In 2015, the manifesto played up Britain's international role as the only country that was a member of the UN Security Council, North Atlantic Treaty Organisation, G7, G20, the Commonwealth and European Union (Labour Party, 2015). It repeated the commitment to meet global challenges, also highlighting the need to work with 'allies in Africa and Latin America' (*ibid.*: 74). It pledged that Labour would sustain the 0.7 per cent of GNI commitment while ensuring value for money and focusing aid on the poorest countries (*ibid.*: 80). It reflected Ivan Lewis's previous work and Mary Creagh's three key themes by emphasising the SDGs, prioritising tackling inequality, putting human rights at the heart of development and focusing on conflict-affected states (*ibid.*). The manifesto also reflected existing policy threads, pledging Labour to set up a Centre for Universal Health Coverage to promote free healthcare for all; addressing tax avoidance and ensuring supply chains that were sustainable and protected workers' rights (*ibid.*).

The 2017 manifesto – *For the Many Not the Few* – revisited several of these themes and policies.[12] It pledged to realise Ivan Lewis's earlier aim of 'an integrated strategy on defence, diplomacy and development' (Labour Party, 2017: 116) and reaffirmed an earlier focus on conflict prevention and resolution but making a new pledge to create a Minister for Peace and Disarmament (*ibid.*: 117). The Party gave strong support to the SDGs and to reporting annually to Parliament on progress towards achieving them. Citing the loss of £46 billion to African economies through corruption and tax evasion, the manifesto repeated earlier Labour policy on improving transparency and regulation of tax havens (*ibid.*: 122). It included Osamor's Chatham House pledge on funding civil society organisations and ensuring respect for human rights, workers' rights and sustainability within supply chains (*ibid.*: 123). It also repeated Mary Creagh's 2015 manifesto pledge to establish a 'Centre for Universal Health Coverage' and to promote universal healthcare (*ibid.*: 123), pledged guaranteed access to the UK market for least developed countries in the wake of Brexit, and to put conflict resolution and human rights at the heart of policy (*ibid.*: 122).

While this process of policy development covered considerable new ground for Labour, and sought to respond to the changing relationships with developing countries, African countries not least among them, it remained a somewhat fragmented process. Though there were efforts to sustain specific policy pledges, the presentation of these, and their place within a wider development vision, was subject to considerable reinvention under different shadow secretaries. As a result, a number of tensions and challenges remained unresolved.

Tensions and challenges

In contrast to its time in office, the considerable policy rethinking Labour engaged in during its years in opposition received much less media attention.[13] Progress was certainly not helped by the rapid turnover of personnel, reforms to the policy process itself and wider political disruptions, including the internal strife in the Party after 2015, the snap general election of 2017 and Brexit. As a result, a number of broader tensions and challenges continued to face the Party as it sought to regain office.

Aid: defence or rethinking?

A key problem for any opposition is how to meet the multiple, often competing, tasks of opposition: to oppose the Government, to think more long term about strategies and policy, and to achieve its own concrete policy outcomes even while in opposition. Following 2010, these tensions played out across the whole range of policy areas, with Labour struggling to position itself on economic policy, deal with its legacy in relation to foreign military interventions and defend public services.

In international development policy this tension was most clearly visible between a need to defend past achievements on aid and take time to rethink development policy more broadly 'beyond aid'. Over the period from 2010, much time and effort was spent on engaging with debates around the overall level of aid spending: defending Labour's achievement, pressuring the Coalition to live up to Cameron's commitment to meet and sign into law the 0.7 per cent of GNI target and latterly defending this commitment against increasing attacks from backbench Conservatives and the right-wing press (for example, Osamor, 2017b).[14] Indeed, the writing into law of the 0.7 per cent pledge via a private member's bill, overwhelmingly backed by Labour MP's votes, was one area where Labour figures felt they achieved real policy outcomes against much foot-dragging, if not outright opposition, from the Government's side (Anderson, 2015).[15] However, the level of aid was only one of several issues that needed to be addressed. The pursuit of other policy achievements, the rationale for aid and how aid related to wider rethinking of development policy, also competed for attention.

Labour did achieve some policy successes beyond the 0.7 per cent aid target. Under Ivan Lewis, Labour commissioned Tessa Jowell MP and Lewis's advisor, Jessica Toale, to run an online campaign to lobby for early years targets to be included in the SDGs (Watt, 2012). Remarkably, this initiative was successful,[16] demonstrating for Lewis the ability of Labour, even in opposition, to achieve changes in policy, a fact he put down to the unique international standing the British Labour Party continued to enjoy on development policy issues.[17] On universal healthcare (UHC) too, Labour claimed success. Mary Creagh's championing of UHC had met with opposition from Secretary of State Justine Greening, who implicitly supported private health provision instead.[18] In international development questions in the House of Commons after the election, Greening changed her position and backed the inclusion of UHC in the SDGs.[19]

However, while the underlying rationale for aid formed part of the Party's campaign in support of the 0.7 per cent target, it remained an area where clearer thinking was elusive. As with the Conservatives' position, and with Blair's own policy towards Africa, aid was supported on a 'dual rationale' of being both morally right and in the national interest. This stance features in almost every Labour statement on international development: NPF policy documents, speeches of shadow secretaries and statements by campaigning groups like Labour Campaign for International Development (LCID) (Harman, 2011a; Labour Campaign for International Development, 2014; Lewis, 2012; National Policy Forum, 2014; Osamor, 2017a).[20] Yet this position not only raises questions about the potential tension between the two rationales, but also reveals differences within each: differing accounts of what is the moral imperative for aid and multiple notions of what aspects of the national interest are served by aid – from curbing migration, to economic growth, to improving security (see for example Harman, 2011a; Lewis, 2013a; 2013b; 2013c;, 2017; Osamor, 2017b).

Some Labour voices urged more policy development 'beyond aid'. The campaign group LCID argued that the 'consensus' on development really only went as far as a consensus on the level of aid spending, and Glennie (2012) wrote that there was a need to bring the politics back into development policy: 'Let's stop pretending development is like a mathematical equation; it is a political battleground.'

The Party did respond to this line of critique, Lewis's work on the post-2015 development agenda and Creagh's focus on the 'meso' level of development interventions among them. A number of figures in the Party were also prominent in debates around the 'beyond aid' agenda. Labour figures such as Stephen Twigg (later to chair the Committee) were key to the Commons International

Development Select Committee inquiry into how to move international development cooperation beyond a simple focus on aid flows (Select Committee on International Development, 2015). Labour MPs Glennys Kinnock and Stephen Doughty edited a 2015 report *Beyond Aid: Labour's Ambition for a Radical Development Agenda*, supported by the campaigning group LCID (Kinnock and Doughty, 2015). While both Government and opposition accepted the general premise that development cooperation should be thought of in terms covering a wide range of policy areas (Glennie, 2014), they did so with considerably different emphases. Where the Conservative Government focused on security and private sector issues, Labour focused on issues of fair trade, tax evasion, inequality and corporate responsibility. Arguably, too, Labour's support for UHC, and the idea of an 'international Sure Start' (Watt, 2012) can be seen as promoting 'international public finance' rather than the 'temporary fix' of aid (Alonso and Glennie, 2015; Glennie, 2014).

Nevertheless, on occasion the need to defend the amount of aid spending has come at the expense of longer-term thinking. For example, Ivan Lewis (2013a) was criticised for arguing that 'ending aid dependency is the right objective for greater equality and the dignity, independence and self-determination of nations and citizens. It should be a core part of the mission of a centre-left development policy.' NGOs felt that it 'sent the wrong signal' on aid in a context where continued commitment to the 0.7 per cent aid target was under threat.[21] More recently, the 0.7 per cent target was the main development-related issue raised in the party's NPF consultations in 2016 and 2017 (National Policy Forum, 2016b; 2017a), and as right-wing attacks on aid increased it dominated the initial policy contributions from Kate Osamor in 2016–17 (Osamor, 2016b; 2017a; 2017b). Notably, in late 2017, Osamor began to speak on this issue, arguing that aid was only ever a 'sticking plaster' and the Party needed to address the 'underlying causes' rooted in a deeply unequal international system (Osamor, 2017c).

Political context

The task of balancing short-term opposition work with longer-term rethinking was made even more difficult, between 2010 and 2017, by the changing domestic and international context. Escalating challenges to aid from right-wing Conservative MPs and media meant that defensive interventions – protecting the aid budget as well as opposing what Labour saw as aid diversion (to defence and foreign office uses), securitisation and privatisation were given greater prominence than longer-term rethinking. This was perhaps more the case for the post-2015 period as Coalition government was replaced by a Conservative-only administration and an ascendant, eurosceptic and aid-sceptic right wing made itself felt. Indeed, in the run-up to the 2017 election there was widespread speculation that the Conservatives would either fail to recommit to the 0.7 per cent target or undermine it by re-categorising aid or diverting it to military or diplomatic budgets. Labour figures such as Ivan Lewis (Lewis, 2017) and prominent international private donors such as Bill Gates weighed in. Early in the campaign, the Conservatives announced they would in fact retain the commitment in their manifesto (Conservative Party, 2017).

However, Labour also had to respond to a wider challenge to international cooperation. Labour has a long-standing commitment to multilateralism in international affairs, within which its development policy and policy towards Africa had always resided. Yet this was a far more promising context in the 1990s, in the post-Cold War push for liberalisation and expansion of a liberal, US-led international order than in the un-cooperative and increasingly mini- or bi-lateralist context of 2017, where the whole direction of US grand strategy appeared to be in doubt. The 2017 NPF policy consultation noted that long-standing Labour values of internationalism, social justice and universal rights were under threat, facing 'seismic challenges' (National Policy Forum, 2017a: 3). Even in 2014, the final policy document of the 'Britain's Global Role' policy commission had noted the challenge: 'bi-lateral diplomacy, or a foreign policy driven solely by short-term commercial interest, is not sufficient to deal with global or regional issues that transcend national borders' (National Policy Forum, 2014: 125). And in its 2016 paper on defence policy, the 'International' policy commission also noted the negative impact of the weakening it perceived of international institutions that have underpinned stability and cooperation for seventy years (National Policy Forum, 2016a: 95). However, while reiterating commitments to international cooperation, internationalism and international justice, its 2017 manifesto and the limited policy work that had preceded it gave little indication of what this would entail in practical terms, nor how such commitments could be framed in a way that shifted the foreign policy and aid debate within Britain (see Cargill, 2017).

Where is Africa?

A third and rather different point relates to the position of Africa within Labour policy. In the Blair and Brown years, much discussion of international development, as well as a host of related policy initiatives, centred quite explicitly on Africa. Indeed, the party manifestos in 2005 and 2010 had explicit commitments relating to Africa, the 2005 manifesto having a sub-section of its own on Africa and committing the Party to focus on 'Africa and the fight against global poverty' (Labour Party, 2005: 90; 2010). After 2010, Africa was far less prominent in terms of specific commitments and much policy discussion, and the 2015 manifesto noted the shift in the global economy from West to East and pledged an 'Asia Step-Change Task Force' (Labour Party, 2015: 75). Although African countries would be affected by a series of policy pledges – on Common Agricultural Policy reform, migration and peacebuilding – these, like international development pledges, were cast in general rather than Africa-specific terms (Bailey and Taylor, 2015). Despite mentioning a series of African conflicts, the 2017 manifesto and the 2017 NPF report were otherwise quiet on specifically African concerns, the NPF report having a section devoted instead to 'Asia' (Labour Party, 2017; National Policy Forum, 2017b: 57).

Even so, it was clear from Africa's constant rhetorical presence in speeches and policy documents, often providing real-world examples within which broader policy points were being made, that it hadn't entirely slipped from view. Mary Creagh argued that there had not been a 'downgrading of Africa' in policy and claimed, 'I was always very clear that Africa was front and centre in my mind when thinking about development' and the Ebola crisis in West Africa shaped her thinking on healthcare in 2015.[22] Moreover, even if less central to Labour policy than under Blair's leadership (which was in any case rather unusual in its focus on Africa), African states continue to be important to Labour policy dilemmas beyond providing rhetorical or anecdotal material to speechwriters.

Perhaps at the broadest this is evident in the desire expressed in some circles to 'forge a new kind of relationship' with developing countries.[23] As noted earlier, despite a language of partnership, Blair-era Africa policy was to some extent still characterised by a Western-centrism placing a liberal morality and conditionality at the forefront of policy (Brown, 2006; Gallagher, 2013). Lewis put this as a need for 'replacing paternalism with dynamic partnerships between North and South, developed and middle-income countries' (Lewis, 2012) and Murphy proclaimed that 'our own economic, political and social advance is not brought about by conquest but the self-advancement of African countries themselves' (Murphy, 2013).

The tension here is not only thinking through what those new relationships might look like, but also how such goals sit alongside other now well-established aspects of Labour foreign and development policy, such as commitments to human rights (including explicitly, LGBT rights), governance and anti-corruption. For its part the Party's NPF noted the violation of human rights in a number of African countries including Zimbabwe and DRC and called on the UK to 'lead by example ... upholding moral and legal obligations at home and supporting the development of free societies abroad' (National Policy Forum, 2013: 141). It went on to say that human rights 'should also be a consideration in our bilateral relationships with other countries, including in our aid relationships and in trade between countries' (*ibid.*). From 2016, Jeremy Corbyn, Shadow Foreign Secretary Emily Thornbury and Kate Osamor all stressed the centrality of human rights to any future Labour Government's foreign and development policy; Thornbury arguing this would go beyond the 'ethical dimension' initially pledged by Robin Cook in 1997.

However, this all implies continued forms of conditionality – whether to cut aid in response to homophobia, oppression of women, abuse of human rights, corruption or absence of democratisation (McNeill and Small, 2014). Several Shadow Secretaries of State – Lewis, Murphy, Abbott and Osamor – all endorsed at least some forms of conditionality. Lewis grappled with the issue most directly, arguing for 'greater up-front conditionality in relation to human rights and corruption' (Lewis, 2013a). Indeed, Lewis argued that the UK should withdraw budget support for Rwanda in the wake of the UN report into eastern Congo, a move that was met with criticism from Rwanda and from the UK Government.[24] Reflecting on the approach, Lewis argued, 'I felt the message too often was "you can do what you want" because these were leaders who had delivered on economic growth and to some extent poverty reduction … [but that] government to government support is essentially a kite mark – I accept you as an acceptable partner.'[25] Lewis also tried to balance conditions on corruption by addressing the actions of Western institutions and countries as well as African Governments, pledging to be 'tough on corruption and tough on the causes of corruption' (Lewis, 2012).[26] Labour policy henceforth contained strong commitments to tackle tax evasion.

Whether such tensions can be managed through a combination of distinguishing between 'poor people and poor countries' on the one hand (McNeill and Small, 2014), perhaps withdrawing direct budget support without withdrawing aid as Lewis suggested, and agile country-specific diplomacy on the other (Lewis 2017), is an open question. Even then, the reactions of ever-more diplomatically assertive African states may still make such tensions difficult to handle (see for example Fisher, 2013).

Africa is also 'front and centre' when thinking about how to spend aid effectively and avoid 'waste' when also committing to focus on conflict-affected states. A focus on conflict-affected countries was part of Labour's policy while in government; this increased under Cameron's Government but was also a key theme of Labour's pre-2015 development policy and, as Creagh noted, 'virtually all the conflict states are in Africa'.[27] Yet how to do that while also combatting corruption and fraud is a tricky prospect (McNeill and Small, 2014). Indeed, there was a claimed quadrupling of fraud cases relating to UK aid following Cameron's move to ensure that half of DFID's budget should go to fragile states and regions (Syal, 2017). Labour's response has not been to question the focus but to accept that greater risks need to be taken with aid money: 'the more we focus our resources in conflict-ridden and fragile states the greater the risks we are taking' (Lewis, 2012). Yet the implications of this, while also trying to shore up the aid budget from critics, are not clear.

Finally, African states are to the forefront when thinking through the relationships between development and broader foreign policy goals. This came to the fore especially in the context of discussions of terrorism and combatting the threat of 'ungoverned spaces', most of which are identified as being in the Middle East or Africa. In response to terrorist attacks in Algeria and Mali in 2013, Ed Miliband highlighted the threats from 'ungoverned spaces and security vacuums' in North Africa and for the need to use 'diplomacy and development in response' (Miliband, 2013). This line of argument was echoed by Jim Murphy, then Shadow Secretary for Defence, calling for 'preventative intervention' in the 'arc of instability across north and central Africa combining military, developmental and diplomatic activity' (Murphy, 2013). In its 2012 report to Conference, the NPF emphasised security, stability and the rule of law as key to making aid effective and for the combination of development, diplomacy and defence policies (National Policy Forum, 2012). In 2013, Lewis asked Lord McConnell to help to coordinate the work of his team and the shadow defence team under Jim Murphy and shadow foreign office work of Douglas Alexander (Lewis, 2013c).[28] This need for coordination was reiterated in the 2017 manifesto, which called for 'an integrated strategy on defence, diplomacy and development' (Labour Party, 2017: 116). Thus, although the Party opposed the Conservative Government's blurring of aid *funding* by channelling overseas development assistance through the Ministry of Defence and Foreign and Commonwealth Office because of the lack of accountability it entailed, it argued for *policy* coordination, and close cooperation between the three areas 'on the ground' (Osamor, 2017c).[29]

Brexit

Finally, there is the challenge of Brexit itself, a set of problems that Labour, like others, had only just begun to think through. Perhaps not surprisingly there was precious little in the 2017 manifesto, nor in policy work since June 2016, on how Britain's international development policy would need to change in the wake of Brexit. The only explicit commitment given in the 2017 manifesto was to protect market access to the UK for the least developed countries (Labour Party, 2017). This pledge relates to one of a number of key problems Brexit poses for UK development policy, namely how to reorganise the UK's trade with developing countries once outside of the EU umbrella.[30] Though rather vaguely phrased, the commitment at least showed an awareness of the issue. Whether the UK stays within the single market and customs union, or not, was not, in 2017, in Labour's hands. If inside, most of the existing trade arrangements with developing countries would remain in place. If outside, then Labour would need to do some considerable work thinking through what a progressive trade architecture ought to look like.[31] It remains to be seen how the Party will fashion a response that addresses the very significant issues this poses for African states.

Brexit also poses difficult issues about how future UK aid is allocated and whether, and how, it can be used in conjunction with European allies (*ibid.*). Several Labour figures have expressed a fear of a loss of British influence in aid circles, not least because the UK was able to exert great influence on development policy within the EU and was able to achieve UK development goals by forging cooperation with European allies.[32] Echoing Lewis's point about the high standing in which the UK was held in development circles, as a legacy of Labour's time in government, Mary Creagh argued that there would be a decline post-Brexit in countries looking to the UK for 'thought leadership' in development policy.[33] Here there were few signs that Labour's policy was catching up with the Brexit timetable: the NPF annual report in 2017 acknowledged the impact Brexit would have on development objectives in very general terms only and there was little specific discussion of how the Party should revise policy towards African states in the light of Brexit (National Policy Forum, 2017b).

Following the better-than-expected 2017 general election result, Labour was arguably in a stronger position to push the Government for commitments on international development issues as Brexit negotiations progressed. Though complicated by changes and uncertainties on the shape of future EU development policy and aid budgets (DG-Ex, 2017), there was arguably a need for Labour to seek to press the Government in the interests of the least developed countries – in aid and trade – in a context where the dominant political and media voices were focused on securing Britain's own interests.[34]

Conclusions

Labour's attempt to rethink its policy on international development, to build on, but not be bound by, its record in government, has shown some successes. A focus on a more universalistic and rights-based approach to development, and an orientation towards the SDGs, provide a promising basis on which to recast the relationships underpinning development cooperation. A number of pledges – on inequality, health, worker rights and conflict-affected states – have become embedded within Party policy. As we have seen, all of these will be key to reshaping relationships with African states. This rethinking has taken place in difficult circumstances. A harsher political context, the difficulties of opposition itself, the frequent changes of key personnel and a rapidly changing international agenda have all impacted on the Party's efforts on international development. The period between the general elections of 2015 and 2017 saw something of a hiatus in policy development, as internal turmoil, Brexit and election campaigning dominated the Party's time. Yet by late 2017, there were signs of a renewed focus on reviewing the overarching strategy of development policy. It remains to be seen whether this will address some enduring tensions and uncertainties in the Party's approach. In a difficult domestic and international political environment, a progressive left-of-centre strategy for Africa specifically, and international development more generally, is both more essential, and tougher to formulate, than ever.

Notes

1. For example, see Abrahamsen (2005); Abrahamsen and Williams (2001); Brown (2006; 2009); Cumming (2004); Porteus (2008); Gallagher (2013).
2. As former Shadow Secretary of State for International Development, Mary Creagh put it (author interview with Mary Creagh MP, via phone, 26 January 2017).
3. It should be noted that publicly available Labour Party documentation is very incomplete and there is no single accessible and up to date Labour archive. Key interviews used for this chapter were conducted by the author in 2017 with former Shadow Secretaries of State, Mary Creagh and Ivan Lewis, and with Linda McAvan MEP.
4. Author interview with Ivan Lewis MP, London, 28 February 2017.
5. Author interview with Ivan Lewis MP, London, 28 February 2017.
6. They were: Douglas Alexander (June–October 2010); Harriet Harman (November 2010–October 2011); Ivan Lewis (November 2011–November 2013); Jim Murphy (November 2013–October 2014); Mary Creagh (November 2014–September 2015); Dianne Abbott (September 2015–June 2016); Kate Osamor (June 2016–December 2018).
7. Author interview with Ivan Lewis MP, London, 28 February 2017.
8. These were: decent jobs and universal social protection; access to universal healthcare and social protection; universal access to basic utilities; quality primary and secondary education; protection of ecosystems and biodiversity; basic food security; women's empowerment; freedom from violence; good governance including from recipient Governments, donors and multinational companies; and active and responsible citizenship including choosing elected representatives (Lewis, 2013b).
9. Author interview with Ivan Lewis MP, London, 28 February 2017.

10 Author interview with Mary Creagh MP, via phone, 26 January 2017.
11 The consultation website was accessible at: www.labour.org.uk/index.php/shapeour manifesto/ [accessed 10 January 2018].
12 At over 120 pages long, the manifesto was felt to be making an ambitious number and range of pledges but was widely regarded as helping Labour to secure a far better result in the election than most had predicted. Labour, at around twenty points behind the Conservatives in most opinion polls and having an eleven-point deficit in the May 2017 local elections, secured 40 per cent of the vote to the Conservatives' 44 per cent (BBC News, 2017).
13 Exceptions here include the 'early years' campaign run by Tessa Jowell (Watt, 2012).
14 Author interview with Ivan Lewis MP, London, 28 February 2017.
15 Author interview with Mary Creagh MP, via phone, 26 January 2017.
16 The target is part of SDG target 4.2 (United Nations, 2018).
17 Because of the high regard that continued in Africa for Blair and Brown, Lewis claimed, 'The British Labour Party had a voice that normally you wouldn't have as an opposition party', author interview with Ivan Lewis MP, London, 28 February 2017.
18 Author interview with Mary Creagh MP, via phone, 26 January 2017 and author email communication with Mary Creagh MP, 5 July 2017.
19 Author interview with Mary Creagh MP, via phone, 26 January 2017 and author email communication with Mary Creagh MP, 5 July 2017. Greening's comment is recorded in 'Sustainable Development Goals. Oral answers to questions', House of Commons, 3 June 2015, www.theyworkforyou.com/debates/?id=2015–06–03d.575.7&s=SDGs+section%3Adebates#g576.5%20 [accessed 10 January 2018].
20 Author interview with Mary Creagh MP, via phone, 26 January 2017.
21 Author interview with Ivan Lewis MP, London, 28 February 2017.
22 Her own background was in working for Oxfam and she had made visits to Burundi, Rwanda and DRC while a backbench MP. Author interview with Mary Creagh MP, via phone, 26 January 2017.
23 As Jonathan Glennie (2014) put it, 'the British remain … somewhat patronising and condescending to people of other countries, especially poorer ones'.
24 Author interview with Ivan Lewis MP, London, 28 February 2017.
25 Author interview with Ivan Lewis MP, London, 28 February 2017.
26 In 2012, Lewis commissioned Hadeel Ibrahim of the Mo Ibrahim Foundation to produce a report on tackling corruption for the shadow international development team (Lewis, 2012 and author interview with Ivan Lewis MP, London, 28 February 2017). Though never published and despite the Foundation's focus on African Governments' performance, the report was highly critical of Western multinationals and banks (author interview with Ivan Lewis MP, London, 28 February 2017).
27 Author interview with Mary Creagh MP, via phone, 26 January 2017.
28 This coordination was limited by the cabinet reshuffle in which both Lewis and Murphy moved positions, author interview with Ivan Lewis MP, London, 28 February 2017.
29 Author interview with Ivan Lewis MP, London, 28 February 2017.

30   See also Lightfoot *et al.* (2017); Mendes-Parra *et al.* (2016); and Chapters 1 and 9 of this volume.
31   Author interview with Linda McAvan MEP, Sheffield, 3 March 2017.
32   Author interview with Mary Creagh MP, via phone, 26 January 2017; author interview with Linda McAvan MEP, Sheffield, 3 March 2017.
33   Author interview with Mary Creagh MP, via phone, 26 January 2017.
34   Author interview with Linda McAvan MEP, Sheffield, 3 March 2017.

References

Abbott, D. (2016) 'Labour is still standing up for international development', *Left Foot Forward*, 15 January 2016, https://leftfootforward.org/2016/01/comment-labour-is-still-standing-up-for-international-development/ [accessed 1 February 2017].

Abrahamsen, R. (2005) 'Blair's Africa: the politics of securitization and fear', *Alternatives: Global, Local, Political*, 30:1, 55–80.

Abrahamsen, R. and Williams, P. D. (2001) 'Ethics and foreign policy: the antinomies of New Labour's "Third Way" in Sub-Saharan Africa', *Political Studies*, 49:2, 249–64.

Alonso, J. A. and Glennie, J. (2015) 'What is development cooperation?', United Nations Economic and Social Council (ECOSOC) Development Cooperation Forum Briefs, February 2015, www.un.org/en/ecosoc/newfunct/pdf15/2016_dcf_policy_brief_no.1.pdf [accessed 28 September 2016].

Anderson, M. (2015) 'UK passes bill to honour pledge of 0.7% foreign aid target', *Guardian*, 9 March 2015, www.theguardian.com/global-development/2015/mar/09/uk-passes-bill-law-aid-target-percentage-income [accessed 28 September 2016].

Bailey, H. and Taylor, M. (2015) 'Election 2015: what's in the party manifestos for Africa?', *African Arguments*, 29 April 2015, http://africanarguments.org/2015/04/29/election-2015-whats-in-the-party-manifestos-for-africa-by-magnus-taylor-and-hetty-bailey/ [accessed 28 September 2016].

BBC News (2017) 'Results', www.bbc.co.uk/news/election/2017/results [accessed 10 January 2018].

Brown, W. (2006) 'The Commission for Africa: results and prospects for the West's Africa policy', *Journal of Modern African Studies*, 44:3, 349–74.

Brown, W. (2009) 'Reconsidering the aid relationship: International Relations and social development', *The Round Table: The Commonwealth Journal of International Affairs*, 98:402, 285–301.

Brown, W. (2016) 'Navigating uneven development: Britain's Africa policy in historical perspective', in K. Matin and A. Anievas (eds), *Historical Sociology and World History: Uneven and Combined Development over the Long Dureé* (London: Rowman and Littlefield), 149–69.

Cargill, T. (2017) 'Labour manifesto pledges on foreign policy', British Foreign Policy Group, 18 May 2017, http://bfpg.co.uk/2017/05/labour-manifesto-pledges-on-uk-foreign-policy/ [accessed 6 September 2017].

Cartmail, G. (2014) 'Putting workers' rights at the heart of international development', *Left Foot Forward*, 10 April 2014, https://leftfootforward.org/2014/04/putting-workers-rights-at-the-heart-of-international-development/ [accessed 1 February 2017].
Casalicchio, E. (2016) 'Kate Osamor: "Britain should no longer be in bed with dictators"', *Politics Home*, 21 September 2016, www.politicshome.com/news/uk/foreign-affairs/house/79175/kate-osamor-britain-should-no-longer-be-bedfellows-these [accessed 28 September 2016].
Conservative Party (2017) *Forward Together: Our Plan for a Stronger Britain and a Prosperous Future* (London: Conservative Party).
Creagh, M. (2015a) 'Inequality and universal health coverage', Speech at the Institute of Development Studies, University of Sussex, 29 January 2015, www.marycreagh.com/speech_to_institute_for_development_studies_inequality_and_universal_health_coverage [accessed 28 September 2016].
Creagh, M. (2015b) 'The role of the private sector in development', Speech in Cambridge, 5 March 2015, www.marycreagh.com/the_role_of_the_private_sector_in_development [accessed 28 September 2016].
Cumming, G. D. (2004) 'UK African policy in the post-Cold War era: from realpolitik to moralpolitik?', *Commonwealth & Comparative Politics*, 42:1, 106–28.
DG-Ex (Directorate-General for External Policies European Union) (2017) *Briefing: Preliminary Assessment of the Impact of Brexit on EU Development and Humanitarian Aid Policies* (Brussels: European Parliament).
Fisher, J. (2013) 'Structure, agency and Africa in the international system: donor diplomacy and regional security policy in East Africa since the 1990s', *Conflict, Security & Development*, 13:5, 537–67.
Gallagher, J. (2013) *Britain and Africa under Blair: In Pursuit of the Good State* (Manchester: Manchester University Press).
Glennie, J. (2011) 'Labour needs to bring its own politics into international development', *Guardian*, 3 June 2011, www.theguardian.com/global-development/poverty-matters/2011/jun/03/uk-labour-international-development-politics [accessed 28 September 2016].
Glennie, J. (2012) 'Finally, the UK's Labour party seems to know its own mind on development', *Guardian*, 4 October 2012, www.theguardian.com/global-development/poverty-matters/2012/oct/04/uk-labour-party-own-mind-development [accessed 28 September 2016].
Glennie, J. (2014) 'Towards a new narrative on aid and international development', paper presented to the BISA Africa and International Studies Working Group and ESRC Seminar Series on UK Africa Policy After Labour, University of Birmingham, 13 May 2014, www.open.ac.uk/socialsciences/bisa-africa/files/uk-africa-policy/Transcript%20of%20Glennie%20presentation.pdf [accessed 6 September 2017].
Haddad, L. (2010) 'Does the Labour Party still care about international development?', *Development Horizons*, 29 September 2010, www.developmenthorizons.com/2010/09/does-labour-party-still-care-about.html [accessed 9 November 2017].

Harman, H. (2011a) 'Growing the aid budget in a time of deficit reduction: moral imperative and political challenge', Speech at London School of Economics, 3 February 2011, www.lse.ac.uk/website-archive/publicEvents/pdf/20110203%20Harriet%20Harman%20transcript.pdf [accessed 6 September 2017].

Harman, H. (2011b) 'Launch of Labour's international development policy review', 20 April 2011, http://labour-speeches.sayit.mysociety.org/speech/599163 [accessed 23 February 2017].

Kinnock, G. and Doughty, S. (eds) (2015) *Beyond Aid: Labour's Ambition for a Radical Development Agenda* (London: Labour Campaign for International Development).

Labour Campaign for International Development (2014) 'Beyond aid: the future UK approach to development. Submission to the International Development Select Committee from the Labour Campaign for International Development', 2 October 2014, https://labour-cid.files.wordpress.com/2014/07/submission-to-the-international-development-select-committee.pdf [accessed 8 February 2017].

Labour Party (2005) *Britain, Forward Not Back: The Labour Party Manifesto 2005*, www.politicsresources.net/area/uk/ge05/man/lab/manifesto.pdf [accessed 8 September 2017].

Labour Party (2010) *A Future Fair For All: The Labour Party Manifesto 2010*, http://news.bbc.co.uk/1/shared/bsp/hi/pdfs/12_04_10_labour_manifesto.pdf [accessed 28 February 2017].

Labour Party (2015) *Britain Can Be Better: The Labour Party Manifesto 2015*, www.labour.org.uk/page/-/BritainCanBeBetter-TheLabourPartyManifesto2015.pdf [accessed 28 February 2017].

Labour Party (2017) *For the Many Not the Few: The Labour Party Manifesto 2017*, www.labour.org.uk/page/-/Images/manifesto-2017/Labour%20Manifesto%202017.pdf [accessed 6 September 2017].

Landsberg, C. (2011) 'Diffused continentally; undermined abroad?', paper presented to the seminar, African Agency: Implications for IR Theory, City University, London, 14 September 2011, www.open.ac.uk/socialsciences/bisa-africa/files/africanagency-seminar4-landsberg.pdf [accessed 6 September 2017].

Lewis, I. (2012) 'Speech', Speech to Labour Party Annual Conference, 1 October 2012, www.politics.co.uk/comment-analysis/2012/10/01/ivan-lewis-speech-in-full [accessed 11 January 2017].

Lewis, I. (2013a) 'Labour's post-2015 development goals', Speech to CAFOD, 30 January 2013, http://labour-speeches.sayit.mysociety.org/speech/596255 [accessed 23 February 2017].

Lewis, I. (2013b) 'Labour's post-2015 vision: equality 2030', Speech to BOND 'Beyond 2015' conference, 14 May 2013, https://lcid.org.uk/2013/05/15/labours-post-2015-vision-equality-2030/ [accessed 23 February 2017].

Lewis, I. (2013c) 'Speech', Speech to Labour Party Annual Conference, 23 September 2013, http://press.labour.org.uk/post/62050072023/ivan-lewis-mps-speech-to-labour-party-annual [accessed 28 September 2016].

Lewis, I. (2017) 'The UK's aid commitments are under threat, it's time to defend them', *Guardian*, 12 February 2017, www.theguardian.com/global-development/2017/

feb/12/the-uks-aid-commitments-are-under-threat-its-time-to-defend-them [accessed 16 February 2017].

Lightfoot, S., Mawdsley, E. and Szent-Iványi, B. (2017) 'Brexit and UK international development policy', *Political Quarterly*, 88:3, 517–24.

McNeill, K. and Small, A. (2013) 'Foreign policy dilemmas for progressives', Progress Online, 15 May 2013, www.progressonline.org.uk/2013/05/15/foreign-policy-dilemmas-for-progressives/ [accessed 3 February 2017].

McNeill, K. and Small, A. (2014) 'Development dilemmas', Progress Online, 20 February 2014, www.progressonline.org.uk/2014/02/20/development-dilemmas [accessed 3 February 2017].

Mendes-Parra, M., te Veld, D. W. and Winters, L. A. (eds) (2016) *The Impact of the UK's Post-Brexit Trade Policy on Development: An Essay Series* (London: Overseas Development Institute).

Miliband, E. (2013) 'Speech', Speech in the House of Commons, 21 January 2013, http://labour-speeches.sayit.mysociety.org/speech/596293 [accessed 6 September 2017].

Murphy, J. (2013) 'Preventative intervention: how the UK responds to extremism in North and West Africa and beyond', Speech to the Henry Jackson Society, 14 February 2013, http://labour-speeches.sayit.mysociety.org/speech/596196 [accessed 6 September 2017].

Murphy, J. (2014) 'DFID under Labour: development and power', Speech to the ONE Campaign, 8 April 2014, http://press.labour.org.uk/post/82096135630/dfid-under-labour-development-and-power-jim [accessed 28 September 2017].

National Policy Forum (2012) 'Labour Party National Policy Forum report 2012', www.leftfutures.org/wp-content/uploads/2012/09/2012-NPF-Annual-Report-to-Conference.pdf [accessed 3 February 2017].

National Policy Forum (2013) 'Labour Party National Policy Forum report 2013', www.policyforum.labour.org.uk/uploads/editor/files/NPF_report_low_res.pdf [accessed 3 February 2017].

National Policy Forum (2014) 'Labour Party National Policy Forum report 2014', www.policyforum.labour.org.uk/uploads/editor/files/NPF_Annual_Report_2014.pdf [accessed online 3 February 2017].

National Policy Forum (2016a) 'Labour Party National Policy Forum report 2016', www.huntingdonlabourparty.org.uk/wp-content/uploads/2016/08/NPF-Report-2016-.pdf [accessed 3 March 2017].

National Policy Forum (2016b) 'Labour Party National Policy Forum International Commission Consultation Briefing', www.policyforum.labour.org.uk/agenda-2020/commissions/international/npf-consultation-2017-international [accessed 3 March 2017].

National Policy Forum (2017a) 'Labour Party National Policy Forum Consultation', February 2017, www.labour.org.uk/index.php/npf-2017/international [accessed 6 September 2017].

National Policy Forum (2017b) 'Labour Party National Policy Forum Report 2017', https://members.labour.org.uk/national-policy-forum [accessed 3 March 2017].

Osamor, K. (2016a) 'Kate Osamor MP, Labour's Shadow International Development Secretary, responding to Priti Patel's speech', www.kateosamor.co.uk/kate_osamor_mp_labour_s_shadow_international_development_secretary_responding_to_priti_patel_s_speech_said [accessed 30 November 2016].

Osamor, K. (2016b) 'Priti Patel must support the 0.7% commitment of aid spending or the Prime Minister must pull her into line', www.kateosamor.co.uk/press_release_kate_osamor_mp_priti_patel_must_support_the_0_7_commitment_of_aid_spending_or_the_prime_minister_must_pull_her_into_line [accessed 30 November 2016].

Osamor, K. (2017a) 'Time to stand up for foreign aid', *Prospect*, www.prospectmagazine.co.uk/world/time-to-stand-up-for-foreign-aid-dfid-international-development [accessed 7 February 2017].

Osamor, K. (2017b) 'Development aid in turbulent political times', Speech at Chatham House, 19 April 2017, www.chathamhouse.org/file/case-foreign-aid# [accessed 10 November 2017].

Osamor, K. (2017c) 'Keynote speech: Labour's vision for international development', Overseas Development Institute, London, 2 November 2017, www.kateosamor.co.uk/keynote_speech_overseas_development_institute [accessed 10 November 2017].

Porteus, T. (2008) *Britain in Africa* (London: Zed Books).

Select Committee on International Development (2015) *The Future of UK Development Co-operation: Phase 2: Beyond Aid*, International Development Committee, Tenth Report, https://publications.parliament.uk/pa/cm201415/cmselect/cmintdev/663/66302.htm [accessed 6 September 2017].

Syal, R. (2017) 'UK foreign aid fraud investigations "quadruple in five years"', *Guardian*, 9 February 2017, www.theguardian.com/global-development/2017/feb/09/uk-foreign-aid-investigations-quadruple-in-last-five-years [accessed 10 January 2018].

United Nations (2018), 'Sustainable Development Goal 4', https://sustainabledevelopment.un.org/sdg4 [accessed 10 January 2018].

Watt, N. (2012) 'Jowell gets role in helping mothers and children in developing countries', *Guardian*, 30 September 2012, www.theguardian.com/politics/2012/sep/30/tessa-jowell-role-international-aid [accessed 6 September 2017].

8

The mixed fortunes of African development campaigning under austerity and the Conservatives*

Graham Harrison

2005 witnessed the rolling out of the Make Poverty History (MPH) development campaign coalition. The general, but not unanimous, view was that MPH made tangible headway on many of its demands. But, after the campaign, a sense of uncertainty about its costs and benefits spread throughout the sector. From 2006 onwards, individual campaign organisations each made a quieter and less celebratory post-mortem of the 2005 moment before returning to organisation-specific campaigning.[1] As a result of economic recession from 2008, the meta-narrative of British politics shifted to crisis and austerity. In 2010, New Labour was replaced by a Coalition Government of Conservative and Liberal Democrats, in which the former were dominant. This election outcome removed a key institutional relationship that development campaigners had come to rely on: a ruling party that shared many of the development norms of the campaign organisations themselves.

Nevertheless, in 2013 a major national development campaign coalition was once again devised: the Enough Food If campaign (EFIF). This chapter explores the motivations and strategies that underpinned the construction of a campaign coalition in such adverse circumstances. It explores the motivations and effects of the EFIF campaign in the context of austerity, Conservative rule, and an ongoing historical conflation of Africa and UK development campaigning.

The road to Enough Food If

The Make Poverty History effect

MPH has attracted a healthy amount of attention within scholarly research (Harrison, 2013; Sireau, 2009). For our purposes, we need not so much to analyse that campaign as consider its effects on campaign coalition-building moving from New Labour to the Conservative-led Coalition Government. The core point to start with here is that since MPH 'the sector has been unable to replicate the scale of previous successes' (Cox, 2011: 4).

The sense of uncertainty after 2005 generated a considerable strategic reflection within development campaign organisations, leading to the emergence of an influential and innovative shift in campaign thinking, manifested in two reports. In *Common Cause*, Crompton (2010) argued that campaigns needed to develop deeper and less goal-oriented activities dedicated to the nurturing of pro-development emotions and values. This refocusing was articulated and developed in a very influential report, *Finding Frames*, which took Crompton's 'deep frames' and presented a more specific model in which emotions, identity and values were categorised into transformative, 'bigger than self', deliberative and justice-oriented ways of thinking and acting (Darnton and Kirk, 2011; Kirk, 2012).

Thus, throughout the period from global financial crisis to the Coalition Government, development campaign non-governmental organisations (NGOs) were moving away from the possibility of an MPH-like campaign, preferring to work on their own core messages, and reflect both individually and in discussion across organisations on the shift in perspective towards a campaign strategy that was more interested in deeper campaign subjectivities than mass popularity and successfully reached goals and targets. Individual NGOs reflected (again) on the nature of their imaging; there were discussions about how best to deploy celebrity endorsement; and the possibility of new sub-coalitions based in deeper and more political work were explored. In sum, there was an institutional mood to move away from MPH. What makes this interregnum (2005–10) important is the contrast with what followed when EFIF was constructed.

Africa's curious presence/absence

But, before we move on to explore EFIF in more detail, we should consider the place of Africa within development campaigning. In a sense, Africa is everywhere and nowhere. From the early 1990s, campaign NGOs declared that they would take more care with their imaging out of a concern that the 'negative images' of the 'starving African child' reinforced post-imperial imaginaries of white saviour, compassion fatigue, charitable virtue and 'bad news' Africa. Nevertheless, the continued use of words such as 'poverty' and 'charity' – as well as the use of images of peasant farmers and children – sustained a kind of cognitive order in which campaign discourses were coded African (Harrison, 2010). In other words, the continued use of major campaign tropes concerning poverty and charity passively and implicitly worked within a kind of 'meta-Africa'.

EFIF's core vocabulary was 'hunger' and 'malnutrition', words that are very strongly integrated into the Africa–charity–development discourse. This association has been powerfully constructed through major famine appeals such as Band Aid and Biafra, and it continues in the charitable appeals of major NGOs in spite of its general unfashionability within campaign circles. Indeed, it is within the fundraising activities of campaign NGOs that Africa often figures most strongly. The best example of this is the Disasters Emergency Committee, a central fundraising body that represents the major NGOs involved in humanitarian disaster emergency relief. These are the same NGOs that are at the heart of campaign coalition activity. As a result of the combination of these activities – campaigning and fundraising – within the same large NGOs, it is easy for the public to associate Oxfam and Save the Children for example with Africa as these organisations carry out high-profile and urgent appeals for money after civil wars and droughts, almost all of which are in Africa. During the interregnum there were major emergency appeals focused on the Horn of Africa, East Africa, West Africa and Southern Africa.

When public attitudes surveys ask relevant questions, evidence emerges of a default Africa–poverty–charity association. In an Oxfam survey, 75 per cent of respondents stated that hunger was Africa's major problem (Dowden, 2013). In a larger survey of public opinion carried out by the Overseas Development Institute/Institute for Public Policy Research (Glennie et al., 2012: 9), the word cloud presenting frequently used words in respondents' qualitative answers to questions on aid, shows that 'Africa' is the only spatial reference and it sits just above the largest words: 'poverty' and 'hunger'. In the absence of a strong geographical repositioning of EFIF, the focus on food, hunger and malnutrition would seem, if anything, *more* likely to be 'Africanised' than MPH's focus on debt, aid and trade.

Furthermore, the campaign issues arranged under the food rubric were in a more empirically tangible sense African issues. The 'land grab' issue, tax evasion, biofuels and transparency are all concerns that have been mainly embedded within the epistemic communities generated by aid professionals, academics and policymakers involved in Africa. It was also heavily reflected in EFIF's

'Executive Summary' in which almost all of the images and geographical references were to Africa (Curtis and Thomas, 2013). In light of all of this, EFIF represented a *more intense* Africanisation of development campaigning.

New Government

Some similarity

It is important to start with a note of moderation. It is not the case that the coming to power of the Coalition Government, or indeed the subsequent Conservative Government, represented any kind of totalising counter-revolution in development policy. Indeed, the short history of Blair's New Labour and David Cameron's Conservatism was one of substantial convergence (Clarke, 2018). Both in terms of public image, leadership style and substantive areas of policy strategy, New Labour and Conservative policy shared a great deal.

In its 2010 manifesto, the Conservative Party publicly affirmed that it would commit to the 0.7 per cent of Gross National Income (GNI) aid target, which was previously a key aspiration of New Labour. Making this commitment publicly allowed the Tories a fairly cheap means of brand decontamination (Heppell and Lightfoot, 2012), emerging as they were from a public image of sleaze and self-interest.

Cameron's Big Society, 'golden thread' in development[2] and quality of life conceptual orientations also fed into a development vision that was moderately distinct from but substantially similar to New Labour's. His approach bears substantial similarity to the Commission for Africa report, a Blair/Brown initiative (Commission for Africa, 2005).

Some difference

But this did not mean that nothing had changed. In the first place, campaign organisations were now faced with a political party that had been culturally and ideologically distant from them. Few Conservative MPs considered international development as a major policy issue and, compared with New Labour, there was a weaker pro-aid constituency. More broadly, the Conservative Party in Parliament and among its membership were ideologically hostile to international development campaigning values, which had been constructed out of a Fabian, socialist and social-democratic Christian bundle of values. More practically, development NGOs simply did not have good advocacy networks with Conservative MPs. All of the celebrity advocates taken up by campaign NGOs were broadly on the left and culturally anti-Tory. The NGOs' policy positions on things like trade, climate change and transnational corporations (TNCs) were clearly more distant from Tory views than they were under New Labour, for all of the convergence at the heart of policy. This new environment was uncertain and potentially adversarial.

Secondly, in some ways the Conservatives *have* shifted international development strategy, although this has not been as publicised as perhaps it should be. The core shift has been away from good governance and partnerships with aid-recipient states, which was at the very heart of New Labour's strategy. In its place is a far stronger focus on private companies as key development partners (Mawdsley, 2015). The Conservative Government has consolidated an aid model based in the contracting of private companies. This was present during the New Labour administration (Taylor, 2012: 454), but there is also a clearer strategic orientation by the Conservatives to present private companies as 'developmental'. Beyond the actual payments to contracted private enterprises, aid strategy has, in a sense, been 'corporatised' in that the kinds of claimed knowledge and skills that private companies have are perceived as part of the international aid project itself. One can see this most clearly in the new Alliance for a Green Revolution in Africa (Kaarhus, 2011). One can also see it in the provision of technological and infrastructural services by large TNCs. Discrete projects to promote microfinance, communications technology connectivity, the introduction of new seeds, and training all involve private corporations as service providers, knowledge holders and aid recipients. The Conservative approach to development was/is more concertedly 'corporate' in that business is seen as a *direct* agent for the promotion of development, not just a source of capital which, according to most economic models (and subject to the right policy environment), generates developmental effects.

And, of course, the shift in the British party system roughly overlapped with the global economic crisis. The crisis fed into the NGO sector in a way familiar to other economic crisis moments previously: it generated a concern that fiscal austerity would impact upon the aid budget, that rising unemployment and stagnant disposable incomes would reduce charitable donations, and that the general public mood would shift against aid because of a concern for the poor 'at home'. The rise of the UK Independence Party was explicitly based in arguments about massively reducing or abolishing aid, laced with barely disguised racism.

It was this context within which Cameron's explicit endorsement of the 0.7 per cent figure and declaration of 'One World' Conservatism opened the door very slightly to a new working relationship between international development NGOs and the Government. Against some currents within his own Party and somewhat against the austerity narrative his Party enthusiastically embraced in most areas,

Cameron's leadership identified overseas development assistance as a diagnostic of its social conscience (see Chapter 6). This rather marginal and protean development within the Tories is vital to understanding the emergence of EFIF.

Enough Food If

A window of opportunity

Campaign coalitions offer an opportunity to understand the nature of campaigning in a way that is especially revealing. Most obviously, one can explore the dynamics of relations between individual campaign organisations because they are having to work together formally as part of a single political project. Secondly, the campaign coalition itself requires coordination, all manner of dialogue, the construction of a shared discourse, and the establishment of an institution that manages, leads and coordinates the efforts of individual NGOs. Thirdly, campaign coalitions' core purpose is to create a high-publicity action that strongly and publicly engages with Government or other official development agencies. As such, campaign coalitions offer a revealing way to explore the place of individual development campaigns within a broader British polity and public space. It is in this light that we shall explore the EFIF campaign of 2013. EFIF emerged shortly after the changes outlined in the previous section, a fact that raises key questions concerning the ability of development NGOs to negotiate a terrain defined by a sense that something similar to MPH was unlikely to happen again and that the relatively amenable political environment of New Labour had been replaced by something more problematic.

EFIF became a coalition of over 200 UK-based NGOs, oriented around issues of global hunger and malnutrition. In 2012, David Cameron hosted a post-Olympics Hunger Summit, a 'summit' that was largely a celebrity-/sportsperson-endorsed expression of concern about global hunger, claiming that this would be a major international issue for the Government leading into its hosting of the G8 the subsequent year. ONE and Save the Children attended the summit and spoke warmly about Cameron's commitment. The EFIF coalition identified this moment as the 'open door' through which Britain's development NGOs might find a revived role in the new political environment. This marked an opportunity for major development campaign NGOs: a statement of government openness to campaigning and a high-profile event in which 'hunger' would be a prominent focus.[3]

The large development NGOs with strong lobbying abilities have always sought the ear of politicians. This was at the heart of MPH. It was also the case that these NGOs sought an audience with Gordon Brown (and him with them) when he became Prime Minister; and it was also the case when the Conservative Party came to power.[4] The purpose of these informal contacts was to secure some common ground between the Government's agenda for the G8 summit and the kinds of campaign goal that the development NGO sector might advocate. There is a symbiosis here in which a ruling party enjoys a 'halo effect' from publicly supporting aspects of development NGOs' campaigns and NGOs can make claims to success based in expectations that some of their 'asks' are informally assured as amenable to the Government.

Thus, it seems reasonable to identify the beginnings of the coalition in 2012 when some NGOs were speaking with each other informally and also in communication with the Government, all around the notion of hunger which had been identified as a strong starting position for 'detoxifying' the Conservative Party. A broad agenda that would reflect a development coalition's common interests and have a reasonable chance of being supported, in part by the UK Government, could serve as a starting point for coalition-building in earnest.

In October 2012, a British Overseas NGOs for Development (BOND) Annual General Meeting was held in which plans for a coalition around food and hunger to focus on the G8 summit were mooted. At this point, a group of prominent and relatively radical NGOs chose to remove themselves from the coalition, expressing concerns about the focus on hunger and the apparent lack of adversarialism concerning the Conservative-dominated Government.[5]

Finding common cause

From November 2012 onwards, EFIF Assembly meetings rolled out a series of actions to focus mainly on the UK-hosted G8 Summit in June 2013.[6] Member NGOs reported on their own actions, and the Organising Committee members shared information about the broader strategy for the UK aid budget and the G8 'moments'. A set of four core themes related to hunger were set out, partly as the outcome of talks with Cameron, partly as important and inclusive campaign themes.

The EFIF campaign was publicly launched at Somerset House, London on 23 January 2013.[7] The event was focused on generating media attention. Its main impact was through a high production value three-dimensional film, beamed onto the façade of the House. The main speaker in the film was Bill Gates. The invitees were EFIF campaign members, some celebrities and people from the media. The event itself made no attempt to convey the demands of the campaign, develop an engagement with a broader public or identify a core problem that needed addressing beyond hunger as a condition.

In March, EFIF carried out a series of actions or 'stunts' to publicise this 'ask', mainly focused around an intense tweet and email operation focused on Chancellor George Osborne, an 'elephant in the room' image campaign and a series of George Osborne 'rush mobs' in which campaigners wearing Osborne masks turned up in public places for photo opportunities. As a result, in April the coalition claimed a success in securing a commitment to achieving 0.7 per cent of GNI aid expenditure. However, because the Government did not commit to include the magic 0.7 per cent as legislation for the Queen's Speech and because this commitment had been supported by Cameron repeatedly before the Budget, perceptions of a campaign success were muted. The commitment to 0.7 per cent and a general increase in Department for International Development (DFID) expenditure had been ongoing since 2010. Nevertheless, in the April meeting it was presented as a campaign success.

After April, EFIF focused on the G8 meeting to be hosted by the British Government. The G8 'moment' was conceptualised as a week-long period, commencing with a large public assembly which aimed to coincide with Cameron's hosting of a Nutrition for Growth pre-summit meeting. Following on from that date, smaller publicity events would keep public attention until a smaller rally took place on 15 June in Enniskillen to coincide with the G8 meeting. Between April and June, EFIF propounded its four demands to be addressed by the G8. These were: a commitment to 0.7 per cent of GNI dedicated to official development assistance; a move to ensure international companies pay 'fair' levels of tax in poor countries; a halt to 'land grabbing' in poor countries; and transparency in development aid and practice. It is striking how (with the exception of land grabbing) these demands closely mirrored the Conservative Party's own development strategy, embedded in the golden thread notion mentioned earlier, but also Cameron's more recent 'three Ts' of transparency, tax and trade which had each become core parts of EFIF demands.

Transparency and tax were foregrounded by the Conservative Party at a time when Cameron was still centrally concerned to introduce a more socially minded image to his Party. This was a period when public attitudes towards government and big business were relatively negative. There was not only concern about the fraud and collusion by banks in the aftermath of the financial crisis and associated rescue packages; but this was also a period in which large companies like Amazon, Google and Starbucks were revealed to be paying no or extremely little tax to the British Government. The Tory focus on tax and transparency and its connection to a morally positive international development campaign addressed the bad publicity emanating from tax evasion within big business.

The Big If

The London 'Big If' rally took place on 8 June. Attendees were invited to plant a flower-windmill in a way that resembled a commemoration of a single death. A pathway from this field to a stage with band and film clips brought people into the main event. Geographically removed from the G8 meeting which was to take place a week later, the experience of the rally was complex: a mixture of expressions of concern or lamentation about hunger; sociability; spectacle; and in an indirect way an address to next week's meetings in Lough Erne. There was a sizeable attendance from people who were already members of development NGOs: in a survey carried out by Harrison and Grasso, 67 per cent of respondents identified as members of development organisations.[8]

The assembly at Hyde Park coincided with Cameron's hosting of a Nutrition for Growth Summit which had an overlapping agenda, based in a project to address hunger through business and science. This was the epitome of the Conservatives' DFID vision. Cameron's summit laid heavy emphasis on the role of corporate technologies – this was the essence of the meaning of 'business and science'. This meeting, held at Unilever House, was not mentioned throughout the day, although Bill Gates, the major video speaker, propounded his usual messages about the benefits of technology and big business.[9] On 7 June at Number 10 EFIF staged a hand-in by schoolchildren of empty plates with 'messages for leaders' written on them which was aimed at the Nutrition for Growth Summit.[10]

The Lough Erne G8 Declaration starts: 'Private enterprise drives growth, reduces poverty, and creates jobs and prosperity for people around the world'. It then proceeds to itemise an agenda that precisely overlaps with the Conservative international development world-vision. The media generally reported on the G8 outcomes with an exclusive focus on Cameron, adding in some imagery of EFIF visual stunts of G8 leaders as chefs, or anonymous fat cats in a tax haven.[11] The G8 did not commit to clear and concrete measures to ensure transparency in tax reporting and to prevent tax evasion, something that authoritative experts stated clearly and critically. Nevertheless, the EFIF spokesperson spoke of a 'step in the right direction' and the 'right ambition'.[12]

The loose and generalised connection between the EFIF assembly and the G8 made it difficult to discern in any concrete way the effects of the EFIF campaign on the G8, especially in light of the closeness of the agenda of EFIF to Cameron's own. Although EFIF campaign managers were pleased with the profile afforded to the campaign in the media, the content itself is less reassuring, based as it was on the association of campaign images with a generally government-focused and uncritical reportage on what were fairly moderate and vague commitments.

A final wrap-up meeting was held in July. The main content of that meeting was an enthusiastically delivered general assessment of the campaign by the Chair of the Policy and Advocacy Working Group which awarded gold, silver and bronze to general areas of the campaign's aims. This was delivered in a very positive fashion but was not accompanied by any organised critical reflection. In place of this, attendees were invited to write on post-its and pin them to boards under different themes. The exact purpose of this exercise was not clear. The impression – at least for this attendee – was that the primary purpose was to ensure positive feelings about the campaign. The person reporting to the meeting on the overall performance of the campaign declared 'we got every single thing!'[13] It is worth bearing in mind that this meeting was of coalition members only; it was not 'outward-facing' and did not require 'spin' for the purposes of messaging and brand. In this context, it seemed clear that the meeting was driven strongly by a therapeutic sense of ensuring positive closure to the campaign after the difficulties that had defined the period from 2006 to 2013.

Throughout the campaign, EFIF's policy aims were flexible and broad. They revolved around vague causal premises. There was no clear idea of how the campaign or indeed the G8 might arrest 'land grabbing'. An emphasis on biofuels early on was de-emphasised. The issue of tax reform rose in importance, in spite of an opaque causation with hunger and malnutrition which seemed to boil down to an expectation – naïve by any analytical standards – that increased tax revenues from foreign direct investment would create larger resource for investment in agriculture. Furthermore, the strong emphasis on smallholder farming and local technological change that came from early meetings and the small member organisations of the campaign was lost. Through the Tories and the G8, the 'solving hunger through business and science' and new Green Revolution corporate–state project garnered highly publicised commitments of resource.

The fact that the campaign took care to establish aims which did not require specific targets of achievement connected to metrics or discrete policies not only raises questions about the way one might evaluate campaign success; but it also opens up a deeper analytical question about how success and failure are constructed. In essence, EFIF was set up *not* to fail. The demands it made were sufficiently broad and integrated into government initiatives as to make it possible to put a positive spin on practically any outcome from the G8 in terms of commitments to address hunger and malnutrition. The breadth, generality and creeping moderation of EFIF's demands necessarily left space for those who wished it to declare success. This might be considered not so much as a 'failure' of the campaign to get certain things achieved, but rather as a *strategy* elaborated within the specific conditions of the time. We shall now explore other ways in which this was so.

Constructing success

Success for EFIF was framed in a specific way. The framing of success was not strongly oriented towards the policy achievements and resource commitments emanating from the campaign's pressure on the G8 which, we have argued, was difficult to discern. Success in terms of G8 action was, at best, broadly implied, partial or affirmed rather than demonstrated. The concrete outcomes of the campaign were only positive in the sense of possibly leading to action by G8 states in areas that had already been identified by the British Government as possible areas for action. The G8 (which saw global hunger as one issue among others) did not make strong clear commitments for action in any case. Since 2013, it is fair to say that those who drove the EFIF campaign have not followed up or campaigned to ensure that the areas of success have been realised. It is also very obvious that, to date, little has been achieved in reducing mass hunger and malnutrition and what success has been achieved can hardly be accounted for by G8 agency.

But there was very positive *affect* in the wrap-up meeting which put a kind of seal on a campaign that had worked well enough to establish a kind of besieged *modus operandi* for coalition campaigning: strategically cautious, aware of the difficulties of coalition-building, and in some sense therapeutic for an NGO sector that was looking for a sense of renewal in hard times. Principally this message was directed towards those within the coalition itself. Although entirely subjective, this observer was struck by how much time and energy were spent in assembly meetings talking up the project itself in ways that seemed to border on motivational speaking.

EFIF did not achieve a brand or legacy in the way that Band Aid, Jubilee 2000 or MPH did. Even the most sympathetic reading would not claim that EFIF had a big impact on British Government development practice. It did not become part of Britain's 'ribbon culture' (Moore, 2010).

Although there was broad and positive media coverage of the campaign's 'event' high spots, there was less media reporting of mission accomplished or success. There was no high-profile media event to relate the campaign's successes to the general public. The campaign coalition's main success comes from its achievements in organising a campaign coalition, establishing a relationship with government and re-energising its existing members during a politically depressing period. This kind of success derived from strategic decisions made by the coalition's managers.

The EFIF campaign: short and sweet

The campaign itself was effectively six months long. Aware of how MPH had tailed off after the G8 and that coalition member commitment had waned, EFIF focused on the G8 Summit in June and then held a wrap-up meeting for coalition members in July. As noted, the wrap-up meeting was overlain with a 'success' message which was not strongly evidenced and left no space for clear critical reflection. There was no 'next steps' moment either, although an evaluation consultancy was commissioned (Tibbett and Stalker, 2014).

The first campaign meeting was *in camera*. Some campaign organisations attended this first meeting and then left the coalition on the grounds that it reproduced the moderate and (in their view) apolitical strategy that came to dominate MPH.[14] In this sense EFIF had, by making its first meeting open to all organisations, defined itself around the 'BOAG' NGOs and without the larger 'radical' NGOs. This had the effect of reducing the political tensions that had for a time pervaded MPH.

The first open general assembly of EFIF (16 November 2012) commenced with some scene-setting addresses from those in the coordination team. There was a strong affective content in these addresses that aimed to produce an affirmative and encompassing feeling in the venue. One key speaker related how good it felt to be back together again, implicitly referencing the sense of break-up left by MPH. Even in this first general meeting, there was a strong framing of the campaign around what one speaker called 'ending well' and 'celebrating'. This is, of course, entirely understandable at the start of a project to build a coalition. But it was also noteworthy that there was no sense of contention (Tarrow, 2005), uncertainty, struggle or opposition upon which a mobilisation might be constructed. One representative who asked if hunger and malnutrition could be meaningfully addressed in the absence of demands to end the 'War on Terror' was pointedly excluded, although the points he made were quite reasonable.[15]

Beyond the '0.7 per cent', there was no specific target-setting, identification of a basket of specific policy 'asks' from G8 governments or clear identification of the problem of hunger. The four themes of investment, land, tax and transparency were announced as the orientations of EFIF. As the assembly meetings proceeded and campaign material and activity emerged, it was clear that the evocations of the campaign were designed not to rely on specific, ambitious but realistic targets in the way that MPH and Jubilee 2000 had. Rather, these themes served as the aspirational focus for the campaign, each framed with a more or less specific cause and effect: stop land grabbing to protect smallholders; invest and give aid to improve agricultural productivity; reduce tax avoidance to improve revenues that could be invested in agriculture; and 'force governments and investors to be honest and open about the deals they make in the poorest countries that stop people getting enough food'.[16] These themes are presented with very vague causations, no specific demands and – especially in the case of the final theme – stretch a clear sense of cause and effect.

Within assembly meetings, the coalition was theme-driven, not target-driven in terms of its demands. The bulk of meeting content was oriented towards the management of media (electronic and print) and public attitudes. As a result, the meetings were mainly concerned with the processes and progress of coalition-building. The complex questions about campaign demands, and the causations behind hunger and malnutrition were not mooted.

The shortness and sweetness structured into the campaign makes sense from a post-2010 campaign recovery point of view; but as a way to deal with the massive and complex issue of hunger and malnutrition, it raises a very important issue. The campaign's organisation and duration made it constitutively unable to address global malnutrition and hunger in any meaningful fashion. The core issues relating to hunger and malnutrition are at least as complex as those of international debt, apartheid and slavery, and in each of those campaign areas coalitions endured for years and even generations. There is no amount of campaign success that can be compressed into a six-month period that would come close to addressing global hunger and malnutrition.

EFIF was a coalition that was sensitive to the plurality of its coalition members but, in the absence of the larger 'radical' NGOs, it worked through the larger and well-resourced mainstream development NGOs. EFIF was inclusive, open-ended, not tied to any specific achievements and *de facto* dominated by the large campaign organisations. It was designed in a strictly time-constrained fashion that ensured it did not collapse or lose energy. It worked well in generating a campaign coalition but far less so as a vehicle to identify clear targets and exacting actions attached to them.

Adjusting expectations

Ensuring success also required the construction of a strong policy and vision overlap with government. The absence of contentious or adversarial content in the campaign would make it highly likely that the campaign could be broadly positive about government actions and, as a result, narrate the campaign as having had a positive effect on government action.

During the first open assembly meeting – and repeated throughout subsequent meetings – a message was related that the Conservative Government was amenable to EFIF and that there was a real window of opportunity for the campaign. In the words of the Chair of the Policy and Advocacy Working Group,

Cameron was 'saying some really good stuff'. This framing effectively removed the notion of an adverse political environment from the campaign. One might suppose that NGO campaigns often tag on to larger and more 'official' and governmental initiatives (Hilton *et al.*, 2013), but in this case the window of opportunity afforded by the moments from the Olympic 'summit' to the G8 meeting was narrow indeed, and no explicit reflection on this fact or the dangers of attaching hope to a political party strongly wedded to neoliberal values can be found in any of the materials from the campaign or the discussions within the assembly meetings.

The major NGOs in BOND were meeting with senior members of the Conservative and Liberal Democrat parties as soon as possible after the election victory. In this period, Cameron's strategy for the Tories was based in what were at the time judged to be relatively 'liberal' political ideas, revolving around well-being and the 'Big Society'. The Conservatives were also well aware that a certain kind of presentation of international development had worked well for New Labour as a way to represent a political aesthetic of national grandeur and moral purpose. Positive signals about international development offered a fairly straightforward way to address the issue coined by now-Prime Minister Theresa May, of being perceived as the 'nasty party'.

There was, in effect, a mutual desire by major campaign groups and the new Coalition Government to find cohabitation within which both could claim a moral virtue as progressive development actors, and an agenda was discovered to enable this comity. Hunger was the venue within which this was achieved. David Cameron articulated his 'golden threads' of development; the campaign coalition interpreted this core directive within Cameron's declared development vision as positive and fairly easy to work with. One can readily see how it maps quite extensively onto the four themes of EFIF. In none of the meetings I attended was Cameron's golden thread notion articulated in a critical fashion, in spite of its obvious ideological and neoliberal facets.

Cameron generated a strong formulation of both problem and solution in regard to hunger that fulsomely fitted with a liberal and globalist Conservative worldview in which well-meaning TNCs, supported by governments and amenable scientists, would disseminate technologies, techniques and financial mechanisms that would engineer peasant households into petty entrepreneurs able to upscale their own well-being. This agenda went under the rubric 'solving malnutrition and hunger through business and science'. The 'science' part of this phrasing effectively meant corporately owned technologies such as improved seeds, fertilisers and pesticides.

EFIF reconciled itself to this vision. It invited Bill Gates to speak at its event and it did not make any strong critical statements of Cameron's vision for solving hunger. EFIF 'wished the leaders well' in their meetings. Beyond the main stage performances, the main event was the planting of a field of 'windmill' flowers to represent the number of children who died from malnutrition, an event that could hardly have been more apolitical.

As the G8 event approached, the campaign's messages on hunger and malnutrition and the those of the UK Government came to overlap. Cameron's explicitly pro-business, technocratic and financialised model of change was devised within his Government, did not change and was announced as the agenda for his leadership of the G8. It was accompanied by a broad and open-ended EFIF coalition, which was based on thematic overlaps with government, broad aspirations rather than demands, and a lack of critical positions on the Conservatives' vision of development. These properties ensured that any outcomes from the G8 could feasibly look like success.

In sum, 2013 saw EFIF briefly generate an effective international development coalition in the teeth of inter-organisational trepidation and a broader political environment defined by austerity and a shift to the right in UK governance. Inasmuch as one judges EFIF a success in managing a coalition that worked and did not generate a problematic legacy, one has also to understand its failure to make any kind of 'historic' progress with regard to hunger and malnutrition.

Conclusions

The EFIF campaign can be understood as a response by development NGOs to a particularly challenging environment. In the teeth of a shift to the right and a recession, NGOs set out a coalition that had as its primary aim establishing the beginnings of a *modus vivendi* in a new period. This did not translate into new, strong and ambitious campaign demands.[17] But its success can be identified in its more internalised focus on making campaign coalitions based in a relationship with government possible. This explains why the organisation of the campaign was based in broad thematic aspirations that enjoyed a substantial overlap with government agendas that were devised by and large independently from the development NGOs. It also explains why the campaign itself was highly time-constrained, generalised and articulated in ways that did not expect specific outcome 'wins'.

EFIF failed entirely to commence the construction of new values or frames with regard to Africa. The social categorisation Africa remains as it was: a shallow but resilient association with charity, poverty and hunger. Since EFIF, the campaign sections of development NGOs have once again returned to their own projects, and within these endeavours more challenging and richer public addresses have emerged. It would seem that the success of the campaign coalition is based in the relegation of Africa's representation to that of post-imperial artefact, a means to generate broad appeal and comity with government. This representational mode is substantially removed from the realities of Africa, and the real problem with this is that it does not seem to matter.

Notes

* This chapter draws significantly upon Harrison, G. 'Post-wristband blues: the mixed fortunes of UK development campaigning under austerity and the Conservatives', *British Journal of Politics and International Relations*, 20:2, 409–24. Copyright © 2018 by the Author. Reprinted by permission of SAGE Publications, Ltd.
1. See for example Oxfam (2013).
2. Like many of Cameron's attempts to disseminate 'big ideas', the golden thread notion was rather opaque and not especially prominent. In Cameron's words: 'you only get real long-term development through aid if there is also a golden thread of stable government, lack of corruption, human rights, the rule of law, transparent information' (Cameron, 2012). One can see that this fits with the 'three Ts' and with facets of the EFIF agenda.
3. Although I shall dispense with the quotation marks, it is important to note that the notion of hunger is a heavily constructed political term more than it is a specific calorific requirement. In the UK, its normative content and the kinds of identity it produces have tended to gravitate towards the charitable image of the famine victim. This concern that hunger evoked old-fashioned charitable appeals was expressed on numerous occasions during the EFIF coalition meetings.
4. The British Overseas Aid Group (BOAG) Chief Executives met with David Cameron before EFIF was commenced (notes from coalition meeting, 16 November 2012). BOAG consists of ActionAid, Oxfam, CAFOD, Save the Children and Christian Aid.
5. Author interviews with War on Want and the Jubilee Debt Coalition.
6. The BOAG campaign NGOs had been meeting informally since mid-2011. The author attended general assembly planning meetings throughout 2012 and 2013. Much of the information in this section derives from the notes of those meetings.
7. The author attended this launch meeting.
8. N=476. The coalition expected 30,000 to attend, and some estimates were as high as 40,000. This did not reflect my own observations. The survey team distributed 3,000 surveys through a purposive sampling of one in ten and covered the entire field.
9. Bill Gates's relation to international development campaigning is controversial and, in the context of this chapter, revealing. See McGoey (2015).
10. The Nutrition for Growth Summit was protested by NGOs which had decided not to participate in EFIF.
11. This was clear from EFIF's own collating of G8 media coverage, seen by the author.

12 These comments were reported in the *Guardian* and the *Telegraph* respectively, both 18 June 2013.
13 From research notes of the meeting held on 5 July 2013.
14 Notable examples here include War on Want and Global Justice Now (formerly World Development Movement).
15 The relationship between war and hunger is a common theme within livelihoods and famine research. See for example Keen (2008); Macrae and Zwi (1994).
16 Taken from Tearfund (2013). Note: I have directly quoted this last theme because it is difficult to paraphrase in a clear or concise fashion. I am not sure what it means.
17 It is worth noting that a broadly read reflection on MPH that argued for the construction of 'positive deep frames' was absent throughout the campaign (Darnton and Kirk, 2011). See also Hampson (2006).

References

Cameron, D. (2012) 'Transcript of David Cameron Q&A at New York University', 15 March 2012, www.gov.uk/government/speeches/transcript-of-david-cameron-qa-at-new-york-university [accessed 27 February 2018].
Clarke, G. (2018) 'UK development policy and domestic politics 1997–2016', *Third World Quarterly*, 39:1, 18–34.
Commission for Africa (2005) *Our Common Interest* (London: Commission for Africa).
Cox, B. (2011) *Campaigning for International Justice: Learning Lessons (1991–2011) Where Next? (2011–2015)* (Seattle, WA: Bill and Melinda Gates Foundation).
Crompton T. (2010) *Common Cause: The Case for Working with our Cultural Values* (Edinburgh: World Wildlife Fund).
Curtis, M. and Thomas, C. (2013) *Enough Food for Everyone: The Need For UK Action On Global Hunger*, Report, Christian Aid, http://curtisresearch.org/wp-content/uploads/enough_food_if_-_the_report.pdf [accessed 3 January 2019].
Darnton, A. and Kirk, M. (2011) *Finding Frames: New Ways to Engage the UK Public in Global Poverty* (London: BOND).
Dowden, R. (2013) 'Africa's image and reality: wealth and poverty sit side-by-side', www.royalafricansociety.org/blog/africa%E2%80%99s-image-and-reality-wealth-and-poverty-sit-side-side [accessed 27 February 2018].
Glennie, A., Straw, W. and Wild, L. (2012) *Understanding Public Attitudes to Aid and Development*, Report (London: Institute for Public Policy Research and Overseas Development Institute).
Hampson, T. (2006) *2025: What Next for the Make Poverty History Generation?* (London: Fabian Society).
Harrison, G. (2010) 'The Africanization of poverty: a retrospective on "Make Poverty History"', *African Affairs*, 109:436, 391–408.
Harrison, G. (2013) *The African Presence: Representations of Africa in the Construction of Britishness* (Manchester: Manchester University Press).

Heppell, T. and Lightfoot, S. (2012) '"We will not balance the books on the backs of the poorest people in the world": understanding Conservative Party strategy on international aid', *Political Quarterly*, 83:1, 130–8.

Hilton, M., McKay, J., Crowson, N. and Mouhout, J.-F. (2013) *The Politics of Expertise* (Oxford: Oxford University Press).

Kaarhus, R. (2011) 'Agricultural growth corridors equals land-grabbing? Models, roles and accountabilities in a Mozambican case', paper presented at the International Conference on Global Land Grabbing, 6–8 April 2011, Institute of Development Studies, University of Sussex.

Keen, D. (2008) *Benefits of Famine: A Political Economy of Famine and Relief in Southwestern Sudan, 1983–9* (Oxford: James Currey).

Kirk, M. (2012) 'Beyond charity: helping NGOs lead a transformative new public discourse on global poverty and social justice', *Ethics & International Affairs*, 26:2, 245–63.

Macrae, J. and Zwi, A. (eds) with Duffied, M. and Slim, H. (1994) *War and Hunger: Rethinking International Responses to Complex Emergencies* (London: Zed Books).

Mawdsley, E. (2015) 'DFID, the private sector and the re-centring of an economic growth agenda in international development', *Global Society*, 29:3, 339–58.

McGoey, L. (2015) *No Such Thing as a Free Gift* (London: Verso).

Moore, S. (2010) *Ribbon Culture* (London: Routledge).

Oxfam (2013) 'Make Poverty History and G8 promises: was it all really worth it?', Press Release, 30 May 2013, www.oxfam.org.uk/media-centre/press-releases/2013/05/make-poverty-history-and-g8-promises-was-it-all-really-worth-it [accessed 27 February 2018].

Sireau, N. (2009) *Make Poverty History Political Communication in Action* (Basingstoke: Palgrave Macmillan).

Tarrow, S. (2005) *The New Transnational Activism* (Cambridge: Cambridge University Press).

Taylor, I. (2012) 'Spinderella on safari: British policies toward Africa under New Labour', *Global Governance*, 18:4, 449–60.

Tearfund (2013). 'Enough food for everyone IF', www.tearfund.org/about_you/around_the_uk/northern_ireland/northern_ireland_news/archive/enough_food_for_everyone_if/ [accessed 27 February 2018].

Tibbett, S. and Stalker, C. (2014) *Enough Food For Everyone If: Campaign Evaluation* (London: The Advocacy Hub) (commissioned by the Enough Food for Everyone IF campaign).

9
British campaigns for African development: the Trade Justice Movement

Stephen R. Hurt

With the rise of neoliberal thinking during the 1980s and the associated preference for export-oriented development strategies, trade liberalisation became a firmly established orthodoxy within policy elites. The idea of 'special and differential' treatment for developing countries, within the rules of global trade, came under increasing pressure as a result. In the context of UK policy towards Africa, this is a view that was entrenched during the period that followed the end of the Cold War. As Williams noted, 'both the Conservative and Labour governments have subscribed to … the ostensibly mutually beneficial nature of international trade and FDI' (2004: 52).

However, at the turn of the century and the period beginning with the protests at the World Trade Organization (WTO) Ministerial in Seattle in 1999, it seemed like the emergent global justice movement could offer an avenue for counter-hegemonic struggle which would be able to challenge the ideas and institutions of global governance, particularly those governing world trade. Hence, the theoretical concerns of this chapter are to investigate the extent to which these new social movements have been able to shift both the material and ideational terrain of global trade. Existing critical literature suggests this has proven difficult. For example, Paterson has argued that in the case of the WTO, it has been able to employ a strategy of *trasformismo* so that any changes implemented are simply 'cosmetic and designed to assimilate and absorb counter-movements and ideas to make them consistent with the demands of the global economy' (2009: 57).[1] In a more general sense it has been argued that 'one of the disappointments of NGOs has been their tendency to identify more readily with alternative forms of interventions than with more systemic changes' (Bebbington *et al.*, 2008: 5). McSweeney (2014: 280) goes further, in raising the question of whether the problem is simply one of focusing too much on lobbying and policy reforms rather than structural changes, by reminding us that civil society represents a terrain where hegemony can be reproduced as well as resisted.

Within the context of UK–Africa relations, the Trade Justice Movement (TJM) has been at the centre of attempts to challenge the hegemonic assumptions of the developmental benefits of trade liberalisation. TJM became one of the three pillars of the Make Poverty History (MPH) coalition, which played such a key role in 2005 in shaping understanding within the UK of what the main barriers to African development are. Often perceived as the poor relation of the MPH coalition, TJM's focus on the rules of global trade added a crucial structural dimension to the diagnosis of African poverty and underdevelopment. Hence, this chapter's focus on the role played by TJM within the broader context of British campaigns for African development (see Chapter 8 for a discussion of the Enough Food If campaign, which was the next major development campaign coalition after MPH).

The research for this chapter included a series of twenty-two qualitative semi-structured research interviews with relevant individuals, which were conducted during the period from July 2015 until September 2016. Interviewees were selected with two key criteria in mind. First, that a range of the most important organisations within TJM were represented, and secondly that the entire period since TJM's formation in 2000 was covered.

TJM was created at a time when a nascent global justice movement was just emerging. In the UK, non-governmental organisations (NGOs) were starting to take advantage of the relaxation of charity law constraints that had been achieved in 1995, which enabled them to adopt more overtly political campaigns (Saunders, 2009: 50). TJM is a coalition of NGOs (at the time of writing nearly seventy),[2] which sought to build on the approach taken by the Jubilee 2000 movement that campaigned for the cancellation of Third World debt. Its founding statement published in June 2002 focused on the need to rebalance the rules of international trade. Its central argument was that:

> The international trade regime needs fundamental change if it is to succeed and benefit us all. The world needs international trade rules, but to date these have favoured the narrow commercial interests of the most powerful trading nations and the largest corporations, at the expense of the wider public interest and smaller economic enterprises. (Trade Justice Movement, 2002)

This initial statement was complemented by a huge mass lobby of Parliament on 19 June 2002, which gave TJM a real sense of initial momentum (BBC News,

2002). At the time, the focus of TJM was on the multilateral rules being negotiated within the WTO. Its formation was a direct response to the launch of the Doha Round of the WTO, which claimed to have the aim of making the rules of global trade fairer for developing countries as its core remit. Since the early 2000s, things have changed quite significantly and the focus of TJM's attention has shifted, as trade liberalisation has been largely enacted through bilateral and regional agreements.

The rest of this chapter is organised as follows. The first section discusses the term 'trade justice' itself and considers both how it has been framed by actors within and outside of TJM and its relationship with 'fair trade', which has often been uneasy. The second section then interrogates the network approach adopted by TJM and how this has both helped and hindered aspects of its work. The third section discusses the evolution of TJM's campaigning and particularly the extent to which African development has featured within its work. The chapter then concludes with some thoughts on the extent to which NGOs can influence the agenda on trade and how this relates to the British debate on African development.

The overall argument of the chapter is that given the peculiarities of development campaigning in the UK and the centrality of Africa to some of its key campaigns, the work of TJM has often been bound up with broader campaigns for African development. While TJM's campaigns have undoubtedly been important in highlighting the broader structural dynamics underpinning the challenges to development in Africa, due to a range of factors outlined below its direct impact on policymaking has been somewhat limited. The UK Government's commitment to the developmental benefits of free trade has remained consistent throughout the period of TJM's existence, despite different political parties having been in power. What has changed, however, since the election of the Coalition Government in 2010, is a significant reduction in the close links to policymakers that TJM had enjoyed under New Labour. Nevertheless, TJM has had what can be understood as a discursive impact, by continually problematising the assumption that free trade promotes development, and in doing so attempting to rearticulate the debate on African development within the UK.

The framing of 'trade justice'

During the debates that resulted in the creation of TJM, there was of course significant discussion about what an appropriate name would be. One interviewee recalled that 'there was quite a lot of debate about what phrase to use, but there weren't many obvious alternatives, because it was about trade and people felt very strongly that justice was a more powerful concept than fair trade'.[3] Since its formation the understanding of the relationship between trade and development, within TJM's member organisations and the wider policymaking community, has traversed three distinct positions. First, a liberal conception of trade justice informed by the idea that a rules-based system of free trade will promote development in the Global South, if the world's major trading powers also commit to opening their markets. Secondly, a view rooted in the contemporary Fair Trade movement, which suggests that by adopting an alternative way of doing trade, producers in the Global South can be fairly rewarded for their goods, which in turn will promote development. A third, more radical understanding, views the structural inequalities within the system of global trade as the main obstacle to broad-based human development in the Global South.

Given these competing frames, there remains a common misperception that 'trade justice' and 'fair trade' are one and the same.[4] Sharman (2007: 385) highlights that there are also overlaps in terms of some of the organisations involved, with some fair trade producers (e.g. Traidcraft) also campaigning for trade justice. The fact that the two terms are often used almost interchangeably also highlights the attempts at co-optation by policymakers which have to some extent served to neutralise the progressive power of the term 'trade justice'. The stance of the UK Government has been largely consistent. Its view of trade justice has been a liberal one, where the emphasis is fairness combined with a belief in the power of free trade as a tool for development. For example, Tony Blair in his landmark speech to the Labour Party Conference in 2001 argued that the problem for Africa was that free trade was not being fairly implemented. He argued that Africa needed 'access to our markets so that we practise the free trade we are so fond of preaching' (Blair, 2001). In 2011, then Prime Minister David Cameron outlined that trade, rather than aid, was of greater significance in relation to Africa's future development. Adopting a similar stance to that of Blair a decade earlier, he called for free trade governed by rules 'that must be open and fair to all' (Cameron, 2011).

Despite its more radical beginnings, the dominant contemporary conceptualisation of fair trade is focused on improvements to market access for producers from the developing world. This contrasts with the emphasis of TJM's founding statement on the broader structural changes to the global trading system that are needed, rather than simply fair access to Western markets. This has been described by Fridell as the shaped-advantage perspective of fair trade, which simply offers 'capability enhancement to a limited number of Southern partners' (2006: 23). Reflecting on these tensions between trade justice and fair trade, some of the interviewees felt that the latter acts as a positive example of how trade can work differently and in the interests of social development. An interviewee from the Fairtrade Foundation summed up this argument by suggesting that 'fair trade can be a gentle introduction … fair trade campaigners are more likely to want to campaign on trade justice because they are interested in trade and they're interested in supply chains and they are interested in access of African people to European markets'.[5] However, a number of interviewees questioned this premise. For example, one interviewee said that although there is a case to be made 'that buying a fair trade product in a supermarket is a very easy first step to starting to take action, what I'm not at all convinced about is the journey that people make from buying that product to … actively participating in building a group of people who are going to take action in a stronger way'.[6]

The liberal approach focusing on market access and specifically the removal of agricultural subsidies in the US and the EU was adopted by Oxfam International in its own campaign in 2002 entitled 'Make Trade Fair'. This campaign, which received several celebrity endorsements, focused on a global petition that attracted 17.8 million signatures before being submitted to Pascal Lamy, the WTO's Director-General at the time, at the Hong Kong Ministerial in December 2005 (Mallet and Lau, 2005). This caused some tensions in TJM at the time and there was some debate within Oxfam about whether it should continue to support the activities of TJM, given the power of its own brand and the differences in its approach to conceptualising 'trade justice'.[7]

Hence, there have been, and remain, a variety of opinions over the framing of 'trade justice' as a unifying concept for TJM and particularly how 'fair trade' sits within this. The original goal of some of the key advocates of fair trade within the UK was to create a model of alternative trade based on a more direct relationship with developing countries. However, the Fairtrade Foundation with its emphasis on increasing sales and ethical consumers has become 'ever more reliant on [multinational companies] and supermarkets in order to sustain this growth' (Anderson, 2009: 237). This has recently resulted in the problematic decision taken by some major food companies to replace their use of the official Fairtrade Mark with their own certification schemes. In May 2017 it was revealed that the supermarket chain Sainsbury's was going to drop the use of the Fairtrade Mark for its range of own-brand teas and replace it with the label 'fairly traded' based on its own set of criteria (Rivera, 2017). This has led to a coalition, coordinated by the Catholic Agency For Overseas Development (CAFOD), which also includes the Fairtrade Foundation itself, launching a campaign trying to put pressure on Sainsbury's not to ditch the Fairtrade Mark. Meanwhile, Cadbury's is also reported to be switching to the use of the Cocoa Life scheme of certification, which is run by Mondelez International who are the new owners of Cadbury's (Murphy, 2016). In both cases the concern is that these alternatives lack the independence ensured through the Fairtrade Mark given that they are organised directly by the companies themselves.

It is unsurprising, therefore, that many of the interviewees expressed concerns about the increasing tensions and confusions of framing between 'fair trade' and 'trade justice'. One interviewee noted that 'there's an interesting dynamic with … fair trade in its kind of purest form and the kind of emergence of the Fairtrade Mark and movement at the same point in time and the dynamics within that, which I think were never properly understood or resolved'.[8] Another observed that in recent years the Fair Trade movement in the UK has negotiated relationships with a wide range of corporate suppliers, whereas TJM has campaigned against proposed trade deals, like the Transatlantic Trade and Investment Partnership (TTIP) because there is a concern about an advancement of corporate interests over the rights of citizens.[9]

In sum, on the issue of framing, the initial idea behind 'trade justice' was to make a moral or ethical case against the current structures of global trade. The overall aim of TJM has been to raise awareness of the problems with the existing structures and then use popular pressure to get the UK Government to seek to change them. While MPH found it relatively easy to make an accessible case to the public for debt cancellation and more aid, the case for regulatory reform of world trade by its very nature has always been relatively underspecified. One interviewee noted that even at 'the high watermark of Make Poverty History where the public were engaged with at some level the issues of global poverty, the trade bit never really came through. It was mentioned quite a lot but … people never made the leap of understanding as to what that really meant.'[10] Africa, meanwhile, has featured quite strongly in the way that the issue of trade justice has been framed, particularly during the period of MPH. This compounded the difficulties of trying to define trade as a social justice issue. As Harrison argues, given the longer history of British campaigns for African development, 'MPH illustrated how difficult it is to frame Africa within a British campaign for global social justice' (2013: 178). The difficulties of framing 'trade justice' are also related to the organisational challenges faced by TJM, to which I now turn.

Organisational challenges and TJM's network approach

As a network of NGOs, TJM encompasses a wide variety of organisations, including trade unions, Friends of the Earth, and a range of both large and small development NGOs. As Saunders has argued, the adoption of organisational arrangements based on coalitions of NGOs, as in the case of TJM, 'ha[s] allowed once conventional humanitarian, aid and development NGOs to be active in both the global justice movement and the more staid arena of conventional NGO politics simultaneously' (2009: 55). TJM currently has a coordinator employed directly by the network itself and then a Board made up of representatives who are elected annually by the member organisations themselves. It is quite a loose network and organisations within TJM can opt in, as and when they choose, depending on the campaign issue. It grew out of a more informal arrangement known as the UK Trade Network, which one interviewee described as 'trade policy people from each of the main NGOs ... it was literally just a group, it was pretty much the same people who then became the policy group of the TJM'.[11]

The creation of TJM followed the first significant development coalition campaign, Jubilee 2000, which was formed in October 1997. Many of the interviewees noted that the organisational set-up of TJM was directly influenced by the experience of Jubilee 2000, which was focused on the cancellation of the external debts of developing countries. It had a much larger secretariat than TJM and it effectively became an organisation in itself, with a recognisable identity, rather than being a looser coalition of existing NGOs. One interviewee summed up quite starkly some of the issues related to how Jubilee 2000 had been organised: 'Ann Pettifor, who was the Director of Jubilee 2000, was a very strong character, she's high profile and she led the movement and the NGOs didn't like that, and so when they came to constructing new movements ... like TJM and Make Poverty History they deliberately looked for models where there wasn't a clear leader.'[12]

Within networks of NGOs it tends to be the case that a limited number of organisations play a leading role in setting the overall agenda (Pianta, 2014: 215). This has certainly been true in the case of TJM. Reflecting on his time as the coordinator of TJM and the range of views of different member organisations, one interviewee concluded that 'there were times where the different priorities at different organisations were difficult to work out politically ... TJM itself became a place of contestation and tension and that was largely welcome because it meant we needed to sort of sharpen what we were doing and sharpen our communication'.[13] In particular, there were debates within TJM about the balance to strike between pursuing incremental changes and the more fundamental vision of trade justice articulated in its founding statement. More recently, the way TJM has worked has reduced the potential for such conflicts because member organisations are more able to pick and choose which campaigns they wish to support. It is suggested that 'people do work in less formal ways now, so that we kind of know that if we tried to get a massive sign on statement that everyone can sign up to, people are probably not going to be that happy with it'.[14]

TJM is also a domestically based network within the UK. However, within Europe it has been argued that domestic trade justice campaigns have found it particularly hard to have an impact on policy because trade is an area that is delegated to the EU (*ibid.*: 219). There were attempts, particularly during the campaign on Economic Partnership Agreements (EPAs), to work across Europe and with African civil society organisations (CSOs) as part of a wider 'Stop EPAs' campaign (discussed below). One interviewee suggested that when a coalition is extended even more, in this fashion, the range of views becomes broader and this can make political agreement and decision-making even more difficult.[15] More recently, TJM has worked with the Seattle to Brussels Network, which operates across Europe, in contributing to the publication of an 'Alternative Trade Mandate', which was launched in November 2013 by a European-wide alliance of CSOs (see Alternative Trade Mandate Alliance, 2013). However, given the broad nature of actors involved in drafting this document it has been viewed as 'an exercise in, not exactly futility, but in just being all things to everybody'.[16]

In sum, what TJM has been able to do over the course of its existence is keep trade on the agenda in the UK campaigning context, despite some of the bigger member organisations not having persisted with it as a priority for any significant length of time. As an established coalition it has been able to preserve access to domestic policymakers.[17] After the dissolution of MPH in early 2006, Oxfam and Christian Aid in particular shifted their focus to other campaign issues, most notably climate change.[18] However, the work of smaller organisations like War on Want and Global Justice Now (formerly World Development Movement), and the impact of TJM as a coordinating network, have meant that some of the peaks and troughs in terms of interest among the big NGOs have been smoothed out.[19] What TJM creates is both a knowledge base on trade and a ready-made structure so that when trade issues come to the fore again (as in the recent cases of TTIP and Brexit) a wider coalition can easily be re-formed.[20] In the next section, I explore in more detail how African development has featured explicitly within TJM's campaigning since its formation.

African development and TJM's campaigning

TJM's initial focus was a campaign aimed at advancing the issue of agricultural subsidies in the North within the WTO and in particular a call for reforms to the EU's Common Agricultural Policy. In part, this was justified on the basis of supporting African farmers by seeking to improve their market access. However, this was an agenda that was somewhat limited in its critique of existing structures. In fact, the UK Government was at times able to frame it as an issue that could be seen to be allied to the broader push in favour of, rather than critical of, trade liberalisation (Sharman, 2007: 387). It was felt within TJM at this point that while there was some traction in terms of the UK Government listening to what it had to say, there was a concern that there seemed to be 'an intention to portray the TJM as pro-trade liberalisation'.[21] Developing countries remained an important part of TJM's campaigning during 2003 as it switched its emphasis to the WTO Ministerial in Cancún. In response to efforts by both the EU and the US to extend trade liberalisation into new areas such as investment, competition policy and government procurement, TJM aligned itself with several governments in the Global South which sought to block the introduction of these new issues into the WTO's negotiating agenda.

In the UK, trade justice as an idea became more familiar during 2005 as it became one of the three key demands made by the MPH coalition. The other two central aspects of this campaign coalition were the cancellation of the external debts of poor countries and a demand for more and better aid. The idea of MPH was first conceived in October 2003, with the plan being to focus on 2005 given that the UK Government was both hosting the G8 Summit in July and would be holding the presidency of the EU during the second half of that year (Saunders, 2009: 52). During 2004 the MPH campaign then set out its key demands, and throughout this period, as Harrison suggests, 'the issues remained generic and transnational – that is, based on broad moral arguments with little reference to specific situations, and with no spatial focus beyond that of the Global South' (2010: 394).

However, as the MPH campaign developed, we saw an explicit Africanisation of the agenda. Harrison convincingly argues that despite initial attempts not to focus specifically on Africa, 'MPH consciously selected a historical narrative (abolition, apartheid, and debt) within which to place itself which was to all intents and purposes "African", which then became a synonym for poverty' (2013: 165). TJM's position within MPH meant it was unavoidably drawn into this framing.[22] One of the members of the MPH coordination team concurs with Harrison's reading, suggesting that, during 2005, trade was 'framed within the context of Africa ... instead of a focus on the ... sweep of neoliberal trade agreements and WTO'.[23] This was all a very long way from the broader rules and structures identified by TJM at its foundation. As a result, it was possible for MPH to be co-opted into New Labour's 'year of Africa' in 2005 and the idea of trade justice was redefined in terms of access to Northern markets. This is evident in the findings of Blair's Commission for Africa, which focused its trade recommendations on the removal of agricultural subsidies to allow African economies to realise their 'true' comparative advantage (Hurt, 2007: 360).

Following the formal dissolution of the MPH campaign coalition in 2006, TJM entered a new era with fewer resources and a significantly reduced public profile. This period saw TJM respond to the shift away from the WTO and multilateral trade governance towards bilateral and regional trade agreements, and specifically the EU's negotiation of EPAs with African, Caribbean and Pacific (ACP) states. EPAs constituted an attempt by the EU to move away from its system of non-reciprocal trade preferences for ACP states, to a series of regional free trade agreements that would be compliant with WTO rules. However, the EU also sought to introduce its new trade issues that went far beyond what was required for WTO compatibility (Hurt, 2012: 501–2). Together with NGOs across Europe and Africa, TJM was involved in the launch of a new campaign, organised by the 'Stop EPAs' coalition. This highlighted the difficulties for UK-based trade campaigners because of the central role played by the European Commission in trade policymaking. TJM had to adopt a two-step approach by first trying to convince the UK Government to alter its policy stance and then encouraging it to push for a change in the EU's negotiating mandate on EPAs.

The central focus of the campaign on EPAs was to prevent the EU introducing the new issues that had been successfully resisted a few years before at the WTO's Cancún Ministerial. It was felt that their inclusion reflected the EU's strategic trade interests, rather than the development needs of ACP states (Trade Justice Movement, 2007). The other main aim was to slow the process of negotiations down beyond the initial deadline of 31 December 2007, which had been set by the EU. In this sense, the work of TJM was effective given that, aside from the EPA negotiated with the Caribbean region, the negotiations were extended well beyond this deadline. As part of this campaign, on 19 April 2007 TJM organised a simultaneous lobby of every European embassy in the UK, which was supported by roughly a thousand activists (Saunders, 2009: 51). Moreover, the UK Government both accepted that the new trade issues should not be included in EPA negotiations, unless ACP states specifically requested them, and committed to work with other member states to change the European Commission's stance on this (Sharman, 2007: 389).

One of the key points about the campaign on EPAs is that it was part of a wider action that involved CSOs across Europe and Africa. An interviewee from the Fairtrade Foundation highlighted how 'certainly around EPAs there was a whole period when organisations were quite actively bringing concerns being expressed by developing countries'.[24] It has been convincingly argued that this wider campaign had an impact on the discursive nature of the EPA negotiations by questioning EPAs' developmental potential, making them 'a politically contentious issue instead of a technical-administrative affair' (Del Felice, 2014: 159). The discursive impact of this NGO campaign helped enable African states to engage in a process of 'rhetorical entrapment of the EU' during the EPA negotiations (Hurt et al., 2013: 83).

Following the high-water mark of 2005, the work of TJM has become much less visible. Its focus on bilateral trade agreements has continued although this has shifted away from Africa and towards the EU's negotiation of both TTIP with the United States and a Comprehensive Economic and Trade Agreement with Canada. The main emphasis of this work has been on the potential consequences of regulatory harmonisation for upholding socio-economic and environmental rights within the EU. Of concern for TJM and the wider campaign against TTIP has been the potential inclusion of an Investor–State Dispute Settlement mechanism, which would allow transnational corporations to sue governments that introduce measures which they deem to be detrimental to their ability to make profits.

Even during this campaign, TJM has sought to try to articulate the precedent TTIP might have for future trade agreements with developing countries. For example, in February 2014 it submitted written evidence to the inquiry into TTIP organised by the EU Sub-Committee on External Affairs within the House of Lords. Here it was suggested that any rules contained in a deal between the EU and US are likely to become the template for future trade negotiations with developing countries.[25] Moreover, in a report on TTIP's relationship to the UN's Sustainable Development Goals, it concluded that:

> As the blueprint for multilateral trade, it undermines the global partnership for sustainable development and directly challenges the ability of individual countries to develop their own strategies for poverty reduction and sustainable development. Instead, it sets a powerful precedent that promotes privatisation and liberalisation as the de facto policy option and seeks to 'discipline' state involvement in key sectors such as public service delivery and industrial strategy, (Trade Justice Movement, 2015: 30)

One of the most significant recent developments in relation to the work of TJM has been the referendum result of 23 June 2016 in favour of the UK leaving the EU. It now seems clear that Brexit will result in the UK leaving the customs union and becoming independently responsible for trade policy. As Langan notes in Chapter 2, during the referendum campaign some leading Brexiteers suggested a good reason for leaving the EU was that it would allow the UK to develop a more progressive trade policy with Africa. Such claims have provided a new urgency and contemporary relevance to TJM's campaigning. Given the focus on securing a trade deal with the EU itself, and other key partners like the US, it seems inevitable that Africa will not be a priority for the UK Government, as it begins to formulate an independent trade policy. The Government's recent White Paper suggests that for future trade with developing countries the main aim will be to ensure continuity of market access, whereby the UK adopts a preference scheme that at least matches what the EU currently offers (Department for International Trade, 2017: 31–3).

Brexit has therefore provided a context for NGOs in the UK to once again combine a focus on trade with development issues. TJM has argued that Brexit provides an opportunity for the UK to adopt a trade policy that guarantees for countries in the Global South 'the best possible development outcomes by supporting regional integration and market diversification, and by strengthening local industries that develop value-added products' (Trade Justice Movement, 2017: 1). On this basis they are much closer to the Labour Party's emerging position on future trade with Africa. In a recent speech, Barry Gardiner, Shadow Secretary of State for International Trade, acknowledged how controversial the negotiation of EPAs has been and that the UK should avoid forcing African countries to liberalise in the future (Gardiner, 2017).

In sum, what this review of TJM's campaigns demonstrates is the reactive nature of much of its work. Rather than determine a definitive blueprint for trade justice it has, to some extent understandably, fallen into a pattern of reacting to ever-changing empirical developments. In part, this is the nature of the issue area and without TJM it is unlikely that trade would have retained the profile it has in relation to campaigning on African development. One interviewee neatly encapsulated how trade is rather different from other key campaign areas for development NGOs, by noting that 'debt and aid are quantitative campaigns, they are saying we want more of something or less of something, trade is not quantitative, it's a qualitative campaign and they are harder, you know because there are shades of grey. But there ought to be shades of grey on the aid and debt one but there weren't.'[26]

Conclusions: can NGOs influence the agenda on trade?

As other scholars (e.g. Bendell and Ellersiek, 2010) have noted, it is hard to make a quantitative assessment of the impact of NGO campaigning on policy. In some cases, it may even be that policies change broadly in line with NGO demands, but for other reasons, not directly related. Koenig-Archibugi (2014) suggests that one way to reflect on what aspects might determine the potential influence of NGOs is to consider internal and external factors. Internal factors include the effectiveness of coalition-building and the extent to which there are other interest groups providing opposition to the arguments being advocated, whereas external factors would acknowledge the important role played by states and the structures of global governance. The analysis presented in this chapter suggests that, in the case of TJM, while internal factors are not insignificant, external factors are of greater importance.

Similarly, different positions exist in the literature on the potential impact of NGOs in the specific area of trade. Pianta (2014) provides quite an optimistic assessment by focusing on longer-term attempts to reframe the issue. He suggests that since Cancún in 2003 the speed of multilateral trade liberalisation has slowed, as a direct result of NGOs forming coalitions with like-minded governments in the Global South, although as a result we have seen the rise of bilateral agreements (*ibid.*: 219). In contrast, De Bièvre focuses more on the 'day to day' of trade policymaking and highlights the effective lobbying of firms and business organisations, which for him results in the conclusion that 'CSO influence on global trade policy is a glass quite empty rather than half full' (De Bièvre, 2014: 227).

At the European level a formal process of engagement does now take place between policymakers and NGOs, via the Civil Society Dialogue. However, it has been suggested that this has not been translated into meaningful influence on the outcomes of trade policy (Orbie *et al.*, 2016: 532). Historically, the delegation of trade policy from the UK Government to the EU has made TJM's work that bit harder, given that without European coordination it is hard to have any impact.

At the core of TJM's work since 2000 has been the idea of 'trade justice' as an alternative to free trade, which remains the ultimate and ambitious goal of the coalition. If we use this as our yardstick for measuring TJM's impact, then we would have to conclude it has been limited. The UK Government's support for trade liberalisation remains at least as strong as it was at the time of TJM's formation. Reflecting on this, one interviewee questioned whether this is 'a failure of the movement, I think it's a reflection of how hard it is'.[27]

During their time in power, New Labour were very effective in promoting a position of common cause with the work of TJM, and subsequently the broader MPH alliance during 2005. These rather close links appear to have been far less evident during both the Coalition Government of 2010–15 and Conservative rule since the general election in May 2015. In fact, one could argue that in relation to Africa the 'prosperity agenda' advanced by both the Coalition Government and its Conservative successor is even more resolutely in favour of trade liberalisation; with the emphasis on the benefits trade can bring to both economic growth in Africa and UK exporters. As a result, on the issue of trade, where the gap between policymakers and NGOs is much wider than on other issues like aid (where there is a broad consensus among the main political parties on the 0.7 per cent of Gross National Income target), lobbying can be a rather ineffective tool.

Nevertheless, TJM has done much to mobilise UK citizens on the issue of trade. Although the mass lobbies of Parliament and European embassies took place some time ago, without the important coordination role performed by TJM, trade would have struggled to retain a place on the agenda of many development NGOs in the UK. By introducing the concept of 'trade justice', TJM has helped to frame African development within the broader structural logics of the global economy, rather than the more familiar frame based on aid. This has not been consistently achieved, however, and particularly during the era of MPH the message on trade justice was, to a large extent, drowned out. With Brexit likely to result in an independent UK trade policy, it is an issue area which will become increasingly important to the debate on African development in the future.

Notes

1 The term *trasformismo* is a key concept in the work of Antonio Gramsci and is used in this context to explain how potentially transformative ideas are neutralised by policy-making elites.
2 The TJM website (http://tjm.org.uk/our-members) as of 24 October 2017 listed a total of sixty-eight different groups as members.
3 Author interview with Polly Jones (Global Justice Now), London, 23 October 2015.
4 A good example of this is how the *Guardian* newspaper reported TJM's mass lobby of Parliament on 19 June 2002 under the headline 'Fair trade rally to lobby Westminster' – see www.theguardian.com/politics/2002/jun/19/foreignpolicy.uk [accessed 11 June 2017].
5 Author interview with a Fairtrade Foundation representative, London, 9 September 2015.
6 Author interview with Polly Jones (Global Justice Now), London, 23 October 2015.
7 Author interview with Richard English (Oxfam GB), Oxford, 21 October 2015.
8 Author interview with Tom Baker (Bond), London, 1 September 2016.
9 Author interview with Jenny Ricks (Action Aid, UK), London, 10 August 2015.
10 Author interview with Steve Tibbett (Independent advocacy, policy and campaigns consultant), London, 16 September 2015.
11 Author interview with John Hilary (War on Want), London, 27 August 2015.
12 Author interview with Steve Tibbett (Independent advocacy, policy and campaigns consultant), London, 16 September 2015.
13 Author interview with Glen Tarman (Action Against Hunger), London, 20 October 2015.
14 Author interview with Ruth Bergan (Trade Justice Movement), Bristol, 9 July 2015.

15 Author interview with former TJM activist, via Skype, 15 September 2015.
16 Author interview with Liz May (Traidcraft), London, 16 September 2016.
17 Author interview with Ruth Bergan (Trade Justice Movement), Bristol, 9 July 2015.
18 Author interview with John Hilary (War on Want), London, 27 August 2015.
19 Author interview with Benedict Southworth (Independent strategic advisor), via Skype, 22 September 2016.
20 Author interview with Sam Lowe (Friends of the Earth UK), London, 14 September 2016.
21 This comes from confidential notes of a meeting held between TJM's directors and Secretary of State for Trade and Industry, Patricia Hewitt and her advisors on 11 June 2002.
22 Author interview with John Hilary (War on Want), London, 27 August 2015.
23 Author interview with Benedict Southworth (Independent strategic advisor), via Skype, 22 September 2016.
24 Author interview with a Fairtrade Foundation representative, London, 9 September 2015.
25 For details see House of Lords (2014).
26 Author interview with Duncan Green (Oxfam), Oxford, 20 September 2016.
27 Author interview with Ruth Bergan (Trade Justice Movement), Bristol, 9 July 2015.

References

Alternative Trade Mandate Alliance (2013) *Trade: Time for a New Vision. The Alternative Trade Mandate*, www.s2bnetwork.org/trade-time-new-vision/ [accessed 30 June 2015].

Anderson, M. (2009) 'NGOs and Fair Trade: the social movement behind the label', in N. Crowson, M. Hilton and J. McKay (eds), *NGOs in Contemporary Britain: Non-state Actors in Society and Politics Since 1945* (Basingstoke: Palgrave Macmillan), 222–41.

BBC News (2002) 'Trade lobby gets fair hearing', *BBC News*, 19 June 2002, http://news.bbc.co.uk/1/hi/uk_politics/2053120.stm [accessed 24 October 2017].

Bebbington, A. J., Hickey, S. and Mitlin, D. C. (2008) 'Introduction: can NGOs make a difference? The challenge of development alternatives', in A. J. Bebbington, S. Hickey and D. C. Mitlin (eds), *Can NGOs Make a Difference? The Challenge of Development Alternatives* (London: Zed Books), 3–37.

Bendell, J. and Ellersiek, A. (2010) 'Advocacy for corporate accountability and trade justice: the role of "noble networks" in the United Kingdom', in P. Utting, M. Pianta and A. Ellersiek (eds), *Global Justice Activism and Policy Reform in Europe: Understanding When Change Happens* (Abingdon: Routledge), 140–63.

Blair, T. (2001) 'Leader's speech', Labour Party Conference, Brighton, www.britishpoliticalspeech.org/speech-archive.htm?speech=186 [accessed 24 October 2017].

Cameron, D. (2011) 'The time has come for African free trade', *Guardian*, 18 July 2011, www.theguardian.com/world/2011/jul/18/africa-free-trade-david-cameron [accessed 25 October 2017].

De Bièvre, D. (2014) 'A glass quite empty: issue groups' influence in the global trade regime', *Global Policy*, 5:2, 222–8.

Del Felice, C. (2014) 'Power in discursive practices: the case of the STOP EPAs campaign', *European Journal of International Relations*, 20:1, 145–67.

Department for International Trade (2017) *Preparing for our Future UK Trade Policy* (London: Her Majesty's Stationery Office).

Fridell, G. (2006) 'Fair Trade and neoliberalism: assessing emerging perspectives', *Latin American Perspectives*, 33:6, 8–28.

Gardiner, B. (2017) 'Speech on trade and Africa at Labour conference', 26 September 2017, www.barrygardiner.com/barry_speaks_on_trade_and_africa_at_labour_confer ence [accessed 29 September 2017].

Harrison, G. (2010) 'The Africanization of poverty: a retrospective on "Make Poverty History"', *African Affairs*, 109:436, 391–408.

Harrison, G. (2013) *The African Presence: Representations of Africa in the Construction of Britishness* (Manchester: Manchester University Press).

House of Lords (2014) 'The Transatlantic Trade and Investment Partnership – evidence', EU External Affairs Sub-Committee, 12 May 2014, www.parliament.uk/documents/ lords-committees/eu-sub-com-c/TTIP/TTIPoralandwrittenevidencevolume120514. pdf [accessed 12 June 2017].

Hurt, S. R. (2007) 'Mission impossible: a critique of the Commission for Africa', *Journal of Contemporary African Studies*, 25:3, 355–68.

Hurt, S. R. (2012) 'The EU–SADC Economic Partnership Agreement negotiations: "locking in" the neoliberal development model in southern Africa?', *Third World Quarterly*, 33:3, 495–510.

Hurt, S. R., Lee, D. and Lorenz-Carl, U. (2013) 'The argumentative dimension to the EU–Africa EPAs', *International Negotiation*, 18:1, 67–87.

Koenig-Archibugi, M. (2014) 'Introduction: civil society influence on global policy', *Global Policy*, 5:2, 212–13.

Mallet, V. and Lau, J. (2005) 'Diverse groups tell WTO what they think about trade terms', *Financial Times*, 13 December 2005, www.ft.com/content/831bfcc6–6b51–11da-8aee-0000779e2340 [accessed 11 June 2017].

McSweeney, J. (2014) 'The absence of class: critical development, NGOs and the misuse of Gramsci's concept of counter-hegemony', *Progress in Development Studies*, 14:3, 275–85.

Murphy, H. (2016) 'Cadbury cocoa plan raises questions for future of Fairtrade', *Financial Times*, 28 November 2016, www.ft.com/content/2d3967b4-b571–11e6–961e-a1acd97f622d [accessed 25 October 2017].

Orbie, J., Martens, D., Oehri, M. and Van den Putte, L. (2016) 'Promoting sustainable development or legitimising free trade? Civil society mechanisms in EU trade agreements', *Third World Thematics: A TWQ Journal*, 1:4, 526–46.

Paterson, B. (2009) '*Trasformismo* at the World Trade Organization', in M. McNally and J. Schwarzmantel (eds), *Gramsci and Global Politics: Hegemony and Resistance* (London: Routledge), 42–57.

Pianta, M. (2014) 'Slowing trade: global activism against trade liberalization', *Global Policy*, 5:2, 214–21.

Rivera, L. (2017) 'Sainsbury's to launch "Fairly Traded" tea sparking outrage from Fairtrade', *Independent*, 24 May 2017, www.independent.co.uk/news/business/news/sainsburys-fairly-traded-tea-own-brand-fairtrade-foundation-farmers-producers-a7753561.html [accessed 25 October 2017].

Saunders, C. (2009) 'British humanitarian, aid and development NGOs, 1949–present', in N. Crowson, M. Hilton and J. McKay (eds), *NGOs in Contemporary Britain: Non-state Actors in Society and Politics Since 1945* (Basingstoke: Palgrave Macmillan), 38–58.

Sharman, T. (2007) 'The evolution of British trade justice campaigning', *Review of African Political Economy*, 34:112, 385–92.

Trade Justice Movement (2002) *For Whose Benefit? Making Trade Work for People and the Planet*, http://tjm.org.uk/documents/briefings/For-Whose-Benefit.pdf [accessed 24 October 2017].

Trade Justice Movement (2007) *Economic Partnership Agreements (EPAs): Sustainable Development in Jeopardy*, Policy Briefing, August 2007.

Trade Justice Movement (2015) *TTIPing Away the Ladder: How the EU–US Trade Deal Could Undermine the Sustainable Development Goals*, http://tjm.org.uk/resources/reports/ttiping-away-the-ladder [accessed 12 June 2017].

Trade Justice Movement (2017) *Post-Brexit Trade and Development Policy: Ensuring Trade Justice for the Global South*, http://tjm.org.uk/resources/briefings/post-brexit-trade-and-development-policy-ensuring-trade-justice-for-the-global-south [accessed 28 October 2017].

Williams, P. (2004) 'Britain and Africa after the Cold War: beyond damage limitation?', in I. Taylor and P. Williams (eds), *Africa in International Politics: External Involvement on the Continent* (London: Routledge), 41–60.

10

International development NGOs, representations in fundraising appeals and public attitudes in UK–Africa relations

Danielle Beswick, Niheer Dasandi, David Hudson and Jennifer vanHeerde-Hudson

It is widely recognised that public attitudes and perceptions can play an important role in shaping countries' foreign policies (Holsti, 1992; Risse-Kappen, 1991), and UK–Africa relations are no exception. In this chapter, we consider the UK public's perceptions of Africa and Africans, and how these have been informed by charity fundraising appeals. The British public has long been interested in Africa, and in particular British engagement in Africa. Prior (2007: 1), for example, notes that 'tales of Britons striding purposefully through the jungles and across the arid deserts of Africa captivated the metropolitan reading public throughout the nineteenth century'. Over time, public perceptions of Africa have changed, although they remain significantly influenced by the colonial narrative of Britain as a global power following a missionary purpose to 'civilise' Africa.

In the contemporary era, one of the biggest influences on the UK public's perceptions of Africa has come from development non-governmental organisations (NGOs), particularly through the medium of their fundraising appeals. Such appeals have frequently made widespread use of shocking images of African children, devoid of any broader context, which many argue have negatively impacted UK public perceptions of Africans. We consider why such representations continue despite growing criticism. Through an analysis of a 2017 Oxfam campaign and reporting on new research using survey experiments, we demonstrate that an alternative approach to NGO fundraising is possible. Such a shift would contribute to, and be influenced by, broader changes in UK–Africa relations since 2010.

The chapter is structured as follows. The first section considers the problematic representations of Africans in NGO fundraising appeals, and how they have helped produce a narrative around UK–Africa relations in which the UK public is cast as the 'powerful giver' and Africans are portrayed as 'grateful receivers'. In the second section, we explain how, despite efforts to move away from this approach, NGO appeals continue to use negative representations, and their usage has been particularly noticeable since the 2008 financial crisis when organisations feared a drop in funding and donations. The chapter highlights a tension that NGOs face: on the one hand, negative representations allow organisations to raise funds that enable them to support vulnerable people in Africa and around the world. On the other hand, however, these representations also negatively influence and shape attitudes of the British public towards poverty in Africa more generally. We also discuss the growing criticism of this portrayal of UK–African representations, arguing that NGOs continue to use negative representations based on the belief that appealing to the emotions of pity and guilt is the only way to raise significant amounts of money. In the third section, we challenge this view, through an analysis of a 2017 Oxfam campaign and reporting on new research using survey experiments. We conclude by discussing how this potential to change the narrative fits within the broader shifts in UK–Africa relations since 2010.

NGO appeals and UK public perceptions of Africa

UK-based NGOs working in the international development sector have for many years worked across the developing world, seeking to improve the lives of those living in poverty in these countries. These NGOs have often turned to the British public to raise the funds required to carry out this hugely important work. This has, typically, been done by using fundraising appeals that appear in the media and in public spaces, which provide information about the contexts in which they work and images of those they seek to assist, then ask the public to make a charitable donation.

The images and representations of those living in developing countries and regions, particularly in Africa, have been the subject of recent criticism from academics, the media, civil society organisations and the broader public (Darnton and Kirk, 2011; Hilary, 2014; Hudson et al., 2017). Yet, the issue of the representations of the poor in NGOs' campaigns has a much longer history. Lissner (1977) questioned representations of the poor in NGOs' fundraising campaigns over three decades ago, highlighting the 'negative' images used by international NGOs, generally in the form of shocking depictions of malnourished starving young – and typically African – children with no broader context provided. The manner in which these images objectified those living in the Global South,

Lissner argued, was demeaning, lacking in dignity and inaccurate. Such images – referred to as 'the pornography of poverty' (Plewes and Stuart, 2007: 23) – are used, as Cameron and Haanstra (2008: 1476) explain, 'to induce emotions of pity and guilt on the part of potential donors through images and descriptions of material poverty and images of helpless "others" in the global South'.

These types of representation can frequently be seen in fundraising appeals that appear on television, billboards and public transportation, along with other public spaces. They are frequently associated with large fundraising campaigns, for example the Live Aid campaign, which raised around £150 million to tackle the Ethiopian famine, and Comic Relief, which raised more than £70 million in 2017 alone. The effectiveness of these appeals (an issue we return to below) has enabled NGOs to raise billions of pounds over the years, which has helped alleviate the suffering of the poorest in the world. However, these representations have also had negative, unintended consequences in terms of their influence on the UK public's perceptions of those living in developing countries – and in particular of Africans. These negative images, based on stereotypes, can foster negative and inaccurate views among the UK public of those living in African countries. They may also, as we will see, lead to reduced public engagement and decreasing efficacy of such appeals over time.

A question that arises is how have these representations come to influence UK public perceptions of Africa, specifically, if these NGOs work across the developing world? This is in large part because the overwhelming focus in NGO campaigns has been on Africans as the recipients of the British public's donations. Harrison (2010) describes this in relation to the Make Poverty History (MPH) campaign as the 'Africanization of poverty'. Harrison (*ibid.*: 395) notes that with MPH there was initially an explicit decision not to focus on Africa in the campaign precisely because campaigners felt that 'Africa had been subjected to a long history of pejorative and negative imagery'. However, this left a void in terms of the campaign's imagery, which led to concerns over the ability to motivate the public to engage with the campaign. This eventually led to the 'Africanization' of the campaign 'to "re-fill" the hollowness of poverty imagery and mobilise people to engage with campaigns on behalf of distant others' (*ibid.*: 397). It is worth noting that the prominence of Africa in MPH was also related to New Labour directing its international development efforts on Africa at the time – Tony Blair famously describing the continent as 'the scar on the conscience of the world' (*ibid.*: 401).

This emphasis on Africa in international development NGOs' campaigns is not just limited to major campaigns like MPH. Indeed, there is evidence to suggest that the UK public views 'developing countries' as synonymous with 'Africa'. A study in 2000 by the Department for International Development (DFID), entitled *Viewing the World*, analysed UK television coverage of developing countries and its impact on shaping public attitudes (Department for International Development, 2000), and found that the UK public thinks of Africa as synonymous with 'developing world'.[1] Respondents also associated Africa with 'poverty', 'famine', 'drought', 'war' and 'disaster' (*ibid.*: 11). Elsewhere Darnton (2009) and Darnton and Kirk (2011) have shown that the British public tends to associate Africa with poverty and misery, which reflects the representations used in NGO appeals. The use of these representations in campaigns over several decades has promoted the view among members of the British public that there has been virtually no progress in Africa since the 1980s, and that in terms of charity and aid Africa is a 'bottomless pit' (*ibid.*: 22–3).

Such attitudes towards Africa are not restricted to older people, who have been exposed to negative representations in NGO fundraising appeals for many years. What is perhaps particularly worrying is that these attitudes are also found in young people. A 2009 study of primary school students' perceptions of Africa by the Leeds University Centre for African Studies, as part of its 'African Voices' programme, found that: 'African poverty and underdevelopment were also prominent in the choices pupils made about what Africa looked like. Over seventy-three per cent of all pupils selected a picture of hungry children holding out an empty plate as one of their three images and fifty-three per cent of all pupils selected an image of straw huts in a rural setting' (Borowski, 2014).[2]

A second consequence of the pervasive use of negative representations of Africans in NGO appeals has been to portray Africans as impoverished and helpless, and in need of being saved by the UK. This narrative has been referred to as the 'Live Aid legacy', as Darnton and Kirk (2011: 23) explain: 'The resulting paradigm for relations between the UK public and those in the developing world is encapsulated in the concept of the "Live Aid legacy", which casts the UK public in the role of "*powerful giver*", and the African public as "*grateful receiver*". This dynamic still prevails.' Africans are reduced to isolated individuals, lacking in agency and divorced from context. States and state structures are often also absent from these depictions, separating the images from wider context and locating them outside of, or perhaps above, politics. This is by no means only found in NGO campaigning. Gallagher (2011) and Taylor (2012), among others, documented the portrayal of Africa under the Labour Governments of Blair (1997–2007) and Brown (2007–10) in a similar light. Africa was depicted as an arena empty of politics and agendas, full of suffering, and a place where the UK could unambiguously 'do good'.

There are a number of unintended consequences resulting from this portrayal. One issue is that it perpetuates negative stereotypes about Africans among the British public. Secondly, it also prevents more meaningful public engagement with the complexity of poverty and development in Africa, and more broadly. For example, it downplays the role of richer nations, such as the UK, in creating and perpetuating the (structural) problems faced in many poorer countries (Darnton and Kirk, 2011). Continually presenting an image of Africa as a place full of suffering fails to reflect the diversity across the African continent and the positive developments that have taken place. It also undermines efforts to create new narratives about Africa seeking to promote increased trade and investment, such as 'Africa rising', which seeks to present the continent as a place of growing economic opportunity (see, for example, Mahajan, 2011). Given the influence of NGO appeals on the perceptions of the British public towards Africa, it is important to consider more closely how the representations used in these appeals impact public attitudes.

Emotions and the fundraising dilemma

There has been much criticism of the use of such images in NGO fundraising appeals (Hilary, 2014; Seu and Orgad, 2017), although it is important to note that this criticism is not new (Lissner, 1977; Plewes and Stuart, 2007). Specific aspects of these traditional, pity-based representations have been problematised by scholars and practitioners in recent years (Boltanski, 1999; Chouliaraki, 2012), and has gained new impetus following the large campaigns focused on development, debt and the desire to 'make poverty history' during the 1990s and 2000s.

Scholars have paid specific attention to the effect of race (Burman, 1994; Harrison, 2010; Smith and Yanacopulos, 2004), the use of children (Dogra, 2012; Lissner, 1977; Manzo, 2008) and the 'othering' of those depicted (Harrison, 2010; Lidchi, 1999; Smith and Yanacopulos, 2004). Dogra (2012: 22) has argued that there is 'a dual logic of "difference" and "oneness" in NGO and charity appeals. Negative appeals tend to reproduce a shallow sense of cosmopolitanism because they focus on the differences rather than the similarities between people in the developed and developing world.' However, despite the criticism of negative campaign images, few studies have empirically examined the impact of such imagery, and even fewer have used experiments as a way to test effects of such images on potential donors.

This debate about the effects of negative representations is particularly important for international development NGOs because a parallel literature has highlighted declining levels of public engagement with global poverty, linking the decline to the way development organisations have appealed to the public (Darnton, 2009; Darnton and Kirk, 2011; Smillie, 1999). Here, research has shown that development NGOs' campaign strategies – particularly their pity-based fundraising appeals – act as a catalyst in the decline in public interest in, and engagement with, issues of global poverty (Darnton and Kirk, 2011; Dogra, 2012; Plewes and Stuart, 2007; Sireau, 2009). The issue here is that this stands in direct tension with the conventional wisdom that such fundraising appeals are most effective in eliciting donations from the public.

Criticism of traditional appeals has, since 2010, come from within the NGO community and outside of it. The pervasive use of these negative representations in development appeals has been the subject of growing media focus (e.g. Hilary, 2014; Meade, 2014), as well as being satirised in the popular US comedy sketch show, *Saturday Night Live* (see Grenoble, 2014). The Norwegian Students' and Academics' International Assistance Fund (SAIH) also produced a spoof charity song and video in 2013, calling for Africans to help freezing cold Norwegians by sending them radiators.[3] The video, which went viral on the internet, aimed to highlight the problem of the pervasive use of negative stereotypes about Africans in charity appeals, which, SAIH argued, prevented more meaningful engagement by the public in Western countries with issues in Africa, as well as with international development more broadly.

Since 2013, SAIH has also awarded annual 'Radi-Aid Awards', which celebrate 'the best – and the worst – of development charity fundraising videos'.[4] The award for the worst videos ('the rusty radiator award') has tended to receive most attention, serving to highlight problematic representations in NGO appeals. For example, in 2017 the winner of the 'rusty radiator award' was a Comic Relief appeal to alleviate poverty in Liberia featuring the British musician Ed Sheeran, with a Disasters Emergencies Committee advert to raise funds for the East Africa famine featuring British actor Eddie Redmayne also in contention (see Shepherd, 2017). The appeals, as well as the celebrities involved, received significant media criticism for perpetuating 'poverty porn' (e.g. BBC News, 2017; Hirsch, 2017; Reilly, 2017).[5] This growing criticism of traditional NGO appeals in the mainstream media indicates a greater willingness to challenge the crude stereotypes of Africans used in such appeals, and suggests that NGOs may have to move away from negative representations in their appeals if they are to avoid a public backlash.

Indeed, there have been efforts by the NGO sector to regulate its own members on the use of dehumanising negative representations of Africans, and the global poor more generally. The 1987 report *Images of Africa* started the debate on what imagery was appropriate to use in NGO appeals (van der Gaag and Nash, 1987). It was followed by a series of codes of conduct.[6] Yet, despite these efforts, development NGOs have continued to use shocking images of African children. This was particularly evident following the 2008 global financial crisis, which led to widespread concerns from NGOs about the future of development funding (IRIN, 2008).

One of the clearest examples of the continued use of pity-based appeals by leading NGOs is a televised appeal by Save the Children, entitled 'One Child', which appeared on UK television in 2013.[7] The advert begins with the shocking image of a malnourished and sick African child named Fidosi with a mainline access needle protruding from her head, covered in bandages. Much of her hair appears to have fallen out due to malnutrition and her mouth is covered in ulcers. She is alone, crying and in clear distress as she looks towards the camera. The narrator is a British man who informs the viewer that 'she's just a child; only nineteen months old, and in agony ... a girl who knows nothing but pain'. The narrator goes on to ask the viewer to help save the life of a child like Fidosi. This Save the Children advert is a clear example of a development NGO using negative representations of Africans to induce emotions of guilt and pity among the British public in order to garner donations. It is not only Save the Children that has continued to use negative representations in its appeals, other NGOs, such as CARE International, have also used shocking images of African children – with little wider context provided – in their televised appeals.[8]

An important question, then, is given the well-documented criticism and the negative effects on UK public perceptions of Africans, why do we continue to see the use of shocking and dehumanising images of African children in the fundraising campaigns of development NGOs like Save the Children and CARE International? The answer is that such representations are viewed by many in the NGO sector as the most effective means of raising money for their development work. The fear is that by moving away from these traditional, emotive, pity-based appeals, NGOs risk losing out on much needed public donations. As Burman (1994: 29) noted over twenty years ago, 'the poor starving black child is so central to the idiom of charity appeals that aid campaigns depart from this convention only at the risk of prejudicing their income'.

While NGOs have been subjected to criticism, it is important to recognise that the use of negative appeals allows organisations to raise funds to support some of the most vulnerable people in Africa and around the world. However, what works with respect to fundraising – that is, demonstrating urgent need – and the complex task of portraying the context of global poverty are not easy to reconcile. This is a fundamental issue. NGOs have many objectives which may overlap and compete: challenging the structural inequalities in the global system that adversely impact poorer states and people; increasing public awareness about the lives of people living in developing countries; responding to emerging and chronic crises that threaten the lives and livelihoods of millions of people;

and raising money. These objectives do not necessarily go hand in hand, and NGOs have to prioritise between competing demands. Indeed, this is a point that musician and activist Bob Geldof – a leading figure behind the 1984 Live Aid events and several subsequent development campaigns that have focused on Africa – has made about the tension between the need to save the lives of those who are at risk of dying, and at the same time trying to engage in changing the rules and institutions that foster global inequalities:

> we raised money through Live Aid, through Make Poverty History we raised the issues. And so that's the key difference. Live Aid we needed to get money instantly and to draw attention to the potential death of 30 million people. Now dude even now, if you ask me, Bob, number one, should we immediately start stripping down the institutions or should we instantly try and stop 30 million. Well the first thing is to stop the 30 million.[9]

The urgent need to save lives is seen as a justification for the use of shocking images. The immediacy of the need, with campaigns often citing the numbers of preventable deaths occurring every minute, or hour, alongside shocking images, trumps longer-term aims of public education and challenging unequal global structures. It is important to note that while many African countries have experienced significant economic growth and poverty reduction since the 1980s, there are still crises, linked to conflict, disease and drought occurring across the continent that can have a devastating impact on the lives of many. Development NGOs, supported by the UK public, play a crucial role in responding to such crises and supporting the people affected. For example, since 2011s East Africa has experienced its worst drought in sixty years, which has impacted the lives of approximately twelve million people and led to famine in parts of Somalia. In response, the British public donated £45 million, and, as discussed by Beswick in Chapter 6, the Conservative Party devoted its allocated broadcasting time to making an appeal for the UK public to support East Africa, saying 'some things are bigger than politics'.

As such, development NGOs are faced with a fundamental dilemma which has implications for UK public perceptions of Africans: on the one hand, traditional appeals are highly effective at raising funds through public donations, which enables these NGOs to assist highly vulnerable communities; on the other hand, traditional appeals have a negative impact on the British public's perceptions of Africans, which can also hinder broader development efforts such as pushing the UK Government to improve its policies towards Africa and its advocacy at a global level through, for example, the United Nations, European Union, and other international organisations and institutions.

To address this dilemma, it is necessary to focus on the link between representation, emotion and public response – a shift in the way NGOs frame their campaigns and represent those who benefit from them. A key question is whether tapping into more positive emotions in representations and appeals addresses the trade-off NGOs face: that they are able to raise sufficient money to continue to help people in the world's poorest places *and* engender a positive change in public perceptions of poverty, particularly in Africa. Doing so could have powerful implications: allowing more complex and contextualised images of Africa and development could in turn help to support better informed, and more complex and contextualised, public debate on aid and on UK–Africa relations.

Towards alternative representations and positive emotions

There are two important questions that need to be answered to address the dilemma that development NGOs face in their fundraising appeals in using negative representations of Africans. First, what kinds of representation might help to trigger more positive emotional responses from the UK public, which can help to shift the current perceptions of Africans? Secondly, can triggering positive emotions, such as empathy and hope, ensure both that NGOs raise sufficient funds from public donations to continue their work and transform the British public's perceptions of Africans? Answering these questions will require significant work by researchers and NGOs themselves. In the following sections, we provide some examples and evidence of how this shift might take place, and the potential for NGOs to move towards an alternative approach to fundraising that may help to reshape UK public perceptions of people living in African countries.

One recent NGO appeal, Oxfam's 'See for Yourself' campaign, can be considered as overcoming many of the problematic features of traditional, pity-based appeals – but still shares the same aim – trying to get the public to donate. The appeal provides a clear example of how some international development NGOs have tried to move away from the simplistic representations of Africans that are associated with more traditional NGO appeals. We briefly describe the appeal and consider the important ways in which it differs from the apolitical and agency-free images discussed previously. We then present findings from recent research into whether alternative representations can tap into more positive emotional responses, and explore what effect these emotional responses have on donations and public attitudes.

As with many traditional fundraising appeals, the object of Oxfam's 'See for Yourself' appeal is to encourage the viewer to provide a regular monthly donation.[10] The advertisement is based on the story of an 'everyday' British mother and Oxfam donor, Jodie Sandford, being invited by Oxfam to visit Zimbabwe. While there, she is to observe the organisation's work in the country. The video is centred on Jodie visiting, and spending time with, a Zimbabwean mother, Esther Mananzva, and her family. While we do not claim that the appeal manages to overcome all of the problems associated with NGO fundraising appeals, it certainly represents a significant improvement on the traditional appeals we have so far discussed in this chapter in a number of ways.

First, it moves from a static representation to one based on motion: the individuals featured have agency in their own lives and can be regarded as active subjects, rather than simply objects of pity. Secondly, in sending an ordinary member of the UK public to an African country the campaign makes a clear attempt to physically link the giver and receiver. This helps to break down the 'us and them' division, which occurs in many development appeals. Thirdly, the choice of Zimbabwe as the location for this encounter is also significant. Zimbabwe occupies a particular place in British imagination, strongly linked to colonial legacy. This persistent link has led the Director of the Chatham House Africa Programme, Alex Vines, to describe Zimbabwe in 2017 as having an ongoing 'psychological importance' for the UK (Telegraph, 2017). Moreover, government and media interest in Zimbabwe has remained, even as Africa faded from the global agenda. (This interest grew during 2017 with the removal of Robert Mugabe from power.) Taylor and Williams (2002), for example, have traced the evolution of Zimbabwe policy in the early years of New Labour, demonstrating ways in which policy rhetoric and action on Zimbabwe have been used by UK actors to reflect particular ideas about the power, role and responsibilities of the UK in relation to Zimbabwe in particular and Africa more broadly.[11] Choosing Zimbabwe as a location for the campaign therefore helps Oxfam to tap into an existing level of public awareness of Zimbabwe as a country with a complex history and set of current challenges.

Fourthly, the portrayal of a family, rather than simply an individual, in this campaign is also important: Esther is named, which contrasts sharply with campaigns that do not identify the individuals shown. Even more significantly, it is not just a first name, as is often the case in many charity adverts featuring children, but her full name and the area in which she lives are provided. By providing the viewer with Esther's full name, the appeal works to humanise Esther and her family. It also locates Esther within a family and a community so that she is situated, rather than disconnected and disempowered. This context is important – Esther is not simply another member of the global or African poor – we know that she is embedded, she is from the specific district of Gutu in Zimbabwe.

A number of additional features of the Oxfam advertisement further serve to humanise those living in developing countries. For example, there are several scenes in the video showing the daily life of those living in developing countries, which is in sharp contrast to traditional campaign images. The film shows Esther at home feeding her children. The viewer also sees adults in the community of Gutu working in the fields. The displays of daily life and work are essential in demonstrating human characteristics. Rather than the shocking images of children alone, and showing signs of physical and emotional distress, Jodie and Esther are holding the children and caressing them. This humanisation is also emphasised through the language used throughout the film. Jodie describes Esther's twin baby boys as 'beautiful', which, again, is a departure from the more common portrayal of young children in development appeals as dirty, malnourished and diseased.

While Jodie highlights the problems that Esther and her family face in Gutu, she also describes herself as being 'really, really excited' when she is told she will have the opportunity to travel to Zimbabwe. Again, this moves away from the more typical approach of presenting African countries as places of squalor and daily horrors, places to be avoided. It also avoids the single, 'transactional' nature of most engagement with global poverty. By highlighting everyday human and often mundane activities which link people across the world – caring for children, washing clothes, preparing meals and engaging with others – the campaign emphasises connections and proximity, rather than isolation and distance.

More generally, the Oxfam video differs from typical NGO appeals in the manner in which it emphasises the shared identity between people in the UK and African countries, rather than highlighting differences, which has typically been the case. This emphasis on shared identity is largely demonstrated by the relationship between Jodie and Esther, portrayed as two ordinary mothers with much in common. Unlike traditional appeals, which are narrated from the perspective of the omniscient NGO, often via a celebrity voiceover, the narrator in this case is Jodie, a member of the public who donates to Oxfam. This removes the typical mediation by the NGO, and in doing so brings the UK public closer to the African public, through an individual to whom they can relate.

The decision to focus on a woman as the donor may also be seen as an attempt to connect with other potential donors. A recent study (Gunstone and Ellison, 2017) found that women were more likely to donate to charity than men. In their YouGov survey, 54 per cent of women indicated that they had donated in the past year, compared with 40 per cent of men. Women were also significantly more likely to follow up donations with actions, such as talking to friends about their donations.[12]

As such, the Oxfam appeal demonstrates how the representations used in NGO appeals can avoid some of the problematic features of traditional NGO appeals. While we do not have data on how successful the appeal was in terms of public donations, it is worth noting that the appeal's primary focus remained fundraising. However, by avoiding the portrayal of the relationship between the UK and African publics as based on the 'powerful giver' and 'grateful receiver' relationship, the appeal demonstrates how NGO fundraising appeals might begin to reframe the UK–Africa relationship. As such, it marks a shift from the narratives associated with traditional NGO appeals and campaigns, such as MPH.

While the above example demonstrates how NGOs might move towards alternative appeals, it is important to consider whether such appeals are able to ensure that NGOs both raise funds and promote better engagement with the development agenda among the UK public. Two recent studies have employed experimental research designs to test whether alternative appeals can tap into positive emotions, such as empathy and hope, rather than negative emotions, such as pity and guilt – and what the effects of such positive emotional responses are on public donations and public attitudes. The first study was a lab experiment conducted with university students (see Hudson et al., 2019), and the second was a survey experiment based on a nationally representative sample (see Hudson et al., 2017).

Both studies were based on randomly assigning different appeals to respondents. They each tested a traditional, pity-based appeal with negative representations against an alternative appeal that sought to produce a positive emotional response. The traditional appeal in both studies used the image of a suffering African child devoid of any broader context. The language used in the traditional appeal emphasised the suffering of those living in developing countries, their helplessness, and the separation between the viewing public and those living in African countries. In doing so, the traditional appeal also focused on how the UK public could save the lives of those living in developing countries.

In contrast, the alternative appeal looked to add greater context and to avoid the negative representations associated with traditional development NGO appeals. In the lab experiment, the alternative treatment showed the image of a group of people using a water pump. In the survey experiment, the image showed children with a teacher in class, with one of the children holding a sign saying 'future doctor'. The language used in both of the alternative appeals sought to avoid emphasising the helplessness of those depicted – for example, the use of the image of the child holding up the sign aimed to give voice to those depicted in the campaign. The alternative appeals also sought to use a language highlighting the commonalities of the viewing UK public and the Africans represented, rather than using a language of separation, as tends to be the case in traditional appeals.

It is important to note that neither study directly tested the impact of the different appeals on respondents' attitudes towards the African public. However, both studies examined the effects of the different types of appeal on public attitudes towards global development more broadly, which at least allows us to see whether there is some attitudinal difference between respondents receiving different appeals. Given the prevalence of images of Africans in these campaigns, as already established, the findings can be considered useful in understanding this particular subset of relations.

Two key findings emerge from these two studies. The first is that the traditional appeals tend to trigger negative emotions (e.g. pity, guilt, repulsion) in respondents, and alternative appeals produce positive emotions (e.g. hope and solidarity), and these emotions are significant factors in mediating the relationship between the NGO appeals and public engagement. In both experiments, the traditional appeal triggered (the negative emotion) pity and suppressed (the positive emotion) hope. The analysis also demonstrates that these emotions are significant factors in mediating the relationship between NGO appeals and public engagement. For example, in the survey experiment the mediation analysis demonstrates that these negative emotional responses do not have uniform effects: while guilt and anger increase the likelihood of people donating to the charity, repulsion decreases donations. This suggests that these traditional appeals may have unintended consequences, in that while they may trigger emotions that lead to donations, they may also prime other emotions that drive away potential donors.

The second key finding relates to the effects of the appeals on personal efficacy (in the survey experiment) and sense of cosmopolitanism (in the lab experiment). The results of the survey experiment suggest that traditional appeals lower respondents' sense of efficacy in addressing problems of global poverty, which may serve as a barrier to deeper forms of engagement with global poverty. The lab experiment finds that the traditional appeals lower respondents' feelings of cosmopolitanism by suppressing respondents' feelings of hope.

These findings speak directly to the trade-off that has caused such tension and anxiety for development campaigners. They also illustrate another unintended consequence of the sector's use of traditional appeals: messages that generate revenue via donations may serve to reduce other forms of engagement, by generating feelings that there is little that can be done to address problems of global poverty. However, the news is not all bad: by activating the emotion of hope, alternative appeals increase the likelihood of donation and increase respondents' sense of personal efficacy. Alternative appeals may therefore help bridge the trade-off between fundraising and engagement.

Finally, the analysis in both the survey experiment and the lab experiment suggested there was no overall difference between the two appeals on likelihood of making a donation, or donation amount. This null finding is less surprising in light of the countervailing effects of the appeals, mediated by emotion, discussed above, but suggests that moving away from traditional negative appeals is far less risky than NGOs assume in terms of fundraising. The findings of the two studies suggest that NGOs have more scope for experimenting with appeals that seek to trigger positive emotional responses than is commonly believed, which may in the long term help to promote more positive public attitudes in the UK towards those living in Africa and other developing regions.

Conclusions

This chapter has considered how the representations used in NGO fundraising campaigns influence the UK public's perceptions of Africans. It has outlined how NGOs have undergone a shift in their thinking on the use of images of Africans in fundraising campaigns. It has been suggested that this parallels a wider process in reframing UK relations with Africa which has taken place at the level of the UK Government since 1997. Under Blair and Brown, Africa's profile was raised but Africa was depicted in a relatively simplistic way. Under the Coalition and Conservative Governments, relations with Africa have become more nuanced and, as Brown (Chapter 7) and Beswick (Chapter 6) argue, there is now greater scope for African agency and complexity in depicting the relationships with specific African organisations and states. Indeed, the growing criticism of the representations of Africans in NGO appeals in the mainstream media discussed above suggests that the public has also become less accepting of simplistic depictions of Africa.

Fundraising campaigners have similarly recognised the potential damage to public engagement caused by the use of stereotypical/traditional pity-based images of Africa and Africans in their appeals. Campaigns that challenge these traditional images and seek to elicit donations based on a more nuanced depiction of development challenges are emerging, as seen in the Oxfam example. The experimental data presented here suggest that such campaigns, based on provoking more positive emotional responses, have the potential to raise funds in a sustainable way, avoiding damaging donor engagement with future campaigns.

The chapter also highlights the need for further research on understanding how NGO appeals influence public attitudes towards those living in Africa and other developing regions. In particular, this includes exploring alternative approaches to NGO fundraising that focus on trying to elicit more positive emotional responses from the public, as well as prompting donations. Additional experimental work, particularly field research, validating the mediating role of emotions would provide further insights into how appeals affect attitudes and perceptions. Such alternatives are important if UK public perceptions of Africans are to be transformed.

Notes

1. DFID's 2000 report, *Viewing the World*, was based on three studies conducted over a three-month period in 1999. The analysis of audience perceptions was based on twenty-six focus groups each consisting of six–eight people. The focus groups were convened in England and Scotland and they were undertaken by the Glasgow Media Group.
2. The overall number of primary students included in the survey is not reported.
3. See 'Africa for Norway', www.youtube.com/watch?v=oJLqyuxm96k [accessed 12 December 2017].
4. See www.rustyradiator.com/about/ [accessed 15 December 2017].
5. It is worth pointing out that some in the media questioned the negative coverage that Ed Sheeran had received due to the Comic Relief video. See, for example, Mitchell (2017).
6. For example the 1989 General Assembly of the Liaison Committee of Development NGOs to the European Communities, *Code of Conduct: Images and Messages relating to the Third World*; the 1994 *Code of Conduct of British Red Cross and Red Crescent Movement and NGOs in Disaster Relief*; and the 2006 CONCORD: the European NGO confederation for Relief and Development, *Code of Conduct on Images and Messages*.
7. Save the Children, 'One Child' advertisement, 13 January 2012, www.youtube.com/watch?v=99pQ0KJfdoE [accessed 22 November 2017].
8. See CARE International, 'Who Cares?' advertisement, 17 September 2012, www.youtube.com/watch?v=hFHORe4sChI [accessed 22 November 2017].
9. This is taken from an interview with Bob Geldof conducted by Owen Barder for the *Development Drums* podcast in 2013, http://developmentdrums.org/wp-content/uploads/DD38-and-39-transcript.pdf [accessed 8 August 2017].
10. The Oxfam 'See for Yourself' advert is available at www.youtube.com/watch?v=UE-ex7peAfw [accessed 17 August 2017].
11. This is reflected in Chapter 6 by Beswick, showing that Zimbabwe was a point of focus for Conservative politicians in opposition and government.
12. The decision to focus on women in the campaign, specifically Jodie and Esther, may therefore also make sense from a fundraising point of view, allowing an easy point of identification for the group most likely to donate and to advocate for the cause (see also Charities Aid Foundation, 2017).

References

BBC News (2017) 'Did Ed Sheeran commit "poverty tourism" in charity film?', *BBC News*, 7 December 2017, www.bbc.co.uk/news/world-africa-42268637 [accessed 18 December 2017].

Boltanski, L. (1999) *Distant Suffering: Politics, Morality, and the Media* (Cambridge: Cambridge University Press).

Borowski, R. (2014) 'Media influences on young people's perceptions of Africa', 2014, http://16g8433chtiw3m2ge9203ed9.wpengine.netdna-cdn.com/files/2014/01/Africa-UK-Journalism-Conference-Paper.pdf [accessed 12 February 2018].

Burman, E. (1994) 'Poor children: charity appeals and the ideologies of childhood', *Changes: An International Journal of Psychology and Psychotherapy*, 12:1, 29–36.

Cameron, J. and Haanstra, A. (2008) 'Development made sexy: how it happened and what it means', *Third World Quarterly*, 29:8, 1475–89.

Charities Aid Foundation (2017) 'CAF charitable giving 2017: an overview of charitable giving in the UK', April 2017, www.cafonline.org/docs/default-source/about-us-publications/caf-uk-giving-web.pdf [accessed 12 February 2018].

Chouliaraki, L. (2012) *The Ironic Spectator: Solidarity in the Age of Post-humanitarianism* (Cambridge: Polity Press).

Darnton, A. (2009) 'The public, DFID and support for development – a rapid review', report for the Department for International Development, 1 December 2009, https://celebrityanddevelopment.files.wordpress.com/2011/02/darnton-rapidreview_ad011209.pdf [accessed 7 January 2019].

Darnton, A. and Kirk, M. (2011) *Finding Frames: New Ways to Engage the UK Public in Global Poverty* (London: BOND).

Department for International Development (2000) *Viewing the World: A Study of British Television Coverage of Developing Countries*, July 2010, https://celebrityanddevelopment.files.wordpress.com/2012/06/2000viewing-the-world-dfid.pdf [accessed 22 November 2017].

Dogra, N. (2012) *Representations of Global Poverty: Aid, Development and International NGOs* (London: I.B. Tauris).

Gallagher, J. (2011) *Britain and Africa under Blair: In Pursuit of the Good State* (Manchester: Manchester University Press).

Grenoble, R. (2014) '"SNL" nails important point about aid programs in Africa with spot-on, hilarious sketch', *Huffington Post*, 17 October 2014, www.huffingtonpost.co.uk/entry/saturday-night-live-39-cents-african-aid_n_5999612 [accessed 22 November 2017].

Gunstone, B. and Ellison, G. (2017) *Insights into Charity Fundraising* (London: Institute of Fundraising and YouGov).

Harrison, G. (2010) 'The Africanization of poverty: a retrospective on "Make Poverty History"', *African Affairs*, 109:436, 391–408.

Hilary, J. (2014) 'The unwelcome return of development pornography', *New Internationalist*, December 2014.

Hirsch, A. (2017) 'Ed Sheeran means well but this poverty porn has to stop', *Guardian*, 5 December 2017, www.theguardian.com/commentisfree/2017/dec/05/ed-sheeran-poverty-porn-activism-aid-yemen-liberia [accessed 18 December 2017].

Holsti, O. (1992) 'Public opinion and foreign policy: challenges to the Almond–Lipmann consensus', *International Studies Quarterly*, 36:4, 439–66.

Hudson, D., Laehn, N. S., Dasandi, N. and vanHeerde-Hudson, J. (2019) 'Making and unmaking cosmopolitans: an experimental test of the mediating role of emotions in international development appeals', *Social Science Quarterly*, forthcoming.

Hudson, D., vanHeerde-Hudson, J., Dasandi, N. and Gaines, N. S. (2017) 'Emotional pathways to engagement with global poverty: an experimental analysis', Working Paper.

IRIN (2008) 'NGOs pare down in face of financial crisis', *IRIN*, 28 October 2008, www.irinnews.org/news/2008/10/27/ngos-pare-down-face-financial-crisis [accessed 23 December 2017].

Lidchi, H. (1999) 'Finding the right image: British development NGOs and the regulation of imagery', in T. Skelton and T. Allen (eds), *Culture and Global Change* (Abingdon: Routledge), 87–101.

Lissner, J. (1977) *The Politics of Altruism: A Study of the Political Behaviour of Voluntary Development Agencies* (Geneva: Lutheran World Federation).

Mahajan, V. (2011) *Africa Rising: How 900 Million African Consumers Offer More than You Think* (Upper Saddle River, NJ: Pearson Prentice Hall).

Manzo, K. (2008) 'Imaging humanitarianism: NGO identity and the iconography of childhood', *Antipode*, 40:4, 632–57.

Meade, A. (2014) 'Emotive charity advertising – has the public had enough?', *Guardian*, 29 September 2014, www.theguardian.com/voluntary-sector-network/2014/sep/29/poverty-porn-charity-adverts-emotional-fundraising [accessed 8 August 2017].

Mitchell, V. C. (2017) 'Ed Sheeran versus the super-idiots', *Guardian*, 10 December 2017, www.theguardian.com/commentisfree/2017/dec/10/ed-sheeran-versus-the-super-idiots [accessed 18 December 2017].

Plewes, B. and Stuart, R. (2007) 'The pornography of poverty: a cautionary fundraising tale', in D. A. Bell and J. M. Coicaud (eds), *Ethics in Action: The Ethical Challenges of International Human Rights Nongovernmental Organizations* (Cambridge: Cambridge University Press), 23–37.

Prior, C. (2007) 'Writing another continent's history: the British and pre-colonial Africa, 1880–1939', *eSharp*, issue 10, 2007, https://www.gla.ac.uk/media/media_64283_en.pdf [accessed 7 January 2019].

Reilly, N. (2017) 'Comic Relief film starring Ed Sheeran slammed as "poverty porn"', 4 December 2017, *NME*, www.nme.com/news/tv/comic-relief-film-starring-ed-sheeran-slammed-poverty-porn-2167835 [accessed 18 December 2017].

Risse-Kappen, T. (1991) 'Public opinion, domestic structure, and foreign policy in liberal democracies', *World Politics*, 43:4, 479–512.

Seu, I. B. and Orgad, S. (2017) *Caring in Crisis: Humanitarianism, the Public and NGOs* (Basingstoke: Palgrave Macmillan).

Shepherd, J. (2017) 'Ed Sheeran's comic relief film labelled "poverty porn" by aid watchdog', *Independent*, 4 December 2017, www.independent.co.uk/arts-entertainment/music/news/ed-sheeran-comic-relief-poverty-porn-aid-watchdog-a8091016.html [accessed 18 December 2017].

Sireau, N. (2009) *Make Poverty History Political Communication in Action* (Basingstoke: Palgrave Macmillan).

Smillie, I. (1999) 'Public support and the politics of aid', *Development*, 42:3, 71–6.

Smith, M. and Yanacopulos, H. (2004) 'The public faces of development: an introduction', *Journal of International Development*, 16:5, 657–64.

Taylor, I. (2012) 'Spinderella on safari: British policies towards Africa under New Labour', *Global Governance*, 18:4, 449–60.

Taylor, I. and Williams, P. D. (2002) 'The limits of engagement: British foreign policy and the crisis in Zimbabwe', *International Affairs*, 78:3, 547–65.

Telegraph (2017) 'Zimbabwe must reform after Mugabe, says first British minister to visit country in two decades,' *Telegraph*, 23 November 2017, www.telegraph.co.uk/news/2017/11/23/zimbabwe-must-reform-mugabe-says-first-british-minster-visit/ [accessed 12 February 2018].

van der Gaag, N. and Nash, C. (1987) *Images of Africa: UK Report*, 1987, www.imaging-famine.org/images_africa.htm [accessed 8 August 2017].

Conclusions: aspects of continuity and change after New Labour

Danielle Beswick, Jonathan Fisher and Stephen R. Hurt

The chapters in this collection provide a rich, empirically informed picture of contemporary UK–Africa relations and a comprehensive assessment of how far UK Africa policy has changed since the New Labour Government's loss of power in May 2010. What we find is that the overall picture is deeply ambiguous, with assessments differing according to the aspect of the relationship under study. On the one hand, development assistance and security concerns have continued to be important drivers of the UK–Africa relationship since 2010, as they were under the Labour administrations of Tony Blair and Gordon Brown. On the other hand, trade and UK economic opportunities in Africa have moved much higher up the domestic agenda during the ministries of David Cameron and Theresa May. Africa in general has also been of increasingly marginal concern to post-2010 UK Governments, in contrast to the Blair era, where it was often a high priority – at least discursively. In fact, as Vines suggests in Chapter 1, this process of retrenchment was already in train during New Labour's final term of office. As a result, we have seen the UK become a less significant and more pragmatic actor on the continent, during a period when other external actors, particularly China, have considerably increased their engagement with Africa.

This concluding chapter offer a synthesis of the wide-ranging claims made throughout the preceding chapters. In doing so, we return to the four main questions that have guided the research for this book:

1. What are the domestic and foreign policy determinants of contemporary UK Africa policy?

2. How far do these build on or challenge the conclusions of previous analyses of UK Africa policy and relations, particularly those which focused on the periods of Labour Government from 1997 to 2010?
3. What are the potential implications of these continuities and emerging trends for the UK and for Africa, in relation to each other and to wider developments in the sub-fields of security, development, trade, party identity, civil society campaigning and regionalism?
4. What are the power dynamics within UK–Africa relations? To what extent is the UK's relationship with Africa forever shaped by its colonial past?

The key drivers of contemporary UK Africa policy

In explaining the core drivers of contemporary UK–Africa relations, Vines argues in Chapter 1 that development and humanitarianism remain central, echoing the priorities of the Blair and Brown Governments. As many of the chapters demonstrate, however, both security (Chapters 3, 4 and 5) and trade (Chapters 2 and 9) have become increasingly significant issues for UK policy-makers since 2010. What the collection demonstrates, in this regard, is how the UK Government's evolving security agenda and trade interests have become more explicitly tied to the ambitions of its development policy towards Africa since 2010, as Petrikova and Lazell note in Chapter 4.

As this collection demonstrates, the UK Government's relationship with Africa is increasingly driven by a narrative that justifies development policy not as an end in itself but as a strategy for ensuring national security. This is an approach that can be traced back to Blair's 'scar on the conscience of the world' speech in 2001, though this security logic was generally combined with a humanitarian rhetoric during New Labour's period in office. As Petrikova and Lazell demonstrate in Chapter 4, since 2010 this justification of aid to Africa has continued, but with the balance tilted more firmly towards pragmatism and security. Their analysis highlights how, during the five years of the 2010–15 Conservative–Liberal Democrat Coalition Government, the UK developed a preference for targeting aid to those countries in Africa that are perceived to be of greater strategic interest.

This UK approach to security issues in Africa is also driven by continuing support for the idea of 'African solutions to African problems'. Since 2010, as Apuuli reveals in Chapter 3, the UK has continued to support the African Peace and Security Architecture (APSA) led by the African Union (AU). However, in recent years this support has also been matched by a direct commitment of UK troops to peacekeeping missions in Africa. As Curran argues in Chapter 5, this is an approach that has been viewed more favourably by the current Conservative administration than its predecessors. As a result, troops were sent to both Somalia and South Sudan with the justification being couched very clearly in terms of the UK's national security.

Trade and investment links have also become an increasingly important driver of UK–Africa relations. Since the Brexit vote in 2016 and the ensuing debate on a future independent UK trade policy, this aspect of the relationship has only become more significant. Conversely, Brexit has also complicated the EU's existing trade relations with Africa. For example, Tanzania has refused to sign the Economic Partnership Agreement (EPA) between the EU and the East African Community, with officials citing Brexit as one of the key reasons (Hurt, 2016).

At the same time, and as Part II of this volume demonstrates, a range of UK actors – both inside and outside government – continue to portray and frame Africa in terms of development. Both Chapter 6 and Chapter 7 show how the two leading political Parties in the UK – the Conservative and Labour Parties – continue to privilege Africa in the way they frame their thinking on international development. Meanwhile, Chapters 8 and 9 highlight that Africa continues to feature strongly in the campaign focus of civil society coalitions, which include the UK's major development non-governmental organisations (NGOs). Chapter 10 also discusses how perceptions of Africa within the British public in general have been significantly shaped by the approach to fundraising adopted by these NGOs.

Shifts in emphasis since 2010

The legacy of New Labour's period in office from 1997–2010 is clear to see from much of the analysis provided in this volume. Both the Conservative–Liberal Democrat Coalition and Conservative Governments have taken key decisions to ensure some significant aspects of continuity in policymaking to Africa. As Chapter 6 by Beswick, on the Conservative Party, makes clear, the changes the Party has made to its approach to international development policy, and Africa in particular, were a direct response to New Labour's agenda. A process that Beswick traces back to the early 2000s has seen Africa feature within a broader re-imagining of the Conservative Party. During the 2005 election campaign the Conservative Party promised in its manifesto to match Labour's commitment to meeting the United Nations target on aid spending of 0.7 per cent of Gross National Income, while the Liberal Democrats even promised to reach the target quicker than Labour (Clarke, 2018: 24). This emerging consensus among all the major parties in Westminster over the UK's commitment to spending on aid subsequently resulted in Parliament making this UN target legally binding in 2015. Another key continuation of the New Labour legacy enacted by the Coalition Government was the decision to maintain the Department for International Development as a separate ministry after Labour's 2010 defeat, as opposed to downgrading it to a section within the Foreign and Commonwealth Office as it had been under previous Conservative Governments.

Even where there are significant continuities in *approach* from the Governments led by Blair and Brown, both rhetorically and in practice there have been important changes in *emphasis* identified in this volume. Since 2010, the UK Government's engagement in Africa, whether through development assistance or support for peacekeeping, has been more explicitly couched in terms of the 'national interest'. Clarke (*ibid.*: 25–6) confirms some of the findings in this volume, by arguing that while the key principles of UK development policy enshrined by New Labour have survived after 2010, aid has been increasingly focused on fragile states and the purported national interest. These changes in emphasis have become particularly apparent since the Brexit vote in 2016. Trends identified in this volume, such as an increasing securitisation of UK aid policy to Africa (Chapter 4), are likely to be exacerbated in the coming years. As has been recently argued, 'Brexit will reinforce an already obvious realignment in the UK's international development policy towards a more explicit and expanded focus on UK economic and geopolitical interests' (Lightfoot *et al.*, 2017: 517).

There have also been more substantive disruptions to the nature of UK–Africa relations since 2010, many of which have become particularly apparent in the period since the Brexit referendum. As Vines argues in Chapter 1, trade is a policy domain where, in contrast to aid, there is a greater divergence between the leading political parties. In Chapter 2, Langan considers the impact of Brexiteers within the current Government on debates on UK–Africa trade. He evaluates the claims they have made with respect to the UK's withdrawal from the EU and how it will result in an approach to trade with African members of the Commonwealth, which will enable a more developmental arrangement. He also demonstrates how the Conservative Government has suggested it should use the influence afforded through its aid programme to try to help secure future free trade deals with Africa. Langan disputes the claims of the Brexiteers' narrative and convincingly argues that their plans will instead reinforce a neo-colonial pattern of trade. Meanwhile, in Chapter 9, Hurt considers the role of the Trade Justice Movement (TJM), a coalition of civil society organisations, in how trade between the UK and Africa is understood. He argues that TJM continues to challenge the neoliberal assumptions behind the logic of the developmental benefits of free trade. Historically, its work relating to Africa had been focused on resisting the negotiation of EPAs between the EU and regions within the African, Caribbean and Pacific (ACP) states. Hurt also suggests that trade is a policy domain where civil society organisations have renewed their focus given the firm commitment made by the Theresa May-led Conservative Government that in response to the Brexit vote the UK plans to leave the customs union.

In addition to trade, Brexit will have consequences for the UK's wider relationship with Africa. The apparent political consensus on UK development policy is fracturing. As Clarke (2018: 28) notes, since the referendum prominent Brexiteers have taken on important roles in government. Of relevance to UK–Africa relations was the appointment of Priti Patel as Secretary of State for International Development from July 2016 until November 2017, leading a department of government that she had previously argued should be abolished. The UK's current commitments to EU development assistance, delivered by the European Development Fund, will expire in 2020. Historically, as an important player in EU development policy, the UK has been able to extend its reach beyond its traditional sphere of influence in Africa. As Price (2016: 504) has convincingly argued, 'this prime position at the EU level has in turn secured the UK's position as a global leader in development'. Once the UK has left the EU, however, it will not continue to be a participant in the EU's development assistance programmes. This raises two inter-linked questions as to 'whether the level of aid given by the EU to Africa will be sustained, and whether the current British contribution will actually be reinvested in aid when its current commitments expire' (Ansorg and Haastrup, 2016: 4).

Moreover, outside of the EU the UK will not be part of the institutional framework of cooperation that has been developed by the EU and the AU. This includes the EU–AU Summits, the most recent of which took place in November 2017 in Côte d'Ivoire. The approach to the EU's Common Security and Defence Policy action in Africa is also likely to change following the implementation of Brexit. Ansorg and Haastrup (*ibid.*: 6) argue that in contrast to France, which has tended to support a more conventional military approach, the UK has advocated for more of a focus on conflict prevention and peacebuilding. In sum, the UK's immediate future outside of the EU appears to put it out of step with ongoing regional and continental initiatives within Africa. These plans include APSA and the African Continental Free Trade Area (CFTA), which are both being led by the AU.

Another noticeable shift since 2010 has been the altered context for UK-based development NGOs. During New Labour's time in power the relationship between some of the UK's leading development NGOs became increasingly close. As Harrison has noted, this process reached its peak during the Make

Poverty History (MPH) coalition when some leading NGOs 'had no reservations in appealing to New Labour's self-representation as working in Africa's best interests' (2013: 172). In Chapter 8, Harrison contrasts this period with the political context faced by NGOs since 2010. He outlines how, despite the changes within the Conservative Party noted by Beswick in Chapter 6, development NGOs have had to operate within a less conducive domestic political environment. Given this change in situation and following the lessons of the MPH coalition, Harrison then outlines how in 2013 the mainstream development NGOs formed a new coalition, the Enough Food If campaign (EFIF). Harrison suggests that EFIF was able to develop a focus and approach such that it enabled sufficient areas of mutual interest with the Conservative–Liberal Democrat Coalition Government. In contrast to EFIF, Hurt notes in Chapter 9 that TJM, given its calls for more fundamental changes to the way trade works, has found it much harder since 2010 to have a meaningful dialogue with the UK Government.

Finally, the period since 2010 has also seen a process of internal debate within the Labour Party as to how it might renew its understanding of the UK's relationship with Africa after the Blair/Brown era of New Labour. As Brown notes in Chapter 7, during its time in opposition Labour has been partially successful in such a process. He argues that there has been an emphasis on moving the Party away from an agenda dominated by development assistance to one that engages more critically with the nature of Africa's integration into the global political economy. This has resulted, as Hurt notes in Chapter 9, in a much closer alignment between TJM's vision for what the UK's trade relationship with Africa should look like and the evolving policy position within the Labour Party.

In sum, during the period since 2010 we have witnessed aspects of continuity in UK–Africa relations since the era of New Labour. At the same time, however, there have been noticeable and significant shifts in aspects of this relationship, which have resulted particularly from the impact of the Brexit vote in 2016. The final sections of this chapter now turn to some brief reflections on our other two research questions. First, the wider consequences of the findings from this volume for relevant disciplinary sub-fields. Secondly, the evolving nature of power relations that underpin the UK's relationship with Africa and the extent to which they remain forever defined by the legacies of colonial rule.

Power dynamics and the wider lessons for research on UK–Africa relations

Some of the points raised in this volume in relation to the developmental impacts of Africa's future trade arrangement with the UK (Chapter 2) are relevant to much wider debates on how Africa can achieve development through trade policy. Brown's discussion of the Labour Party in Chapter 7 highlights how the Party's thinking is shifting in relation to these debates. He argues that there is now an acknowledgement of the need to think through what a progressive trade relationship between the UK and Africa might look like, although he concedes the Party has much work to do in this regard. As Hurt argues in Chapter 9, TJM continues to challenge the dominant assumptions of the developmental benefits of trade liberalisation. At the same time, this is also a wider debate to which African actors are contributing; one notable example is a recent report by the UN Economic Commission for Africa. It outlines how African states might employ smart trade and industrial policies within current and future trade agreements to encourage industrialisation (United Nations Economic Commission for Africa, 2017).

There are also some broader lessons from this volume for debates on civil society campaigning. Chapter 10 considers the problematic way that many development NGOs have continued to use extremely passive imagery of Africa to raise money for their campaigns. Similarly, Harrison in Chapter 8 demonstrates how the EFIF campaign's focus on hunger and malnutrition fitted rather neatly into this long-standing approach of many UK-based development NGOs. This contrasts with Hurt's analysis of TJM in Chapter 9 and its attempts to switch attention to the underlying structural causes of Africa's development challenges. Chapter 10 does, however, refer to Oxfam's 'See for Yourself' campaign, which the authors argue offers an alternative model whereby development campaigning can be based on positive emotions of hope and solidarity, rather than pity and guilt.

Throughout the chapters in this book, we also get a sense of the ways in which colonial perceptions of Africa continue to shape contemporary understanding within the UK. We are also, though, provided with an indication of how Africa might be able to exert influence in its relations with a multitude of actors within the UK itself. Langan, for example, argues in Chapter 2 that the discourse of Brexiteers within the UK Government on future Africa trade policy has an explicitly neo-colonial dimension to it. The preference of the UK Government, it is suggested, is to replicate the EU's existing EPAs with ACP states (Department for International Trade, 2017). This will almost certainly prove controversial given the difficulties the EU has faced in negotiating EPAs. Of course, this vision is not only challenged by civil society organisations like TJM, as discussed by Hurt in Chapter 9, but, as Langan suggests in Chapter 2, it is also likely to face contestation from African states. Given the apparent limitations of working within sub-regions in negotiating EPAs with the EU, and given the development of the CFTA, Langan suggests a more effective approach to negotiating post-Brexit trade arrangements with the UK would be for the ACP to operate as a collective group. Moreover, African initiatives like the CFTA are seeking to challenge a situation whereby for the period from 2012–14, 76 per cent of Africa's exports to destinations outside the continent remained extractives, which compares with only 39 per cent of exports to other countries within Africa (United Nations Economic Commission for Africa, 2018: 2).

Within the realm of security, we can also see the legacies of colonialism shaping current practice. In Chapter 5, Curran demonstrates how the UK developed a sceptical view of UN peacekeeping operations in Africa, that has to some extent endured. This has resulted in a preference for African solutions to the continent's security challenges. As Apuuli's discussion of the UK's support of the AU's APSA in Chapter 3 reveals, however, there remain some significant limitations in the ability of the AU to meet these challenges. From a financial perspective, at least, there are plans to address this, not least the decision taken in July 2016 to place a tariff of 0.2 per cent on all eligible imports into Africa to help fund the AU. In advance of the signing of the CFTA some African states have already begun to implement this levy (Apiko and Aggad, 2018: 6–7).

The framing of Africa within a broader international development context also serves to reinforce understandings that can be traced back to the colonial era. As the authors of Chapter 10 argue, public perceptions of Africa retain a link to the colonial narrative of Britain's missionary role in the continent. This view is then argued to have been reinforced by the approach of many UK-based development NGOs. Hurt's discussion of TJM in Chapter 9, on the other hand, suggests that it is possible for civil society organisations within the UK to work with partners, both across Europe and Africa, to empower African states in their EPA negotiations with the EU.

Future research on UK–Africa relations

Overall, this edited collection demonstrates both the continuities and important changes to relations between the UK and Africa that have emerged since New Labour lost power in 2010. It notes how domestic political developments in the UK, most notably the Brexit vote, combined with broader global changes, have resulted in a very different context from the one that existed at the beginning of the twenty-first century. In doing so, it focuses largely on the role played by UK actors. The impacts and consequences of the emerging trends highlighted here will not affect such a varied and diverse continent in equal measure. Future research on the UK's relationship with Africa may therefore wish to consider in more depth both the potential African agency in relations with the UK and the more specific consequences for different regions and nation-states across the continent.

References

Ansorg, N. and Haastrup, T. (2016) 'Brexit beyond the UK's borders: what it means for Africa', *GIGA Focus Africa*, 3, 1–10.
Apiko, P. and Aggad, F. (2018) 'Analysis of the implementation of the African Union's 0.2% levy: progress and challenges', ECDPM Briefing Note, February 2018, http://ecdpm.org/wp-content/uploads/BN98-Apiko-Aggad-November-2017.pdf [accessed 25 February 2018].
Clarke, G. (2018) 'UK development policy and domestic politics 1997–2016', *Third World Quarterly*, 39:1, 18–34.
Department for International Trade (2017) *Preparing for our Future UK Trade Policy* (London: Her Majesty's Stationery Office).
Harrison, G. (2013) *The African Presence: Representations of Africa in the Construction of Britishness* (Manchester: Manchester University Press).
Hurt, S. R. (2016) 'Why African states are refusing to sign on to EU trade deals', *World Politics Review*, 9 November 2016, https://worldpoliticsreview.com/articles/20411/why-african-states-are-refusing-to-sign-on-to-eu-trade-deals [accessed 25 February 2018].
Lightfoot, S., Mawdsley, E. and Szent-Iványi, B. (2017) 'Brexit and UK international development policy', *Political Quarterly*, 88:3, 517–24.
Price, S. (2016) 'Brexit, development aid, and the Commonwealth', *Round Table: Commonwealth Journal of International Affairs*, 105:5, 499–507.
United Nations Economic Commission for Africa (2017) *Transforming African Economies through Smart Trade and Industrial Policy* (Addis Ababa: Economic Commission for Africa).
United Nations Economic Commission for Africa (2018) *Continental Free Trade Area: Questions and Answers* (Addis Ababa: Economic Commission for Africa).

Index

0.7 % aid spending pledge 6, 21, 27, 29
   changing the rules of definition 4, 29
   Conservative Party policy on 92, 123, 124–5, 133, 135, 149, 164–5, 216
   Labour Party policy on 132, 140, 144, 146–9
   Liberal Democrat Party policy on 129, 216
0.7% aid target 123–6, 129, 132, 140, 142, 144–9, 168, 192
9/11 4, 55, 57, 60

Abbott, Diane 143–4, 151
ACP (African, Caribbean and Pacific Group of States) 36, 38–9, 41, 46–9, 188, 218
ACPP (Africa Conflict Prevention Pool) 63
African agency 7, 8, 141, 209, 221
African, Caribbean and Pacific Group of States *see* ACP
Africanisation of poverty 6, 7, 198
African Peace and Security Architecture *see* APSA
'African Solutions to African Problems' 54–5, 57, 60, 62–3, 215, 221
African Standby Force *see* ASF
African Union *see* AU
African Union Mission in Somalia *see* AMISOM
African Union Mission in Sudan *see* AMIS
aid
   aid securitisation 74,77–9, 80, 83, 86, 88–9, 92
   aid ties 35–7, 45
   democratisation aid 78–9, 82–3, 86
   development aid 73–7, 91–2, 94, 144, 168
   importance of aid 20–1
   tying to trade agreements 42, 48–9
   UK aid 73, 79–80, 82, 86, 132–4, 153, 217
   UK aid to Africa 4, 56, 131, 215
   UK contributions to EU Development Assistance 152–3, 218
Alexander, Douglas 22, 152
al–Shabaab 62

Alternative Trade Mandate 186
AMIS (African Union Mission in Sudan) 58
AMISOM (African Union Mission in Somalia) 59, 67
Amos, Baroness Valerie 22
Ancram, Michael 124, 125
anti-corruption 81, 86, 89, 93, 143, 150
anti-poaching 17, 26
APSA (African Peace and Security Architecture) 54–5, 58–9, 62–3, 68, 215, 218, 221
   UK support for 62–3
'arc of instability' 134, 152
ASF (African Standby Force) 59, 63
AU (African Union) 9, 48, 54, 55–9, 62–7, 86, 111, 215
AU Mission in Burundi 63

Baldwin, Harriet 28
Belgium
   and 1960 Katanga secession 101
Benn, Hilary 22, 73
'beyond aid' 146–8
bilateral aid review
   (2011) 132
   (2016) 134
Blair Government (UK)
   and 2000 military intervention in Sierra Leone 57, 106
   and 'African Solutions to African Problems' 54–5, 57, 62–3, 215
   and securitisation of development 54–5, 60, 73, 75, 77
Blair, Tony 1–6, 21–3, 25, 40, 54–9, 60, 63, 68, 106, 122, 124–7, 142–4, 147, 150, 164, 182, 198, 209, 214–5, 217
BOAG (British Overseas Aid Group) 172, 176
Boko Haram 62
   counter-insurgency and UK support 62
BOND (British Overseas NGOs for Development) 167, 174

Boxing Day Tsunami (2004) 126
BPST (British Peace Support Team)
   East Africa 26, 63
   South Africa 26
Brahimi Report (Report of the Panel on UN Peace Operations, 2000) 105
Brexit 152–4
   implications for UK–Africa trade 35–50, 153, 189–90, 192, 216
   implications for UK aid allocations 153
Brexiteer 35–9, 40–1, 43–5, 48, 189, 217, 218, 220
Brexit referendum (2016) 1, 3, 25, 55
   impact on David Cameron 25
   impact on UK–Africa trade relationship 5, 8, 15, 16, 20, 28–9, 44, 218–9
   impact on UK engagement with peacekeeping in Africa 67
   see also Brexit; EU membership referendum (2016)
British Overseas Aid Group *see* BOAG
British Overseas NGOs for Development *see* BOND
British Peace Support Team *see* BPST
Brown, Gordon 3, 4, 5, 6, 23, 40, 68, 76, 122, 127, 139–40, 141, 149, 167, 209, 214
Brown Government (UK)
   and 'African Solutions to African Problems' 54, 63
   and securitisation of development 54, 59, 63, 68, 92
budget support 22, 151
Burundi 63

CAFOD (Catholic Agency for Overseas Development) 183
Cameron, David 6, 25–6, 55, 60, 121, 130, 134, 141, 146, 151, 164, 166–9, 174–5, 182, 214
   and 2011 UK intervention in Libya 65
   and AMISOM 62
   and Nelson Mandela 25, 132
   speech in Lagos (2011) 130–1
   visit to Nigeria 25
   visit to South Africa 25
   visits to Africa 127–30
Cameron Government (2015–16) (UK)
   continuity with New Labour Government policy on Africa 133, 164
   Free Trade Initiative 61

   and the 'national interest' in UK–Africa policy 111, 123, 133
   and securitisation of development 73, 75, 77
Cameroon
   limited UK strategic interests in 79, 80, 86
   UK aid programmes in 74, 82–4, 92
CAR (Central African Republic)
   limited UK strategic interests in 79, 82, 86
   UK aid programmes in 74, 82–4, 92
CARE International 202
Catholic Agency for Overseas Development *see* CAFOD
Central African Republic *see* CAR
CfA (Commission for Africa) 16, 22–3, 60, 61, 131, 164, 187
Chad 28, 58, 62, 65, 69
charitable appeals 163, 197
China 23, 41, 112, 130, 214
Christian Aid 186
civil society organisations *see* CSOs
Cleverly, James 37
Coalition Government (UK) 21, 24–5, 27, 30, 55, 59, 61–2, 83, 86, 88–9, 93, 113, 122–3, 129–31, 146, 162, 164, 174, 181, 191, 209, 215
   continuity with New Labour Government policy on Africa 216–17, 219
   and deploying to UN peacekeeping missions in Africa 59, 62
   and the 'national interest' in UK–Africa policy 59, 61
   and securitisation of development 61, 74
   UK Aid: Tackling Global Challenges in the National Interest (2015) 4, 76
Coffey International 91
Comic Relief 198, 201
Commission for Africa *see* CfA
Common Agricultural Policy 44, 150, 186
Commonwealth 8, 29, 30, 35–40, 44, 48–9, 56, 100, 113, 145, 217
   Heads of Government Meetings 29
   increased prominence under Conservatives 124
Comoros 63
Congo, Republic of 65, 69
Conservative Party (UK) 6, 65–6, 121–35, 164, 168, 203, 216, 219
   compassionate Conservatism 122, 129, 131, 135
   'detoxification' 123, 167
   manifesto (2001) 124

manifesto (2010) 164
manifesto (2017) 4, 29, 113, 144, 149
Party Conference
  (2004) 125
  (2011) 131
  (2015) 66
  (2016) 134
party modernisation 122–4, 127
place of Africa in international development policy 1, 162
see also Project Umubano
Cook, Robin 57, 151
and 'ethical foreign policy' 57
Corbyn, Jeremy 143–5, 151
Creagh, Mary 143–5, 147, 150, 153
CSOs (civil society organisations) 1, 6, 86, 145, 186, 197, 217, 218, 220, 221
Cyprus
  UN Peacekeeping Force in Cyprus 102, 104

Daily Mail
  and Girl Effect Ethiopia 90
Darfur crisis 58, 126
  AU peacekeeping 58, 63
  UK engagement 58
DFID (Department for International Development) 16, 20, 21–2, 24, 27–8, 42–4, 49, 65, 73–94, 133–4, 140, 144, 151, 168–9, 198–9
  outsourcing 27
  relative growth compared to FCO 20, 24
  staff cuts 24
  support to Deepening Democracy programme in Uganda 91
  support to Girl Effect Ethiopia project 89, 90, 93
  support to SSR in Kenya 90–1, 93
diaspora 15, 16, 17
  and 2001 UK Census 16
  African living in UK 16–18, 31
  and British electoral politics 17
  impact on UK economy 17, 18
  impact on UK politics 15
  impact on UK services 17, 18
  and remittances to Sub-Saharan Africa 17
  and UK electoral constituencies 17
Djibouti 28, 63
donors (Western aid)
  and fragile states 77, 151
  funding to democratisation programmes 77
  security interests of 73, 77

Douglas-Home Government (UK) 56
Duddridge, James 61, 67
Duncan, Alan 126
Duncan Smith, Iain 123–6, 131

EASF (East African Standby Force) 59, 63
East Africa famine 201
East African Standby Force see EASF
EBA (Everything But Arms) 40, 41
Ebola crisis 60, 134, 150
Economic Community of West African States see ECOWAS
Economic Partnership Agreements see EPAs
ECOWAS (Economic Community of West African States) 59, 63
Eden, Anthony 101
EFIF (Enough Food If) campaign 6, 161–4, 166–9, 170–5, 219, 220
  'Big If' rally 169
Ellwood, Tobias 39
'Empire 2.0' 39, 40, 43, 45
Enough Food If see EFIF
EPAs (Economic Partnership Agreements) 29, 38, 42–3, 46, 48–9, 50, 186, 188–9, 190, 216, 218, 220–1
Eritrea 63
Ethiopia 24–6, 28, 63, 65, 74, 79–80
  UK aid programmes in 74, 80–4, 92
  UK strategic interests in 79
EU (European Union)
  development assistance 67, 218
  EU–AU Summits 28, 66, 218
EU membership referendum (2016) 122, 133, 135
European Commission 35, 37, 46, 49, 188
Everything But Arms see EBA

fair trade 126, 148, 181–4
Fairtrade Foundation 183
Fallon, Michael 62, 111
farm subsidies
  US and EU 127
FCO (Foreign and Commonwealth Office) 20, 22–4, 27–9, 39, 134, 152, 217
  budget and staff cuts 24
  diplomatic missions and high commissions closed 23–4, 31
  diplomatic missions and high commissions (re-)opened 20, 24
  prosperity officers 24

FDI (Foreign Direct Investment) 19, 20, 29, 179
financial crisis (2008) 7, 9, 162, 168, 197
   impact on NGO fundraising 197, 202
Foreign and Commonwealth Office *see* FCO
Foreign Direct Investment *see* FDI
Fox, Liam 28, 35–8, 43, 45, 49
fragile states 73, 75–7, 143, 151–2, 217
France 19, 28–9, 31, 66, 67, 100, 102, 108, 112, 218
free trade 37–9, 42–5, 47, 49, 61, 126, 181–2, 188, 191, 217–8

G8 2, 21, 22, 60, 166–8, 170–2, 175, 187
   Genoa summit (2001) 21
   Gleneagles summit (2005) 2, 187
   Lough Erne Declaration 169
   Lough Erne summit (2013) 167, 172
Gardiner, Barry 190
Gates, Bill 149, 167, 169, 174
Geldof, Bob 203
Generalised System of Preferences *see* GSP
Germany 16
Ghana 24, 29, 39, 42, 44, 59, 63
Girl Effect Ethiopia 89, 90, 93
Global Britain 48, 49, 50
Global Justice Now 186
Global War on Terror 2, 4
'golden thread' 76, 141, 164, 168, 174
Gove, Michael 35
Greening, Justine 75, 132, 147
GSP (Generalised System of Preferences) 41

Hague, William 25, 27, 123–5, 132
Hammerskjöld, Dag 101
Hammond, Phillip 25, 28, 42
Hannan, Daniel 38, 40, 43
Harman, Harriet 142, 147
Houghton, Sir Nicholas 110
Howard, Michael 123, 125–7
human rights 4, 57, 76, 81, 86, 88, 140, 144
   and aid conditionality 150–1, 144–5
   and budget support 151

ICAI (Independent Commission for Aid Impact) 88, 91, 93
   review of Girl Effect Ethiopia (2012) 89
   review of UK security and justice programmes (2015) 91
Independent Commission for Aid Impact *see* ICAI

International Aid Transparency Initiative 88
International Military Advisory and Training Team 26
Investor–State Dispute Settlement 189
Ireland
   training of Malian Army 110

Japan 16, 19
Johnson, Boris 28, 35–9, 45, 49, 134
   using UK aid budget to support foreign policy aims 73
Jubilee (2000) 40, 171–2, 180, 185

Kenya 4, 23–9, 30, 56, 66, 90–3
   election violence (2010–11) 23
   military training relationship with UK 26
   UK aid programmes in 74, 80–4, 86, 92
   UK strategic interests in 79
Ki-moon, Ban 108

Labour Campaign for International Development *see* LCID
Labour Party (UK) 5–6, 9, 21, 55, 57, 124, 126, 135, 139–54, 182, 190, 216, 219, 220
   Labour Party manifesto
      (2005) 149
      (2010) 149
   Labour Party in opposition
      manifesto (2015) 143–5, 150
      manifesto (2017) 4, 29, 113, 145, 149, 150, 152
      National Policy Forum 142, 144–5, 147–9, 150, 152
      policymaking on Africa 139, 140–1, 147, 150, 152–3
      policy reviews 142, 154
      and Universal Health Care 143, 145, 147
   place of Africa in international development policy 1, 162
land grabbing 168, 170, 172
LCID (Labour Campaign for International Development) 147–8
Lewis, Ivan 142–3, 145, 147
   campaign for early years SDG target 145
LGBT rights 150
Libyan intervention 25
Live Aid 198–9, 203
Lomé Convention 39, 47

Index

Macron, Emmanuel 15
Make Poverty History *see* MPH
Mandela, Nelson 25, 56, 127–8, 132
May Government (UK) 28, 55, 133–5, 214, 218
May, Theresa 4, 26, 28–9, 66, 123, 145, 174
MDGs (Millennium Development Goals) 22, 132
Miliband, David 23
Miliband, Ed 142–3, 152
Millennium Development Goals *see* MDGs
Ministry of Defence *see* MoD
Mitchell, Andrew 4, 123, 127–9, 130, 132, 134, 139, 141
MoD (Ministry of Defence)
 and UNAMSIL 106, 107
MONUC (UN Mission in the Democratic Republic of Congo) 108
 UK refusal to deploy troops as part of EU battlegroup 108
moral economy 35–7, 40, 42, 44–5, 47, 49
MPH (Make Poverty History) coalition 6, 9, 126, 161–3, 166, 171–2, 180, 184, 186–8, 191–2, 198, 200, 203, 207, 219
Mugabe, Robert 20, 56, 124–5, 130, 205
Mullin, Chris 5
Multilateral Aid Review (2011) 132
Murphy, Jim 143–4, 150–2

national interest(s) 5, 61, 111–12, 123, 127, 130, 132–5, 147, 217
 economic growth 147, 151
 migration 16, 17, 147
 security 147, 148, 152
National Security Council *see* NSC
NATO (North Atlantic Treaty Organisation) 25, 30, 65, 102, 113, 134, 145
neo-colonialism 35, 41–2, 46, 56, 130
new 'scramble for Africa' 130
NGOs (non-governmental organisations) 74, 89, 141, 143, 148, 162–7, 169, 172–5, 179, 180–1, 184–6, 188, 190–2, 196–8, 200–4, 207, 209, 2016, 218–9, 220–1
 NGO campaigns
  cosmopolitanism 200, 208
  representation of Africans 196–9, 201–2, 204, 207, 209
  representation of children 196, 197, 199
  representations of poverty 197–8
  trade off between fundraising and engagement 204, 208
Nigeria 15–18, 24–6, 28, 30, 62, 130
 and trade 27, 29
Nkrumah, Kwame 42–3, 46
non-governmental organisations *see* NGOs
non-reciprocal trade 47, 49, 188
non-tariff barriers 41
North Atlantic Treaty Organisation *see* NATO
NSC (National Security Council) 27, 28

Obama, Barack 65, 110, 112
ONUC (UN Mission to the Congo) 100–3
Operation Palliser 2, 106
 see also Sierra Leone
Osamor, Kate 144–5, 148, 151
Oxfam 7, 124, 163, 183, 186, 196–7, 205–7, 209
 'See for Yourself' campaign 204–7, 220

Patel, Priti 28, 36, 42, 133–4, 144, 218
peacekeeping 5, 125
 UK assessed contributions 9
 UK contribution in Somalia 59, 133
 UK contribution in South Sudan 133
 UK contributions to AU peacekeeping 9, 55, 68
 UK contributions to UN peacekeeping 21, 26, 29, 62, 215
 UK engagement in capacity building for 26
 UK support for/contributions to peacekeeping in Africa 55, 59
 UN peacekeeping 111
 UN peacekeeping and UK engagement with 8, 104, 107, 130
Peace Support Operation(s) *see* PSO(s)
Pettifor, Ann 185
'pornography of poverty' 198
private sector 132
 role in development 134
Project Umubano 136
prosperity partnerships 24, 61
PSO(s) (Peace Support Operation(s)) 63, 105

Radi-Aid awards 201
RECs (Regional Economic Communities) 36, 46, 48, 50
ring-fencing of aid budget 135
rising powers 130

Rwandan Genocide 5
  impact on UK peacekeeping approaches 104, 105

SADC (Southern African Development Community) 46, 59, 63
Sahel
  UK engagement with 26, 28, 29, 62
Save the Children 124, 163, 166, 202
scrutiny of aid 132, 134
  see also ICAI
SDGs (Sustainable Development Goals) 7, 27, 140, 145, 147, 153, 189
Seattle to Brussels Network 186
securitisation 2, 55, 60, 73, 74
  of aid 79–80, 83, 86, 88–9, 92, 94, 144, 148, 217
  of development 75, 77, 94
Security Sector Reform see SSR
Short, Clare 22
Sierra Leone 16, 21, 26, 28, 57, 105–7, 109–10, 113, 124, 139
  2000 UK military intervention (Operation Palliser) 2, 106
  Ebola 16
  UNAMSIL and UK intervention 106
Solana, Javier 108
Somalia 15, 16, 23, 25, 26, 28, 29, 30, 55, 62, 66, 67, 99, 105, 113, 133, 135, 203, 216
  failed UN operations in and impact on UK peacekeeping approaches 26, 99
  UK contribution to UNSOS 110–11
  UK support for AMISOM 59, 67
Somalia Summits 24, 59
  (2012) 24, 62, 67
  (2013) 24
  (2017) 24, 28, 62
South Africa 25, 27–9, 56, 61, 63, 127–8, 130, 132
  and trade 18–19, 24
Southern African Development Community see SADC
South Sudan
  UK contribution to UNMISS 110–11
SSR (Security Sector Reform)
  DFID support for in Kenya 90–1, 93
Stewart, Rory 28, 135
Stop EPAs campaign 186, 188
Straw, Jack 23, 61

Suez Crisis
  and UK international relations 100, 104
  and UK politics 100–1
supply chains 143, 145, 183
Sustainable Development Goals see SDGs

Tanzania 24, 29, 56, 216
tax evasion 145, 148, 151, 163, 168–9
tax reform 170
TJM (Trade Justice Movement) 6, 180–9, 190–2, 217, 219, 220–1
  founding statement 180, 182, 185
  mass lobby of parliament 180
trade
  independent UK policy 37, 45, 49, 189, 190, 192, 216
  special and differential treatment for developing countries 179
  and UK–Africa relationship 4, 8, 42, 217
Trade envoys 24
Trade Justice Movement see TJM
Traidcraft 182
TTIP (Transatlantic Trade and Investment Partnership) 184, 186, 189

Uganda 18, 28, 63, 104
  UK aid programmes in 74, 81–83, 89, 92
  UK strategic interests in 79–80, 83
  UK support to Deepening Democracy programme 91–2, 93
  UN Development Programme and democracy building programmes in 91
UK Africa Strategy (2018) 15, 21, 26, 28, 30
UK exports to Sub-Saharan Africa 18–19
UK public attitudes 196–7
  to Africa/Africans 163, 199, 200, 202, 208–9
  to aid spending 204
  to poverty 197
UK trade balance with Sub-Saharan Africa 18–19
UN (United Nations)
  Report of the High-Level Independent Panel on United Nations Peace Operations (2015) 109
  see also peacekeeping
UNAMIR (United Nations Assistance Mission for Rwanda) 104
UNAMSIL (United Nations Assistance Mission in Sierra Leone) 106–7
UN Economic Commission for Africa 220–1

UNEF I (United Nations Emergency Force) 100
   UK engagement with 100, 103
UNMISS (United Nations Mission in South Sudan) 110–11
UN Mission in the Democratic Republic of Congo *see* MONUC
UN Mission to the Congo *see* ONUC
UNPROFOR (United Nations Protection Force) 104
   UK contribution to 104, 105
UNSC (United Nations Security Council) 15, 16, 64, 99, 101, 103, 104, 112
   UK scepticism of 102
   UK engagement with on peacekeeping 108–9
UNSOS (United Nations Support Office in Somalia) 110–11

USSR (Union of Soviet Socialist Republics) 4, 102
   and 1960–65 Congo Crisis 103

visas 29

War in Iraq 21, 23, 25, 108, 142
War on Want 186
workers' rights 143–5
World Trade Organization (WTO) 40, 179, 186, 188
   Cancún Ministerial 187, 188
   Doha Round 181
   Hong Kong Ministerial 183
   Seattle Ministerial 179

Zimbabwe 15–17, 20, 23, 29, 56, 124–5, 130–1, 139, 150, 205–6

EU authorised representative for GPSR:
Easy Access System Europe, Mustamäe tee 50,
10621 Tallinn, Estonia
gpsr.requests@easproject.com

www.ingramcontent.com/pod-product-compliance
Lightning Source LLC
Chambersburg PA
CBHW070237240426
43673CB00044B/1826